Access to History for the IB Diploma

The move to global war

Andy Dailey

HODDER
EDUCATION
AN HACHETTE UK COMPANY

To Carol Redmount and Hisham Mehrez with great respect and love.

The material in this title has been developed independently of the International Baccalaureate®, which in no way endorses it.

The Publishers would like to thank the following for permission to reproduce copyright material:

Photo credits: p16 Leonard de Selva/Corbis; **p20** Rykoff Collection/Corbis; **p22** Corbis; **p59** Kent Cartoon Archive/Solo Syndication; **p60** Bettmann/Corbis; **p68** Courtesy of Hoover Institution Library & Archives, Stanford University; **p69** Bettmann/Corbis; **p73** East Asian Image Collection, Skillman Library, Lafayette College; **p75** Kent Cartoon Archive/Express Syndication; **pp79, 80** Courtesy of Hoover Institution Library & Archives, Stanford University; **p84** Llyfrgell Genedlaethol Cymru/The National Library of Wales/Solo Syndication; **p99** Michael Nicholson/Corbis; **p120***t* Underwood & Underwood/Corbis, *b* Kent Cartoon Archive/Express Syndication; **p121** Rickards/Getty Images; **p123** Kent Cartoon Archive/Solo Syndication; **pp128, 134** Kent Cartoon Archive/Express Syndication; **p158** Kent Cartoon Archive/Solo Syndication; **p161** Michael Nicholson/Corbis; **p166** Kent Cartoon Archive/Solo Syndication; **p169** Michael Nicholson/Corbis.

Acknowledgements are listed on page 204.

Every effort has been made to trace all copyright holders, but if any have been inadvertently overlooked the Publishers will be pleased to make the necessary arrangements at the first opportunity.

Although every effort has been made to ensure that website addresses are correct at time of going to press, Hodder Education cannot be held responsible for the content of any website mentioned in this book. It is sometimes possible to find a relocated web page by typing in the address of the home page for a website in the URL window of your browser.

Hachette UK's policy is to use papers that are natural, renewable and recyclable products and made from wood grown in sustainable forests. The logging and manufacturing processes are expected to conform to the environmental regulations of the country of origin.

Orders: please contact Bookpoint Ltd, 130 Milton Park, Abingdon, Oxon OX14 4SB. Telephone: +44 (0)1235 827720. Fax: +44 (0)1235 400454. Lines are open 9.00a.m.–5.00p.m., Monday to Saturday, with a 24-hour message answering service. Visit our website at www.hoddereducation.co.uk

© Andy Dailey 2015

First published in 2015 by
Hodder Education,
An Hachette UK Company
Carmelite House, 50 Victoria Embankment
London EC4Y 0DZ

Impression number   10 9 8 7 6 5 4
Year   2019 2018 2017 2016

All rights reserved. Apart from any use permitted under UK copyright law, no part of this publication may be reproduced or transmitted in any form or by any means, electronic or mechanical, including photocopying and recording, or held within any information storage and retrieval system, without permission in writing from the publisher or under licence from the Copyright Licensing Agency Limited. Further details of such licences (for reprographic reproduction) may be obtained from the Copyright Licensing Agency Limited, Saffron House, 6–10 Kirby Street, London EC1N 8TS.

Cover image © Lebrecht Music & Arts/Corbis
Illustrations by Gray Publishing
Typeset in 10/13pt Palatino and produced by Gray Publishing, Tunbridge Wells
Printed in Italy

A catalogue record for this title is available from the British Library

ISBN 978 1471 839320

Contents

Dedication

Keith Randell (1943–2002)

The original *Access to History* series was conceived and developed by Keith, who created a series to 'cater for students as they are, not as we might wish them to be'. He leaves a living legacy of a series that for over 20 years has provided a trusted, stimulating and well-loved accompaniment to post-16 study. Our aim with these new editions for the IB is to continue to offer students the best possible support for their studies.

Introduction

This book has been written to support your study of Prescribed subject 3: The move to global war for the IB History Diploma. This introduction gives you an overview of:

★ the content you will study for The move to global war

★ how you will be assessed for Paper 1

★ the different features of this book and how these will aid your learning.

 # What you will study

The period from 1931 to 1941 has traditionally been seen as a time in which three nations, namely Japan, Germany and Italy, worked to challenge other nations. In this decade, Japan's military increased its control of its government, conducted two successive wars on China, and demonstrated the weakness of the League of Nations before leaving it and eventually attacking the USA, provoking the Second World War in Asia and the Pacific. Italy and Germany challenged the Great Powers of the time, France and Britain. Italy, ruled by an ultranationalist, sought empire and glory, while Germany, democratically achieving a dictatorship in 1933, worked to ensure its own security, obtain lost lands and become a Great Power itself.

All three nations worked against communism, left the League of Nations, and were opposed to British and French policies of containment. All three would provoke conflicts that led to the Second World War.

You will study the foreign policies, and domestic and ideological issues that contributed to these foreign policies, in two case studies.

Case Study 1: Japanese expansion in East Asia 1931–41

	Chapter 1	Chapter 2
Causes of expansion:		
• Japanese nationalism and militarism in its foreign policies	✓	
• political and economic issues in Japan that affected foreign relations	✓	
• political instability in China that assisted in Japan's expansion	✓	
Events of expansion:		
• invasion of Manchuria and northern China (1931)		✓
• Sino-Japanese War (1937–41)		✓

	Chapter 1	Chapter 2
• Three Power/Tripartite Pact and the outbreak of war with the USA starting at Pearl Harbor (1941)		✓
Responses to expansion:		
• League of Nations, including the Lytton Report		✓
• political developments in China, including the formation of the Second United Front		✓
• international responses, including US initiatives and increasing tensions between the two states		✓

Case Study 2: Italian and German expansion 1933–40

	Chapter 3	Chapter 4
Causes of expansion:		
• impact of fascism and Nazism on the foreign policies of Italy	✓	
• impact of fascism and Nazism on the foreign policies of Germany		✓
• impact of domestic economic issues on the foreign policies of these states	✓	✓
• changing diplomatic alignments in Europe, the collapse of collective security and the policy of appeasement	✓	✓
Events of expansion:		
• Italian expansion in Abyssinia (1935–6), Albania (1939), entry into the Second World War (1940)	✓	
• German challenges to post-First World War settlements (1933–8)		✓
• German expansion (1938–9), the Pact of Steel, Nazi–Soviet Pact and the outbreak of war (1939)		✓
Responses to expansion:		
• international response to Italian expansion (1935–6)	✓	
• international response to German expansion (1933–8)		✓

② How you will be assessed

The IB History Diploma can be studied at either Standard or Higher Level. It has three papers in total: Papers 1 and 2 for Standard Level and a further Paper 3 for Higher Level. It also has an internal assessment which all students must do.

- For Paper 1 you need to answer four source-based questions on one prescribed subject. This counts for 20 per cent of your overall marks at Higher Level, or 30 per cent of your overall marks at Standard Level.

- For Paper 2 you need to answer two essay questions on two different topics. This counts for 25 per cent of your overall marks at Higher Level, or 45 per cent of your overall marks at Standard Level.
- For Paper 3 you need to answer three essay questions on two or three sections. This counts for 35 per cent of your overall marks at Higher Level.

For the Internal Assessment you need to carry out a historical investigation. This counts for 20 per cent of your overall marks at Higher Level, or 25 per cent of your overall marks at Standard Level.

Prescribed subject 3: The move to global war is assessed through Paper 1 and is the third of five prescribed subjects. Paper 1 will contain all five prescribed subjects and questions will be numbered 1–20. There are four sources and four questions for each prescribed subject. Sources are primary and secondary with most being in written form, although there is usually at least one visual source as well.

Questions for Prescribed subject 3: The move to global war will be numbered as 9, 10, 11 and 12 in the Paper 1 booklet. The questions in this book follow the same numbering system. (There are no questions 1–8.)

Examination questions

The four questions on Paper 1 assess different skills and knowledge. You must answer all four and have one hour to do so. The question types are as follows:

Question 9: direct questions

Question 9 is worth 5 marks and has two parts, both of which test your reading comprehension abilities on two different sources. You need to answer both parts of the question by reviewing the source material and paraphrasing information from the sources. There is detailed guidance on how to answer question 9 on page 46. Examples of this type of question might be:

Example 1
a) What, according to Source A, was the importance of the Manchurian Crisis for Japan's military?
b) What is the message conveyed by Source C?

Example 2
a) Why, according to Source B, did Germany reoccupy the Rhineland in 1936?
b) What is the message conveyed by Source D?

Question 10: value and limitations of a source

Question 10 is worth 4 marks and asks you to evaluate a source using the source's origin, purpose and the content you are presented with.

- The origin of a source is its author or creator. This might include the date, publisher and type of delivery, which could be a book, speech, propaganda poster or diary entry.
- The purpose of the source explains what the author was trying to do, such as explaining the impact of an event or conveying a certain type of information.
- The content of the source can indicate many things, such as the point of view of the author, evidence of some historical event or its interpretation or, in the case of a cartoon or other visual source, the audience that the creator wished to reach.

The values and limitations will vary according to each source. A value could be that the author of the source witnessed the event or is an acknowledged scholar. An example of a limitation could be that an author was involved in events and therefore may be less objective. You should try to explain at least two values and two limitations per source, although this may not always be possible. There is detailed guidance on how to answer question 10 on page 48. Examples of this type of question might be:

Example 1
With reference to its origin, purpose and content, analyse the value and limitations of Source A for historians studying international responses regarding Italy's annexation of Albania.

Example 2
With reference to its origin, purpose and content, analyse the value and limitations of Source B for historians studying the effect of the Great Depression on Japan's foreign policy.

Question 11: compare and contrast
Question 11 is worth 6 marks, and asks you to compare and contrast two sources in terms of what information they convey to historians studying some aspect of this prescribed subject. Comparing means that you explain the similarities between the sources, while contrasting explains how they are different. You should aim to have about three similarities and three differences. There is detailed guidance on how to answer question 11 on page 136. Examples of this type of question might be:

Example 1
Compare and contrast what Sources A and D indicate about Japan's government in 1931.

Example 2
Compare and contrast what Sources B and C reveal about the importance of the Abyssinian Crisis for Germany.

Question 12: Essays integrating knowledge and sources
Question 12 is worth 9 marks and requires you to use all the sources in the examination, and to integrate them into an essay that also contains your

own knowledge. There is detailed guidance on how to answer question 12 on page 179. Examples of this type of question might be:

Example 1

Using these sources and your own knowledge, discuss the extent to which you agree that the Ruhr Crisis was a failure for France.

Example 2

Using these sources and your own knowledge, explain why the League of Nations failed to intervene in the Manchurian Crisis.

The appearance of the examination paper

Cover

The cover of the examination paper states the date of the examination and the length of time you have to complete it: one hour. Instructions are limited and simply state that you should not open it until told to do so and that all questions must be answered.

Sources

Once you are allowed to open your examination paper, you can turn to Prescribed subject 3: The move to global war. There you will see four sources, each labelled with a letter. There is no particular order to the sources, so Source A could potentially be a map, a speech, a photograph or an extract from a book. Source A is no more or less important than Source B, or Source C or D. If you see square brackets, [ ], then this is an explanation or addition to the source by the creators of the examination and not part of the original source. Sometimes sources are shortened and you will see an ellipsis, three full stops (…), when this happens.

Questions

After the four sources, the four questions will appear. You need to answer all of them. It is better to answer the questions in order, as this will familiarize you with all the sources to be used in the final essay on question 12, but this is not required. Be sure to number your questions correctly. Do not use bullet points to answer questions, but instead write in full sentences when possible. Each question indicates how many marks it is worth.

About this book

Coverage of course content

This book addresses the key areas listed in the IB History Guide for Prescribed subject 3: The move to global war. The chapters start with an introduction outlining the key questions they address. They are then divided into a series of sections and topics covering the course content. Throughout the chapters you will find the following features to aid your study of the course content.

Key and leading questions

Each section heading in the chapter has a related key question which gives a focus to your reading and understanding of the section. These are also listed in the chapter introduction. You should be able to answer the questions after completing the relevant section.

Topics within the sections have leading questions which are designed to help you focus on the key points within a topic and give you more practice in answering questions.

Key terms

Key terms are the important terms you need to know to gain an understanding of the period. These are emboldened in the text the first time they appear in the book and are defined in the margin. They also appear in the glossary at the end of the book.

Sources

Each chapter contains several sources. These sources indicate the title of work, author or authors, editors where appropriate, publishing company and location, date of publication and which page or pages of that publication this particular source originates from. This source information is included so that you can locate and use these sources to further your own study of history. The sources have accompanying questions and are also used with the practice questions at the end of the chapters. The range of sources used will expose you to many different types of sources that you may find in the examination.

Key debates

Historians often disagree on historical events and this historical debate is referred to as historiography. Knowledge of historiography is helpful in reaching the upper mark bands when you take your IB History examinations. The key debates in Chapters 2 and 4 will help you to develop your understanding of historiography.

Theory of Knowledge (TOK) questions

Understanding that different historians see history differently is an important element in understanding the connection between the IB History Diploma and Theory of Knowledge. Alongside the key debates are Theory of Knowledge style questions which make this link.

Summary diagrams

At the end of each section is a summary diagram which gives a visual summary of the content of the section. It is intended as an aid for revision.

Chapter summary

At the end of each chapter is a short summary of the content of that chapter. This is intended to help you revise and consolidate your knowledge and understanding of the content.

Skills development

At the end of each chapter are the following:

- Examination guidance on how to answer different question types, accompanied by a sample answer and commentary designed to help you focus on specific details.
- Examination practice in the form of Paper 1 practice questions.
- Suggestions for learning activities, including ideas for debate, essays, displays and research, which will help you develop skills needed for Paper 1 and a deeper understanding of the content.

These are all intended to help you develop the following skills in order to achieve examination success:

- *Source analysis.* This book allows you to become familiar with the works of many historians and primary source material. It teaches you to analyse all types of sources and gives you the opportunity to review their strengths, weaknesses, origins, purpose, values and limitations.
- *Integrating sources into essays.* Integrating sources into essays requires that you know how to write a good essay. This book gives guidance on writing good essays that integrate sources.

End of case study material

There are two case studies for Paper 1 prescribed subjects. At the end of each case study in this book you will find:

- a full set of Paper 1 practice questions focused on each case study
- a timeline of important events.

End of the book

The book concludes with the following sections:

Glossary

All key terms in the book are defined in the glossary.

Further reading

This contains a list of books, websites, films and other resources which may help you with further independent research and presentations. It may also be helpful when further information is required for internal assessments and extended essays in history. You may wish to share this list with your school or local librarian.

Internal assessment

A list of potential internal assessment questions for those students wishing to explore a particular topic in more depth.

Case Study 1

Japanese expansion in Asia 1931–41

Causes of expansion

This chapter explores Japan's rapid progression in the late nineteenth and early twentieth centuries from an isolated, undeveloped state to a significant political and military power, especially in Asia. Much of this success was due to industrialization, a strong military and a tightly controlled political system. There were, however, fundamental flaws in the system that would lead to increasing military control of the state, the development of radical nationalism and calls for empire. You will need to consider the following questions throughout this chapter:

★ How did Japan develop into an ultranationalist state with a strong military?

★ How successful was Japan in creating an Asian empire?

★ How did Japan's economic and political issues affect Japan's government?

★ How did instability contribute to Japan's domestic and foreign policy?

Japanese nationalism and militarism

▶ **Key question:** *How did Japan develop into an ultranationalist state with a strong military?*

 KEY TERM

Ultranationalist A belief in which a person or state's nationality is considered superior to that of all others and usually involves racist and discriminatory beliefs against others not of the same nationality.

Meiji Restoration The creation of a new government of Japan after centuries of military government, in which Japan's Emperor held new powers and new, more modern systems of governance were created; it is named after the ruling emperor of that period.

Japan underwent major modernization in the late nineteenth century to become an **ultranationalist** state. The changes, part of the **Meiji Restoration**, were meant to protect Japan from foreign domination. However, modernization placed great stress on Japanese society, especially economic, and many Japanese people would eventually turn to the military to control the state's economy, government and all policies by the early 1930s.

SOURCE A

Excerpt from the Meiji Constitution (1889), translated as part of the Hanover College Historical Texts Collection, USA, located at: http://history.hanover.edu/texts/1889con.html.

Chapter 1. The Emperor

Article 1. The Empire of Japan shall be reigned over and governed by a line of Emperors unbroken for ages eternal.

Article 2. The Imperial Throne shall be succeeded to by Imperial male descendants, according to the provisions of the Imperial House Law.

Article 3. The Emperor is sacred and inviolable.

Article 4. The Emperor is the head of the Empire, combining in Himself the rights of sovereignty, and exercises them, according to the provisions of the present Constitution.

Article 5. The Emperor exercises the legislative power with the consent of the Imperial Diet.

Article 6. The Emperor gives sanction to laws, and orders them to be promulgated and executed.

Article 7. The Emperor convokes the Imperial Diet, opens, closes, and prorogues it, and dissolves the House of Representatives.

> According to Source A, what is the role of Japan's Emperor in the government? **?**

The Meiji Constitution

The **Meiji Emperor** of Japan reigned from 1867 to 1912. This was a period of tremendous reform in Japan, including the abolishment of **feudalism**, industrial development and the creation of a parliament and modern governing systems. The Meiji Emperor declared Japan's constitution, the first such legal document for the country, in 1889.

> **How did the Meiji Constitution organize Japan's government and for what reasons?**

The Meiji Constitution, the work of a special group called the **Privy Council**, stated clearly that the Emperor of Japan was the head of state and that he was a divine individual. Government authority came from the Emperor and government ministers were responsible to him alone, not to the Diet, Japan's newly created parliament. The military was allowed tremendous independence in this document, reporting directly to the Emperor and holding two **cabinet** positions in all governments.

The constitution required all laws and cabinet decisions to be agreed to by all ministers. This meant that if any one minister did not agree with a law or decision, they could simply refuse to sign. This would cause the government to collapse and new ministers to be appointed, or a compromise would have to be reached to accommodate demands of opposing ministers. This increased the power of the military in that they could essentially veto any government decision and could threaten to dissolve a government unless their demands were met.

The Diet

The constitution also created a parliament, called the Diet. This was composed of two divisions: an elected House of Representatives and an appointed House of Peers. The House of Peers was composed of nobility, high taxpayers, famous individuals and special appointments made by the Emperor. The House of Representatives was elected by those with **suffrage** which would eventually include all men over 25 years old. The House of Representatives could create and pass laws which then had to be approved by the House of Peers. If approved, these laws went forward to the cabinet of ministers for consideration. If the cabinet approved, the law went forward to the Emperor and the Privy Council for consideration and possible approval.

🔑 KEY TERM

Meiji Emperor Emperor of Japan between 1867 and 1912 in whose name modernizing reforms were instituted.

Feudalism Form of government in which nobility and their associates, such as warriors, hold substantial governing power.

Privy Council Small government body of elites whose approval was required for laws, major political appointees and more; they controlled access to the Emperor of Japan and were heavily relied on by the Emperor owing to their prestige and experience.

Cabinet Ministers of a government.

Suffrage The right to vote.

Education and loyalty to the state

How did the education system promote nationalism and loyalty to the state?

Modernized Japan required all citizens to attend school for four years; in 1903 this was expanded to six years. The stated purpose of compulsory education was to teach practical skills and the ability to problem-solve, although what it did achieve was increased literacy throughout the country. This led to people reading books, newspapers and journals, including those that criticized the state. Literacy was directly connected to increased awareness of government and its policies, and people's growing opposition to many of these.

Read Source B. What is the 'fundamental character' of the Japanese Empire?

SOURCE B

Excerpt from *The Imperial Rescript on Education* by the Roy Rosenzweig Center for History and New Media, located at *Children and Youth in History*, https://chnm.gmu.edu/cyh/primary-sources/136.

Know ye [you], Our subjects:

Our Imperial Ancestors have founded Our [the Meiji Emperor's] Empire on a basis broad and everlasting, and have deeply and firmly implanted virtue; Our subjects ever united in loyalty and filial piety [respect for elders and those in authority] have from generation to generation illustrated the beauty thereof. This is the glory of the fundamental character of Our Empire, and herein also lies the source of Our education. Ye, Our subjects, be filial to your parents, affectionate to your brothers and sisters; as husbands and wives be harmonious, as friends true; bear yourselves in modesty and moderation; extend your benevolence to all; pursue learning and cultivate arts, and thereby develop intellectual faculties and perfect moral powers; furthermore, advance public good and promote common interests; always respect the Constitution and observe the laws; should emergency arise, offer yourselves courageously to the State; and thus guard and maintain the prosperity of Our Imperial state; and thus guard and maintain the prosperity of Our Imperial Throne coeval with heaven and earth [for as long as heaven and earth exist]. So shall ye not only be Our good and faithful subjects, but render illustrious the best traditions of your forefathers.

The way here set forth is indeed the teaching bequeathed by Our Imperial Ancestors, to be observed alike by Their Descendants and the subjects, infallible for all ages and true in all places. It is Our wish to lay it to heart in all reverence, in common with you, Our subjects, that we may all attain to the same virtue.

October 30, 1890

The Ministry of Education eventually altered the national curriculum, which now emphasized loyalty to the state, family and community. Students were instructed to value Japan's special institution, the Emperor, his divinity and other aspects of Japan's history and culture. The emphasis on Japan's uniqueness was a huge factor in the development of ultranationalism, also called **radical nationalism**, which is closely related to **fascism**.

Offering oneself to the service of the state and protection of the Emperor was also encouraged. Teachers in training had to learn military drills as part of their teaching skills and, by the 1920s, students throughout the country

 **KEY TERM**

Radical nationalism An extreme form of nationalism which can include racism and other forms of discrimination and prejudice against those not part of the nation, which is usually narrowly defined; this belief often justifies violence to achieve certain goals.

Fascism A term derived from the Fascist Party of Italy. It refers to a governing philosophy that glorifies the state, war and sacrificing oneself for the state while de-emphasizing individual rights and freedoms. This term is often used to refer to non-democratic, militaristic governments.

were also required to participate in these. The special connection between the education system and the military would later greatly aid in the military's popularity and eventual control of the political system.

The rise of radical nationalism

Japan had a unique history and, alone among east Asian states, was never annexed to any European or American empire. These factors helped greatly in the creation and propagation of ultranationalism.

← **What factors may have contributed to the rise of radical nationalism?**

A special mission

Many politicians and philosophers believed that Japan was unique among world states and, as such, had a special mission. Some of the things that these individuals believed made Japan unique included:

- It had an Emperor who was divine and descended from the Sun Goddess.
- It had not been conquered by European powers or the USA.
- It had an ancient history of being independent.
- The vast majority of its people were Japanese and shared a common culture and history.
- It was the only non-European state to defeat a European state in modern war (see page 19).
- It was a major military and industrial power by 1920 and one of the most important states at the Paris Peace Conference in 1919, which dealt with the results of the First World War.

SOURCE C

Excerpt from *Fifty Years of Light and Dark: The Hirohito Era* by the staff of the *Mainichi Daily News*, The Mainichi Newspapers, Tokyo, Japan, 1975, p. 11. *Mainichi Shimbun*, or *Daily News*, has been published since 1872 and is one of the largest media companies in contemporary Japan.

Hirohito was now the 'God Emperor' of the almost 2,600-year-old nation, being the 124th in line from the Heaven-descended ancestor called [Emperor] Jimmu. Although scholars found the early part of the Imperial lineage dubious, not a single one of the 'beloved subjects' was expected to question the 'established' godliness of the new Ruler of Japan.

According to Source C, what were Japan's people not to question? **?**

Philosophies developed that Japan not only was special compared to other countries, but should also remove all non-Asian dominance from the region. Since Japan was the only successful, independent modern state, then it was the mission of the Japanese to use these qualities to lead the rest of Asia. Nationalism developed into radical nationalism by the late 1920s. There were many elements to radical nationalism but essentially proponents opposed any policies or politicians that in their view weakened the Emperor and therefore Japan. To this end, assassinations and assassination attempts were a means of terrorizing officials into following and implementing their philosophies. Radical nationalism led to outright racism towards other non-Japanese in Japan's Empire (see page 70).

According to Source D, what would free people from materialism and why?

SOURCE D

Excerpt from *Emperor Hirohito and His Chief Aide-de-Camp: The Honjō Diary, 1933–36* by Honjō Shigeru, translation and introduction by Mikiso Hane, published by University of Tokyo Press, Tokyo, Japan, 1982, p. 25. Honjō was head of the Kwantung Army of Japan from 1931 to 1932 and later served as the military's liaison with Japan's Emperor until 1936. Mikiso Hane was an internationally renowned historian on Japanese history and a professor at Knox College in the USA from 1961 to 1992.

[Ultranationalist ideologist] Ōkawa Shūmei placed the emperor system at the core of his thinking, regarding it as the source of morality and religion. He emphasized the 'way of the Japanese' and the 'Japanese spirit,' which embodies 'statism, idealism, the principle of combat and spirituality.' 'The Japanese spirit,' in Ōkawa's opinion was incompatible with 'the Anglo-American democratic spirit which is the product of individualism, utilitarianism, hedonism, and materialism.' A second Restoration was needed, Ōkawa asserted, to free the people from the oppression of materialism and unite the people and the Emperor. The uniqueness of Japan entitled it to become the leader of Asia …

Growth of militarism

Closely connected to the philosophy that Japan had a special mission or destiny was that of militarism. In order to protect Japan, secure its colonial possession and dominate Asia, which might lead to confrontation with Britain, France or the USA, a large navy and army were required. The military had held a special place in Japanese society for centuries (see below), so the idea of a strong military was not an unusual one. The Meiji Constitution, for example, had also enshrined the special relationship between the military and the Emperor, with the military reporting directly to him (see page 11).

The military was a political force in Japan, holding cabinet positions in the government (see page 11). In this way, the army and navy were able to affect politics and ensure their growth and maintenance. In the late 1920s, as economic crises continued to weaken the civilian government, militarism became increasingly popular as it was tied to expanding the empire, which many hoped would bring economic relief and new lands to settle peasants (see pages 35 and 39).

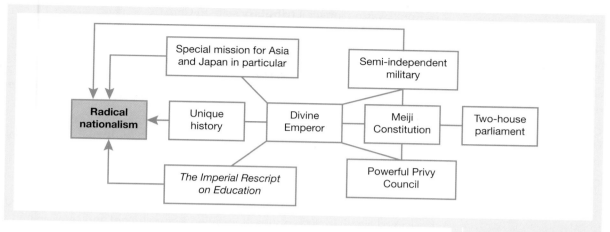

SUMMARY DIAGRAM

Japanese nationalism and militarism

Militarism and foreign policy

▶ *Key question: How successful was Japan in creating an Asian empire?*

Japan had a long history of militarism. The pre-modern government of Japan had been a military dictatorship in which real authority rested with a ***shōgun***; the Emperor was a symbol of national unity and was involved primarily in religious rites, rather than having any power. Industrialization, including the development of factories, railways, ports and international trade, strengthened Japan, allowing, and perhaps requiring, it to expand its empire to include neighbouring states and territories.

Militarism before the First World War

From the late nineteenth century, as Japan modernized and industrialized, its power to dominate and intimidate other nations grew. It acted on long-standing interests in countries such as Korea and engaged in other conflicts with Russia, China and Taiwan. The First World War was its opportunity to demonstrate its strength to the world, especially China and Germany.

Korea 1876–1905

Japan had long had economic and political interests in Korea, the closest neighbouring state. The Mongol Empire launched attacks against Japan from in the years 1274 and 1281, unsuccessfully. Japan invaded Korea in the late sixteenth century but was forced out by Korean and Chinese armies. By 1876, Japan had enough Western military technology and a new desire to export its manufactured goods that it was able to force Korea to sign the Japan–Korea Treaty (1876), also known as the Japan–Korea Treaty of Amity or the Treaty of Ganghwa Island. This document stated:

KEY TERM

Shōgun Hereditary military governors of Japan from 1192 to 1867.

What events resulted from Japan's militarism in the early twentieth century?

KEY TERM

Tributary A state which presents gifts or funds to a stronger state for protection and/or as a sign of loyalty, respect and subservience.

Coup d'état An overthrow of a state's government by individuals within that state.

Qing Dynasty of China The ethnic Manchu family of rulers of China from 1644 to 1911.

- Korea was no longer a **tributary** state to China.
- Japanese citizens could not be arrested or tried in Korean courts.
- Korea could not impose any restrictions on Japanese trade.
- Japan was allowed the use of three ports for its exports.

In 1884, supporters of Japan overthrew Korea's government briefly in a ***coup d'état***. A counter-coup was launched against this new government and supported by Chinese troops. It was clear to other states that Korea was unable to defend itself from other countries and, in 1885, Britain took control of a Korean port city. In 1894, a major peasant revolt erupted against the Korean government, partly in response to the presence of Japan in the country's affairs. When the Korean government asked China for assistance, Japan declared that Korea had violated the Japan–Korea Treaty, and occupied the capital city with 8000 troops. It installed a government and assassinated its main opposition leader, Empress Myeongseong, in 1895. Japanese interference in Korean affairs led to war with China.

First Sino-Japanese War 1894–5

A long series of events, primarily over Japan's interference in Korean affairs but also including assassinations, bans on Japanese imports in China, and other issues, caused increasing tensions between Japan and the **Qing Dynasty of China**. Japan's essential takeover of Korea in 1894 and the gain of even more rights there caused the Qing Dynasty to declare war on Japan in August 1894.

? How does the artist contrast the soldiers of Japan and China in Source E?

SOURCE E

Japanese engraving depicting a scene from the First Sino-Japanese War by Suzuki Kwasson, Tokyo, Japan, early twentieth century. Suzuki (1860–1919) was a prolific artist who depicted battle scenes from the war, along with a variety of other topics and themes.

The war progressed rapidly for Japan, which had a modernized military, complete with ironclad warships, pontoon (floating) bridges and modern rifles. By October, Chinese troops had been driven out of Korea, and Japan began the invasion of Manchuria, a huge province in northeastern China and ancestral homeland of the Qing Emperors of China. Several towns and cities were captured by Japanese troops before winter weather slowed their invasion. In November, Japanese forces captured Port Arthur, a major economic prize; by mid-February 1895, after a long siege, they seized the port of Weihaiwei; then in March, they captured islands off Taiwan.

China requested Japan's terms for peace after suffering nothing but defeat after defeat. The Treaty of Shimonoseki was signed by both countries in April 1895. This treaty:

- granted Korea full independence from China
- gave Taiwan and the Liaodong Peninsula to Japan
- required China to pay a large indemnity to Japan, approximately 13,600 tons of silver
- allowed Japanese ships to operate ships on the Yangtze River, and to have factories in four Chinese ports that would now be completely open to Japanese imports.

Immediately after the Treaty of Shimonoseki was announced, Russia, Germany and France declared that the treaty had to be altered to accommodate their desires. Although Japan clearly dominated China during the war, it was in no way prepared to deal with three of the world's great military powers. In this Tripartite Intervention, as it became known, Russia took control of the Liaodong Peninsula and Port Arthur, leasing them from China. Germany would soon take control of part of the Shantung Peninsula from the much-weakened Chinese government. Japan was humiliated and embittered, but forced to submit to the European powers' demands.

Although the Chinese government gave Taiwan to Japan, officials in Taiwan resisted. On 23 May 1895, Taiwan declared itself the Republic of Formosa, leading to a five-month war that ended with a Japanese victory in October.

Russia

Russian control of the Liaodong Peninsula and Port Arthur in 1895 had revealed that Japan needed more development if it was to protect itself and its interests from European states. Japan's industrialization continued at a rapid rate, leading to increasing exports, increasing revenues to support further military costs, and a larger, better armed military. Japan also sought allies.

SOURCE F

? According to Source F, which country controlled more of China than any other state as a result of the Tripartite Intervention?

Tripartite Intervention results, 1895.

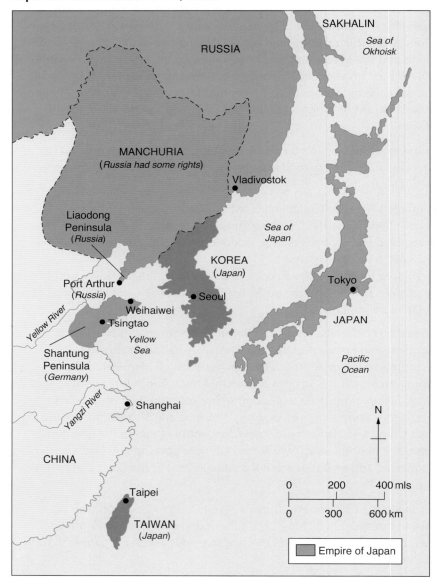

SOURCE G

? According to Source G, what was the purpose of much of Japan's foreign policy?

Excerpt from *Japanese Diplomacy in a Dilemma: New Light on Japan's China Policy, 1924–1929* by Nobuya Bamba, published by University of British Columbia Press, Vancouver, Canada, 1972, p. 35. Bamba specializes in the diplomatic and intellectual history of Japan and is a professor at Tsuda College, Tokyo, Japan.

To catch up to more advanced or superior ones and to supersede them was the individual as well as national goal. Naturally, then, they [Japan] considered the unequal treaties as great national humiliations, and to get rid of them became a major purpose of their diplomacy during the [Emperor] Meiji era. The whole of the national energy was exerted to achieve this goal. Likewise, the people in Meiji [Japan] felt the Triple [Tripartite] Intervention was a great national humiliation. The entire country became enraged. 'Gashin shōtan' (endurance and hard work for the achievement of future revenge) expressed Japan's determination to wipe out this humiliation … The Russo-Japanese War was Japan's 'revenge' against Russia. Russian ambitions toward Korea gave Japan an opportunity to act.

Anglo-Japanese Alliance 1902

Britain was also concerned with Russian expansion in Asia. Russia was rapidly industrializing, clearly expanding towards China, had gained the major port of Port Arthur, and was now building a railway to link the entire Russian Empire with its Asian possessions. Britain had dominated China economically through wars and lopsided treaties throughout the nineteenth century. It had no intention of allowing Russia to expand without a challenge. Unable to afford the expense of a large naval fleet or standing army in China, Britain formed the Anglo-Japanese Alliance of 1902 with Japan. It was the first military alliance for Japan in modern times. Essentially:

- Japan and Britain would aid each other militarily if either was at war with two or more countries.
- If either country was at war with only one other state, then the other would remain neutral.

This alliance was clearly directed at Russia, and Russia's only ally was France. France had no intention of fighting a distant war in Asia since it was more concerned with an increasingly aggressive Germany. The Alliance guaranteed Japan that it needed to deal only with Russia in the case of war, and it was determined to provoke a war and win.

Russo-Japanese War 1904–5

Tensions between Russia and Japan had increased between 1895 and 1904. Russia, leasing Port Arthur and parts of the Liaodong Peninsula from China, stationed a fleet of warships off Port Arthur in December 1897; the port was soon fortified and construction started on railways that would eventually link it to Russia through China's Manchuria. Russia began to pressure Korea to grant mining and forestry rights, further provoking Japan, which felt that Korea was in its sphere of influence.

During the **Boxer Rebellion** in China in 1899 and 1900, approximately 200,000 Russian troops were stationed in Manchuria to protect the railway from Chinese rebels and soldiers. This was also done to prevent Japan from stationing troops there and interfering with Russia's interests in the region. Once the Boxer Rebellion had been crushed, these troops were not withdrawn despite Russia's promises to do so. Both Britain and Japan felt that their interests in China and Korea were threatened by this force.

Japan initiated a series of diplomatic meetings with Russia to resolve the crisis and to clarify the sphere of influence of each state towards Korea and

 **KEY TERM**

Boxer Rebellion An anti-foreign, anti-Christian revolt in China that was eventually joined by government soldiers with support from the Qing Dynasty. The revolt was put down by foreign troops.

'Don't twist in my hands! I want to see how your skin tears on my teeth!!'
Russian postcard from just before the Russo-Japanese War depicting a
Russian Cossack [warrior] eating a Japanese soldier for breakfast, about
1904.

Завтракъ казака.

Врешь, японская натура,
Не вертись въ рукахъ!
Посмотрю какъ ваша шкура
Рвется на зубахъ!!

China; Korea and China were too weak for either power to consider their
input or protests. Eventually, Japan proposed that Manchuria would be in
the Russian sphere of influence and Korea would be in Japan's. Russia did
not respond and so in February 1904, Japan expelled Russia's ambassador
and severed all relations with Russia. Many historians believe that Russia's
government desired war with Japan due to a crippling political crisis in
Russia at the time, in which there were calls for a constitution and governing
reforms which were opposed by the Tsar (Russian Emperor).

Tsar Nicholas II's government hoped that an outpouring of nationalism at Russia's eventual victory over Japan would reinforce the Tsar's popularity and help suppress criticism of his government and its institutions.

Japan attacked the Russian navy at Port Arthur on 8 February 1904 and soon afterwards launched an invasion of Korea. By the end of April:

- A Japanese army had entered Russian-controlled Manchuria.
- The Japanese navy had defeated the Port Arthur-based Russian navy.
- Port Arthur was under siege by land and sea.

SOURCE I

Excerpt from *The Attack upon Port Arthur, 1905* by Lt. Tadayoshi Sakurai, published by the Russo-Japanese War Research Society, www.russojapanesewar.com/sakuri-1.html. Tadayoshi Sakurai was an officer in the Japanese army and participated in Japan's attack on Russian troops at Port Arthur in 1905.

Our objective points were the Northern Fortress and Wang-tai Hill. There was a fight with bombs at the enemy's skirmish-trenches. The bombs sent from our side exploded finely, and the place became at once a conflagration, boards were flung about, sand-bags burst, heads flew around, legs were torn off. The flames mingled with the smoke, lighted up our faces weirdly, with a red glare, and all at once the battle-line became confused. Then the enemy, thinking it hopeless, left the place and began to flee. 'Forward! Forward! Now is the time to go forward! Forward! Pursue! Capture it with one bound!' And, proud of our victory, we went forward courageously.

According to Source I, why were Japanese troops successful in the attack on Port Arthur?

In December, Japanese artillery destroyed most of Russia's navy that was anchored at Port Arthur. The city itself surrendered in January 1905. A Russian army hoping to relieve the siege had been forced to retreat to the city of Mukden in Manchuria, ending all hopes of saving the port city. Mukden fell to Japan in March after a massive battle involving around 500,000 soldiers, one of the largest battles of the twentieth century. Russia's European-based navy finally arrived in May 1905 after months at sea, only to be annihilated in the Battle of Tsushima Straits. Japan then occupied Sakhalin Island, on Russia's Pacific Ocean coast. A revolution erupted in Russia against its government and Russia sued for peace.

Treaty of Portsmouth 1905

Russia and Japan signed the Treaty of Portsmouth that brought the Russo-Japanese War to a close. Negotiated by the USA, the treaty:

- required both Russia and Japan to remove all troops from Manchuria and restore it to China's control
- allowed Japan to lease the Liaodong Peninsula and Port Arthur from China
- granted Japan the right to lease the Russian-built Southern Manchurian Railway from China
- granted Japan the southern half of Sakhalin Island.

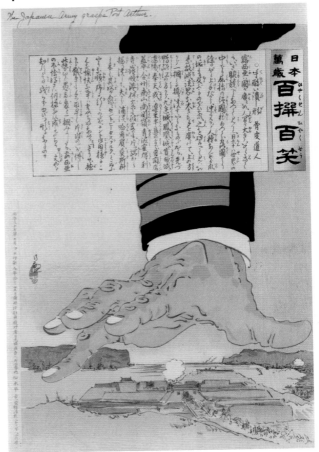

A large Japanese hand crushing Port Arthur, 25 July 1904, from a series entitled 'Long Live Japan: One Hundred Victories, One Hundred Laughs'. A Japanese poster by Kobayashi Kiyochika. Kiyochika was a famous painter and print-maker, living from 1847 to 1915.

How does Source J depict Russian weakness at Port Arthur in 1904?

Japan acquired international respect and authority as the result of the Russo-Japanese War, in addition to the treaty's benefits. The USA agreed to Japanese control over Korea in return for Japan allowing the US full dominance of the Philippines, its large Asian colony. Britain extended the Anglo-Japanese Alliance and recognized Japan's control over Korea as legitimate. The Japanese military's prestige soared and it benefited from increased government spending. Nevertheless, Japan believed that it should have received:

- an indemnity from Russia to pay for the war
- all of Sakhalin Island
- outright control of Port Arthur, the Liaodong Peninsula and parts of Manchuria, instead of having to lease them from China.

SOURCE K

Map of the results of the Treaty of Portsmouth 1905.

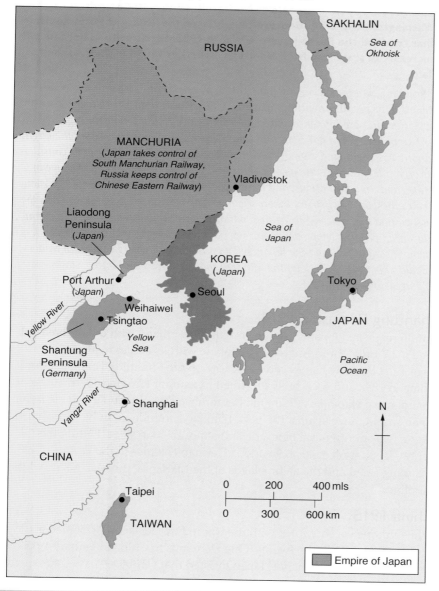

SAKHALIN

RUSSIA

Sea of Okhoisk

MANCHURIA
(Japan takes control of South Manchurian Railway, Russia keeps control of Chinese Eastern Railway)

Vladivostok

Liaodong Peninsula *(Japan)*

Sea of Japan

KOREA *(Japan)*

Port Arthur *(Japan)*

Seoul

Tokyo

Weihaiwei

Yellow River

Tsingtao

JAPAN

Shantung Peninsula *(Germany)*

Yellow Sea

Pacific Ocean

Yangzi River

Shanghai

N

CHINA

0   200   400 mls

0   300   600 km

Taipei

TAIWAN

 Empire of Japan

What were the main results of the Treaty of Portsmouth for Japan, according to Source K?

While Japan was victorious, it seemed that the **Great Powers** were determined to hinder Japanese growth whenever possible.

The First World War

The First World War erupted in 1914 and allowed Japan an opportunity to demonstrate its strength. This strength was directed at Germany and China, although China was ostensibly an ally of Japan during the war.

🔑 **KEY TERM**

Great Powers In this period, primarily European states such as Britain, France, Germany and Russia, but sometimes meant to include the USA, the Austro-Hungarian Empire and Italy.

In Source L, what was Japan's reaction to non-acceptance by European states and the USA?

Excerpt from a *Letter from US President Theodore Roosevelt to Senator Knox*, 1909, Papers of Theodore Roosevelt, Library of Congress, Washington, DC, USA. Roosevelt negotiated the Treaty of Portsmouth that resolved the Russo-Japanese War in 1905. Senator Knox became US secretary of state (minister of foreign affairs) in 1909 for US President Taft.

But with Japan the case is different. She is a most formidable military power. Her people have peculiar fighting capacity. They are very proud, very warlike, very sensitive, and are influenced by two contradictory feelings; namely, a great self-confidence, both ferocious and conceited, due to their victory over the mighty empire of Russia; and a great touchiness because they would like to be considered as on a full equality with, as one of the brotherhood of, Occidental [European states and the US] nations, and have been bitterly humiliated to find that even their allies, the English, and their friends, the Americans, won't admit them to association and citizenship, as they admit the least advanced or most decadent European peoples. Moreover, Japan's population is increasing rapidly and demands an outlet; and the Japanese laborers, small farmers, and petty traders would, if permitted, flock by the hundred thousand into the United States, Canada, and Australia.

Shantung Peninsula 1914

Britain requested Japan's assistance against Germany with the outbreak of the First World War in August 1914, in line with its earlier treaty (see page 19). Germany had leased Kiaochow on the Shantung Peninsula from China in 1898 and soon built a fortified harbour at Tsingtao. Germany kept several naval warships at Tsingtao but removed them when it was clear that Japan would move against the port. Tsingtao surrendered in November 1914 after a two-month naval blockade and a month-long siege. During this period, Japan took control of various German colonies in the Pacific, including Palau and the archipelagos of the Marianas, the Marshalls and the Carolines.

China 1915

While Europe was occupied with the war in Europe, Japan presented a document known as the Twenty-One Demands to China in January 1915. Among the various demands, Japan insisted that China:

- cease leasing territory to foreign countries other than Japan
- agree to Japanese control over the Shantung Peninsula and Manchuria
- allow Japanese 'advisors' to work with various Chinese government officials on its policies
- agree to Japan building railways connecting various ports and areas under its control
- extend Japan's lease on the South Manchurian Railway and allow Japanese citizens to purchase and lease land for economic and agricultural purposes in Manchuria and other northern regions

- allow Japanese citizens to enter and travel freely within Manchuria without any interference from China
- agree to Japan opening mines in Manchuria
- allow Japan to construct its own hospitals, schools and temples anywhere in China
- purchase any needed military equipment from Japan, from where all military training must come.

China delayed responding to the Twenty-One Demands until May 1915, when Japan threatened war unless China agreed. Japan eventually modified the document, reducing the demands to thirteen. China, in no position to resist Japan in the case of war, capitulated. Anti-Japanese and anti-government riots erupted across the country, the first of many. The USA and Britain, both allies of Japan, were now concerned about Japan's aggression towards China and worked to limit Japan's control over it at the Paris Peace Conference.

Paris Peace Conference 1919

Japan was one of the victorious powers that determined the nature of the world's peace after the First World War. Japan, like other participating states, was primarily concerned with its own interests.

During the Conference, the **League of Nations** was formed and Japan was a founding member. Members of the League agreed to the concept of collective security. This meant that a war with one member of the League was a war against all members of the League. League members agreed to settle all disputes through negotiation and arbitration.

SOURCE M

Article 16 of the Covenant of the League of Nations as found in all Paris Peace Conference treaties formulated in 1919 and 1920, located online at Yale University's Lillian Goldman Law Library's *The Avalon Project: Documents in Law, History and Diplomacy,* **http://avalon.law.yale.edu/imt/parti.asp.**

Article 16

Should any Member of the League resort to war in disregard of its covenants under Articles 12, 13 or 15, it shall ipso facto [in fact] be deemed to have committed an act of war against all other Members of the League, which hereby undertake immediately to subject it to the severance of all trade or financial relations, the prohibition of all intercourse between their nationals and the nationals of the covenant-breaking State, and the prevention of all financial, commercial or personal intercourse between the nationals of the covenant-breaking State and the nationals of any other State, whether a Member of the League or not.

When the concept of the League of Nations was presented and various ideas were debated, Japan and other non-European countries demanded a clause against racial discrimination. The Japanese knew that they were considered

KEY TERM

League of Nations
International organization that agreed to resolve international crises through diplomacy and not war that also established groups to address health issues, refugees, workers' rights and more.

According to Source M, what should occur when one League of Nations member declares war on another?

racially inferior by the leaders of many, perhaps most, states because they were not European. China agreed with Japan and also demanded this clause. In the end, other freedoms and rights were included in the document, such as that of religion, but the USA insisted that any statement mentioning racial equality could not be included. There was racial segregation and other forms of discrimination in the USA and most European empires at the time, so these powerful states were not interested in addressing this issue.

🔑 **KEY TERM**

Mandates Lands formerly held by Germany and the Ottoman Empire that were to be administered by Britain, France, Belgium, Australia, New Zealand and Japan after the First World War for the League of Nations.

Annexed Acquired by force.

Conscription Required military service by a government for a specific length of time and usually for men only.

Japan wanted to keep Shantung Peninsula and Germany's former island empire in the Pacific. A system of League of Nations **mandates** was created to govern former territories and colonies of the defeated states of the First World War. Japan was granted supervision, but not outright annexation, of the Mandate of the South Pacific, Germany's islands. The Shantung Peninsula created a problem since Japan occupied the region and China had agreed to allow Japan to control it. Now, however, China demanded its return and the USA clearly wanted it to be part of China to limit Japan's ambitions in the region. In a system of compromises, Japan was able to retain the Shantung Peninsula, but this lasted for only a few years.

Despite not being able to achieve all its demands in Paris, Japan was now clearly an important military power. In a few short years, Russia had been defeated; Korea had been **annexed**; important ports in China, plus neighbouring territories, had been leased; German forces had been defeated; and Japan now sat with the most powerful nations determining the world's future. To secure these new acquisitions and power, and to obtain more, Japan instituted **conscription** and increased the size of its navy.

What were the purposes and results of the treaties signed after the First World War by Japan?

Interwar treaties

Japan was one of the two most powerful states in the Pacific Ocean region. The other was the USA. Both countries worked diplomatically to limit each other's military strength. Japan wanted security initially, and later empire, as well as unrestricted access to US markets and products, especially oil and metals. The USA had no desire for an expensive war in Asia, but also wanted security for its main colony, the Philippines, and other territories such as Hawaii and Guam. The USA wanted unfettered access to China's markets as well. Meanwhile, Japan's government worked to not provoke the USA as any economic response would devastate its economy. Yet Japan was also involved in China, a politically unstable state, with many investments and military units to protect them.

Japan's interwar foreign policy

After the First World War there was pressure by Japan's military to maintain its strength and even expand its size. The military believed that Japan and its newly annexed lands in Taiwan, Korea and the Shantung Peninsula, plus islands that it now supervised as League of Nations mandates, should be protected from foreign states. The military also believed that more lands should be brought under Japan's control and that this would help the

SOURCE N

Map of the Japanese Empire in 1919.

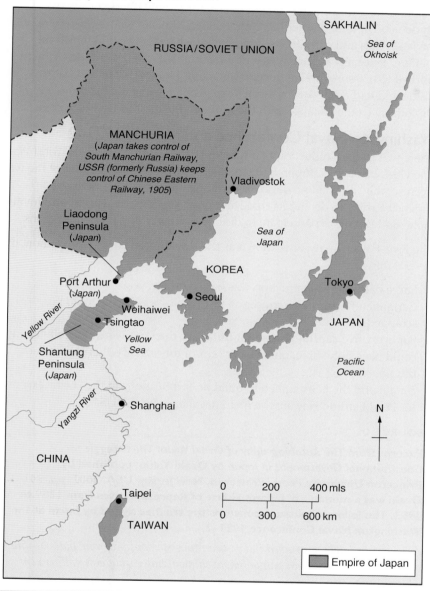

What was Japan's largest colonial acquisition by 1919, according to Source N?

economy of the country. In some way, the army and navy had to be appeased because they were members of the cabinet and could bring down a government at will.

Civilian ministers understood that large militaries were expensive and Japan was economically vulnerable. While many were not opposed to expanding the empire, they were cautious about provoking the USA, Britain and other states, especially over China, which was politically unstable and therefore militarily vulnerable (see page 41). Any economic retaliation by the USA or a European state would severely affect Japan's economy, which relied on exports. The government's foreign policy, commonly referred to as the Shidehara Diplomacy after Japanese Foreign Minister Kijūrō Shidehara of the late 1920s and early 1930s, consisted of a balancing act in which the military, especially the army, was well maintained and Japan's government worked to reassure foreign governments that Japan was not a threat to China and had no desire for further expansion against it. Shidehara Diplomacy would collapse with the Mukden Incident in 1931 (see page 55).

Washington Naval Conference and treaties 1921–2

There was a sharp reduction of armaments at the end of the First World War. The USA, Japan and Britain had large fleets of warships as a result of the war. Even so, the USA had no desire to continue building or maintaining expensive ships to defend its trade and possessions in the Pacific, and invited Japan and Britain to participate in discussions regarding naval limitations.

The Five-Power Treaty, also known as the Washington Naval Convention, did several things:

KEY TERM

Capital ships Large ships such as battleships and heavy cruisers.

- Large battleship construction was halted for ten years.
- Certain battleships and cruisers, a fast type of warship, were to be scrapped.
- For every five **capital ships** that Britain or the USA were allowed, Japan could have only three, only 60 per cent of the size of either the USA or Britain.
- Britain and the USA agreed to build no fortifications in the Pacific except for Pearl Harbor, Hawaii: the main naval base for the USA.

SOURCE O

According to Source O, why should Japan's citizens be pleased with the results of the Washington Naval Conference?

Excerpt from *The Autobiography of Ozaki Yukio: The Struggle for Constitutional Government in Japan* by Ozaki Yukio, published by Princeton University Press, Princeton, New Jersey, USA, 2001, pp. 341–2. Ozaki was a member of Japan's House of Representatives from 1889 to 1953. The following passage concerns the treaties signed by Japan at the Washington Naval Conference 1921–2.

Accordingly, Japan suspended the … fleet [construction] program and was thus able to save the nation an annual naval shipbuilding cost of 500 million yen …

The most ironic part of it all was that both the government and the people, rather than rejoicing that the naval agreement had enabled us to save an annual national expenditure of 500 million yen, shouted 'national crisis!' and 'national shame!' because we were limited to a ratio of three against the British and United States shares of five. They called me by such abusive names as 'traitor' and 'hireling of America.' …

… With the country crying 'national crisis!' I published a booklet titled 'Good Fortune has Befallen our Nation,' in which I explained that arms limitation was the way to save Japan – that far from being a national crisis this was a most felicitous turn of events.

The Four-Power Treaty and Nine-Power Treaty (both 1922) were signed in Washington, DC as well. The Four-Power Treaty ended the Anglo-Japanese Alliance and required Japan, the USA, Britain and France to respect each other's territories. The Nine-Power Treaty required Japan to remove its military from the Shantung Peninsula and called on all nations to respect China's independence and borders.

Japan's military believed that a fleet 60 per cent of the size of the US navy was inadequate for defence. However, the government was mostly relieved at the decisions made in Washington. Japan's economy could not support the building and maintenance of a huge military in the post-First World War economic crisis (see page 33). Japan's government also believed that its foreign policy would be more successful if it was conciliatory and worked through negotiations and compromise during this period (see page 43). It was not in Japan's interest, the government believed, to antagonize its main trading partners.

London Naval Conference 1930

Britain, the USA, Japan and other countries met in London in 1930 to review their earlier naval agreements. All three countries were beginning to feel great financial stress as a result of the **Great Depression** (see page 34) and none desired a renewed, expensive arms race in the form of ships. Japan's navy, however, was now headed by a more aggressive faction than had existed earlier. The navy's leadership insisted that Japan be allowed to have a fleet that was 70 per cent of the tonnage of either the US or British fleet. In a compromise, Japan achieved a 69.75 per cent ratio on battleships, but cruisers remained at 60 per cent. While the government of Japan supported this, the navy objected and threatened to bring down the government. The *genrō* Siaonji (see box) ordered the Privy Council (see page 11) to remove the objecting ministers and to approve the treaty; this was done. In response to the signing of the London Naval Treaty of 1930, Japan's prime minister was shot by an ultranationalist assassin. He initially survived, but died from his wounds several months later.

> *Genrō* is generally translated as 'elder statesman.' These men were initially those that created the Meiji Constitution (see page 11). As they aged, they appointed others. Siaonji was the last powerful *genrō*. It was Siaonji who appointed prime ministers in the name of the Emperor and generally supervised the state on the Emperor's behalf. The *genrō* had direct access to the Emperor and it was assumed by all that they spoke for the Emperor and with his authority. This meant that they were extremely powerful and provided a means to control the state according to their ideas. As Siaonji aged, his participation in government declined and the military was able to assume increasing control over the state until 1936, when most governmental policy was determined according to the military and its needs.

 **KEY TERM**

Great Depression
A worldwide economic depression that led to massive unemployment, political instability, hunger and poverty, among other issues, starting from late 1929 and ending by the early 1940s, depending on the country or region.

To what extent did Japan's budget increase spending on military affairs after 1936?

Military expansion

Japan's army and navy were severely reduced during the 1920s, mainly because Japan suffered a series of economic crises (see page 33) throughout this time. By the end of the 1920s, various factions within the military and in civilian political parties were calling for increased military spending for both defence and offence. Japan wanted to defend its interests in Manchuria, yet also wanted to expand to resolve some of its own domestic issues such as lack of resources and food supply. This expansion would come at the expense of the vast, but weak, neighbouring state of China.

Increased spending

Japan's capital shipbuilding, including battleships, various types of cruisers and aircraft carriers, was limited by the 1922 and 1930 naval treaties (see pages 28 and 29). The army, however, had no limitations in terms of international obligations. The only hindrance to increasing the military was from within Japan's government. The House of Representatives and various ministers believed that a massive military was an expense that Japan could not afford in light of its financial crises in the 1920s.

With the growth of military power in Japan's government (see page 40), army expenditure and expansion increased. Increased spending on the military in the early 1930s was one way the government stimulated economic recovery from the Great Depression (see page 36). Shipbuilding, steel and rubber, as well as other military-related industries, massively increased production.

SUMMARY DIAGRAM

Militarism and foreign policy

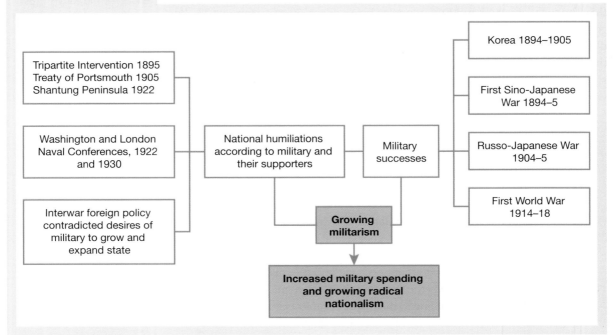

Economic and political issues

▶ **Key question:** *How did Japan's economic and political issues affect Japan's government?*

Economics were a driving force in Japan's domestic and foreign policies. The economy seemed to go through rapid cycles of growth and contraction. When the economy expanded, landless peasants, often women, moved to the cities for factory work and wages. When the economy was less successful, there was mass unemployment and further rural poverty. Failure to stabilize the system meant that **monopolies** expanded to control more of the economy. It also encouraged political groups to try to change the political system.

Industrialization and foreign policy

With the end of the feudal system and the creation of a modern form of government, there was a concerted, intentional effort to industrialize. This would mean not only wealth for many, but also security for the nation, especially protection from the empire-building Europe and the USA. Countries that could build their own industries and export to other nations to pay for needed imports were more independent than countries that could not. This weakness was very clear in nearby China, where the government was unable to prevent foreign powers dominating it, seeking its raw materials and markets for their mass-produced goods created in modern factories.

SOURCE P

Excerpt from *A Modern History of Japan: From Tokugawa Times to the Present* by Andrew Gordon, 2014, published by Oxford University Press, Oxford, UK, pp. 95–6. Gordon is a professor of modern Japanese history at Harvard University, USA.

Industrialization was led by the textile industry. From the 1890s through 1913, output of silk quadrupled. By the eve of World War I, three-fourths of these threads were produced by machine, whereas earlier most silk had been reeled by hand. In addition, about three-fourths of silk output was being exported each year. Production of cotton thread increased at similar rates … about half of the cotton output came to be exported, mainly to China and Korea.

Japan's economy from the late nineteenth century through to the end of the First World War was remarkable. Japan's industrial output increased by 250 per cent between 1895 and 1915 while processing of minerals increased by as much as 700 per cent at the end of the nineteenth century. By 1900, the Ashio coppermine and its refinery were among the top producers of copper in the world. Railways covered 5400 km (3400 miles) by 1900, vastly reducing the costs of goods since transportation was faster and cheaper by rail.

 **KEY TERM**

Monopolies Companies that control entire sections of the economy, such as steel production or shipbuilding.

To what extent did economics drive Japan's foreign policy?

What was the importance of China and Korea for Japan's economy, according to Source P? **?**

Coalmines fuelled the factories and Japan's merchant fleet delivered products to ports throughout the Pacific.

Zaibatsu

Monopolies, called *zaibatsu*, began to form in the nineteenth century and rapidly expanded in the twentieth century. These were enormous corporations owned by individual families that had an impressive economic reach. The *zaibatsu* Mitsui, for example, was involved with banking, mining, paper, textiles and more. The financial strength of the *zaibatsu* meant that large-scale industries could be established relatively quickly and integrated into the economy; they had the capital to invest, and the experts and engineers to design and create industries and ships and markets for distribution. By 1918, the eight largest *zaibatsu* controlled twenty per cent of all manufacturing, mining and trade in Japan.

Zaibatsu increased in size and power as the country suffered economic crises in the late 1920s (see page 34), absorbing smaller companies and banks that were unable to survive. *Zaibatsu* also worked to control the Diet, making sure that economic policies that favoured them were maintained (see Source Q).

?

According to Source Q, to what extent did the *zaibatsu* work to control Japan's Diet?

SOURCE Q

Excerpt from *Dilemmas of Growth in Pre-war Japan* edited by James William Morley, published by Princeton University Press, Princeton, New Jersey, USA, 1971, p. 281. Morley is professor emeritus of political science at Columbia University, New York City, USA.

Some thirty-seven lower house members, eight percent of the membership, held positions with zaibatsu concerns. Another eighteen members had close relatives who were employees of zaibatsu concerns. Thus twelve percent of the lower house was connected with zaibatsu concerns either directly or through relatives … In the House of Peers, eighty-three members, twenty-two percent of the membership, currently held positions with zaibatsu concerns while another twenty-four members had close relations so employed. Thus twenty-eight percent of the upper house was connected with zaibatsu concerns either directly or through relatives.

… The zaibatsu with the most Diet members on its payroll was Mitsubishi … [with] a grand total of sixty-six Diet members. After Mitsubishi came Mitsui, which employed … a grand total of forty-eight.

Eventually, allying with other military factions for survival and business, the *zaibatsu* came to be directly connected to Japan's militarism (see page 40).

Social stresses and employment

Industrialization severely affected the vast majority of people. Impoverished, usually landless, rural families sent their children to cities to work in factories, as clerks, shipbuilders and other salaried jobs. This income allowed many to support their rural families, buy more clothing and other manufactures and increase their food intake. This stimulated the economy to produce further goods and jobs.

The First World War led to higher wages, due to demand for Japanese goods in markets formerly dominated by the USA and European countries, that had suddenly shifted to producing war goods such as weapons. Cotton textile exports, for example, rose by 185 per cent between 1914 and 1918. This led to a shortage of workers and therefore higher wages to attract and keep them. More rural poor relocated to the cities for these factory jobs. In 1920, however, the economy severely shrank as demand for Japanese exports diminished; the USA and other countries resumed full production after the First World War. This meant that millions were suddenly unemployed, reducing their spending power and unable to send money to their rural relatives. Those who owned farmland responded to the lack of demand for farm goods by reducing farm labour. Since the majority of farmers owned no land or only tiny plots, they were negatively affected by every economic downturn.

SOURCE R

Excerpt from *Japanese Diplomacy in a Dilemma: New Light on Japan's China Policy, 1924–1929* by Nobuya Bamba, published by University of British Columbia Press, Vancouver, Canada, 1972, pp. 61–2. Bamba specializes in diplomatic and intellectual history of Japan and is a professor at Tsuda College, Tokyo, Japan.

The effects of the depression were observed in villages as well as in cities. This period is often called the period of 'agrarian panic.' Peasants suffered from the steady decline of farm prices. The price of rice, for example, taking the average for three years from 1911 to 1913 as 100, was 114 in 1925, but dropped to 98 in the next year and to 87 in 1928. The general index of farm prices declined from 118 in 1925 to 93 in 1928. In terms of actual income, the average price of one sack of rice cost only about 6–7 yen in 1928. This meant that about 40 percent of the agrarian population earned less than 60 yen from the rice crop after having paid rent to the landlord. This was worse than even the lowest income group of urban workers.

Read Source R. What was the effect of economic decline in Japan on agricultural workers?

An earthquake and fire destroyed most of Tokyo, Japan's capital, in 1923. The government encouraged banks to lend money at low interest for the rebuilding of Tokyo and other cities. There were suddenly more jobs in construction and factories. With more income, workers spent more on food, clothing and luxuries.

This relative prosperity collapsed again in 1927 with bank failures that resulted from the earlier low-interest loans of 1923. Many who had borrowed to rebuild could not afford to pay the banks. Banks that did not collapse mostly stopped loaning money, even to businesses that required temporary loans for business operations. The economy rapidly contracted, leading to huge numbers of unemployed workers and impoverished farmer labourers. Skilled workers such as mechanics, electricians and carpenters suffered approximately 7.5 per cent unemployment, while over 40 per cent of unskilled workers were also unemployed. Japan's government was unable to address this economic crisis successfully. Then, in late 1929, the Great Depression occurred.

The Great Depression

The Great Depression was a major economic downturn for much of the world. It started in 1929 in the USA and soon spread to other countries. Many countries raised **trade barriers** so that their factories would not compete with those of other states. This meant that Japan, a country that relied on exports, was practically shut off from the USA, its greatest trading partner.

What was the most significant political result of the Great Depression for Japan?

 How did the Great Depression affect silk prices according to Source S?

KEY TERM

Trade barriers Means of restricting trade with other countries, usually by placing high taxes on foreign imports so that domestic goods can be sold more cheaply.

Gross national product (GNP) The value of all goods and services produced by the citizens of a state over one year.

SOURCE S

Excerpt from *A Time of Crisis: Japan, the Great Depression and Rural Revitalization* by Kerry Smith, published by Harvard University Asia Center, Harvard University Press, Cambridge, USA, 2001, pp. 51–2. Smith is an associate professor of history at Brown University in the USA.

The textile industry was hit especially hard, and its experience offers one of the clearest indications of the global market's effects on the domestic economy and on the countryside in particular. Japanese silk that had sold in New York for $5.25 a pound in September 1929 went for $2.50 thirteen months later. Producers kept on making the thread, and exporters kept on selling it abroad, but they made far less money doing so than they had before the start of the America's depression. The dollar value of silk thread exports to the United States fell by almost a third between 1929 and 1931 and by 1934 was less than 25 percent of what it had been five years before. Domestic prices for silk cocoons followed suit, with obviously consequences for the many Japanese farm households that relied on sericulture [silk production] for some or all of their income.

Japan's **gross national product (GNP)** declined by approximately twenty per cent between 1929 and 1931 and stocks on the Tokyo Stock Market lost half their value. Fifty per cent of small- and medium-sized businesses closed permanently. Exports fell by over 40 per cent and unemployment increased dramatically. With fewer consumers of agricultural products, agriculture prices declined by 45 per cent between 1929 and 1931, leaving farmers, most of whom did not own land, in worse conditions than ever before. Landless farmers could not afford manufactured goods and therefore factories remained closed or at severely reduced rates of production.

Unemployment and hunger led to political unrest. There were strikes, riots and a surge in popularity of communist (see page 38) and other groups that demanded a restructuring of government and society. The government crushed many strikes, arresting tens of thousands, but negotiated compromises between striking or terminated workers and factory owners in others. It was clear to most that the governing system simply did not function for the majority of Japanese people: workers and landless farmers. It did, however, function for the *zaibatsu* (see page 32). As banks and other industries collapsed, their share of the economy increased, as it had during earlier crises.

SOURCE T

Japanese farmers' annual income in yen. From *Democratization and Expansionism: Historical Lessons, Contemporary Challenges*, Masayo Ohara, published by Praeger, Westport, Connecticut, USA, 2001, p. 117. The author is an assistant professor in the Department of International Studies at Tokyo Jogakkhan College, Japan.

Year	Owned land	Rented land
1926	1598	987
1927	1421	987
1928	1394	923
1929	1366	874
1930	837	579
1931	641	449
1932	703	538
1933	838	617
1934	837	612
1935	954	683

Analyse Source T. How much did farm incomes decline between 1926 and 1931 for both those farmers who owned land and those who rented?

SOURCE U

Excerpt from *Fifty Years of Light and Dark: The Hirohito Era* by the staff of the *Mainichi Daily News*, The Mainichi Newspapers, Tokyo, Japan, 1975, p. 25. *Mainichi Shimbun*, or *Daily News*, has been published since 1872 and is one of the largest media companies in contemporary Japan.

[During the start of the Great Depression], the number of banks shrank from 1,300 to some 700. Big banks, including Mitsui, Mitsubishi, Sumitomo, Daiichi and Yasuda, strengthened their oligopolistic hold on Japan's economy. The formidable Zaibatsu were steadily solidifying their financial grip on the nation's economic world.

Suffering under persistent depression, the public found its target of patriotic resentment in the large-scale 'buy dollar' policy pursued by Zaibatsu, especially Mitsui, in the second half of 1931. The powerful industrial-financial concern, anticipating the impending ban on gold export, went ahead to buy US dollars on a grand scale ... But patriots and patriotically-inclined press called the Zaibatsu managers 'traitors of the nation' who had handed out national currencies en masse 'in exchange for white men's money.' The government collapsed in the face of public outbursts ...

According to Source U, why were *zaibatsu* labelled as traitors by some?

Japan struggled to create a national policy to deal with the economic crisis. There were efforts to reduce the debt of farmers and to spend government funds in building infrastructure, so that workers would have salaries to spend. There were even plans to send landless peasants and unemployed workers in the cities to Manchuria. This last idea was not accomplished in any magnitude until after 1936. Meanwhile, the government worked to reduce spending to alleviate the tax burden on its citizens and to prevent having to import products and raw materials that it simply could not afford. This policy would change in 1936 with the assassination of the finance minister responsible for this policy, in the 26 February Incident (see page 40); he was replaced by a military appointee. Military needs came to dominate the government.

The military-controlled government adopted a twelve-year plan in 1936 to modernize and expand the armed forces. Spending would continue to increase dramatically with the expansion of the military and further war (see page 72). Military production put new stresses on Japan as the state had few natural resources and exported fewer consumer products to pay for imported materials. Eventually, there were labour shortages. Part of the solution to this was to acquire more territory to supply the war economy. Acquiring more territory led directly to more war.

SOURCE V

Military spending in billions of yen 1929–40. Information from the *Dilemmas of Growth in Pre-war Japan* edited by James William Morley, published by Princeton University Press, Princeton, New Jersey, 1971, p. 250. Morley is professor emeritus of political science at Columbia University, New York, USA.

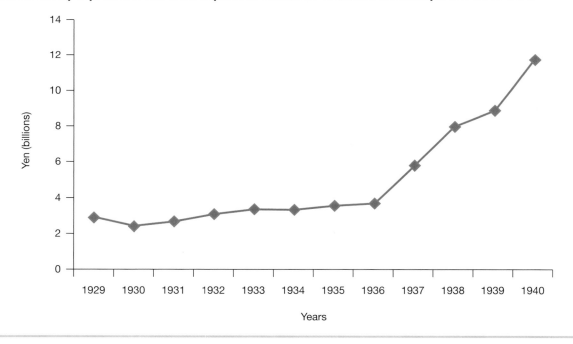

How much more was spent on Japan's military in 1940 than in 1930, according to Source V?

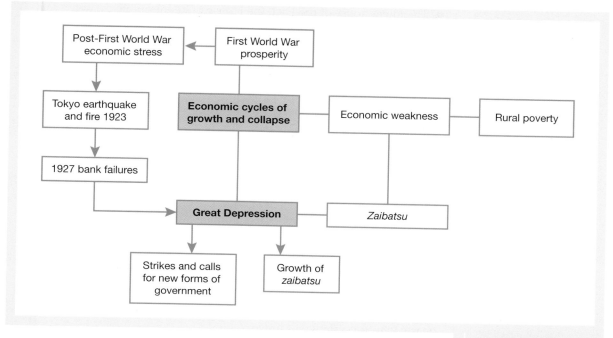

SUMMARY DIAGRAM

Economic and political issues

 # Domestic instability and foreign affairs

▶ *Key question: How did instability contribute to Japan's domestic and foreign policy?*

Economic crises led to instability. The old governing system established by the Meiji Constitution had simply not led to stable economic conditions for the majority of Japan's people. Additionally, the government was unable to create policies to address the Great Depression. China's instability and Japanese interests in Manchuria and other areas meant that there was also a struggle over foreign policy, which was tightly connected to Japan's domestic affairs.

Instability: domestic

Japan's governing system was extremely complex. Some of those complexities included:

- Military authorities had direct access to the Emperor.
- The cabinet worked for the Emperor and could not be removed by the Diet.
- All ministers had to agree to a particular policy or the policy could not be enacted.

> **How did the organization of the Japanese government benefit the military?**

- The lower house of the Diet, the House of Representatives, was responsible for taxation and budgets and could block funding if it disagreed with policies.
- The House of Peers in the Diet often worked against the cabinet and House of Representatives since many of its members were former cabinet members that disagreed on policies.
- The Privy Council and its *genrō* (see page 29) had direct access to and communicated for the Emperor; they had veto power over all government issues.

There were also a great number and variety of political parties, ideologies and even divisions within the army and navy. Much of this struggle centred on social, economic and military policy. The one constant in the entire system was the Emperor, who had ultimate authority, often exercised through the *genrō*.

The diverse and complex government managed to survive throughout the 1920s. This was accomplished through compromise between political factions, suppressing dissent through laws and prison terms, and occasional economic growth. The Great Depression was the crisis that demonstrated clearly that the system was unworkable.

Communism

Communism appealed to the millions of unemployed urban workers, although actual Communist Party membership was very small. Communist, or Marxist, political philosophy advocated the overthrow of all social and economic classes, a complete reordering of society and an end to capitalism. Under communism, all people should be completely equal, have the same rights and receive the same of everything; all property should be owned collectively by all the people. Under the Peace Protection Law of 1925, but amended in 1928 to allow for execution, the government could arrest anyone who wanted to change the governmental system. This clearly meant communists and related **socialists**; over 1000 Japanese advocates of communism or socialism were arrested in 1928.

KEY TERM

Socialists People who believe that society should be as equal as possible financially and in terms of political rights.

? According to Source W, how did government authorities react to the increasing popularity of left-wing political groups?

SOURCE W

Excerpt from *Shōwa: An Inside History of Hirohito's Japan* by Tessa Morris-Suzuki, published by Schocken Books, New York, USA, 1985, p. 166. Morris-Suzuki is a professor in culture, history and language at Australian National University, coordinator of the journal *Asia Rights* and past president of the Asian Studies Association of Australia.

When the first election under the new system of [universal] manhood suffrage was held in 1928, four left-wing [socialist or communist related] parties, one of them closely linked to the Japanese Communist Party, put up candidates. Between them, they won eight seats [in the Diet]: a result which was sufficient to alarm the authorities into redoubling their efforts at suppression. Within a month of the election, over one thousand left-wing sympathizers had been arrested under the Peace Preservation Laws.

From Russian Empire to Soviet Union

The Russian Empire collapsed in stages, starting in February 1917 as a result of political, economic and social stresses from the First World War. The army removed the Tsar in February and established a temporary government to solve the country's problems while it continued fighting the war. This military-supported government was overthrown in October 1917 by a group of communists known as the Bolsheviks, and soon the country was in civil war. By 1921, the communists had won; the Union of Soviet Socialist Republics, or Soviet Union, had formed out of the former Russian Empire; and at least 8 million people had died.

In the world's first communist country, private ownership (of land, businesses and housing, for example) was banned. The state theoretically controlled all assets for the good of all. Millions of former landowners, educated professionals, such as doctors, teachers, lawyers and engineers, government workers and more were imprisoned, exiled or executed. Many countries were alarmed as communist rebellions briefly erupted in Germany and Hungary at the end of the First World War. The Soviet Union encouraged the spread of communism through groups in Europe and Asia. Communism required a complete overthrow of existing governing structures and economic systems, and the destruction of religion. This caused world governments such as Japan's to see the Soviet Union as a major military threat.

Perhaps more importantly, the Soviet Union was the world's only communist state. It bordered Korea (which had been annexed to Japan in 1905; see page 22) as well as the arguably more important Manchuria, where Japan had many interests. Suppression of communism in Japan was part of a larger policy to oppose the Soviet Union.

The Shōwa Restoration

Some conservative members of society wanted to give the **Shōwa Emperor** full power. They called for him to rule directly without a parliament, ministers, a Privy Council or even the *zaibatsu*. Without their influence on policies, they would therefore lose control. This response to the economic and governing crisis was popular with rural farmers, who suffered greatly in times of economic crisis. They believed that the Emperor could and should remove corruption, *zaibatsu*, and anything else that kept the people from being prosperous and safe. With many on the verge of starvation and without the possibility of moving to cities for work, since there were no jobs available, many joined the growing military. Once in the military, they were a powerful, conservative force and were able to support young, ultranationalist officers who held similar views.

Military factions

The military was internally divided. One group was called Tōseiha, or the Control Faction, and they wanted to reform Japan's government rather than destroy it. These reforms would ally the army with the *zaibatsu* and

 **KEY TERM**

Shōwa Emperor Grandson of the Meiji Emperor and often called by his personal name, Hirohito, outside Japan. He was preceded by the short reign of his mentally ill father, the Taishō Emperor.

government officials, suppress political parties, have the government tightly control the economy, and prepare the nation for eventual total war with China and possibly other states.

More radical factions, including Sakurakai (the Cherry Blossom Society) and Kōdōha (the Imperial Way Faction), wanted complete destruction of all political parties, as well as the *zaibatsu* and the government generally, in line with the idea of a Shōwa Restoration. They wanted direct rule from the Emperor, which would destroy what they viewed as a corrupt and incompetent governing system. They also wanted war with the Soviet Union and elimination of socialist and communist groups. Communism was a huge threat in their view as it advocated an end to the institution of Emperor, religion and other aspects of Japanese society and culture. These radical factions attempted a series of *coups d'état*:

- 1931: *March Incident* by Sakurakai; failed when the minister of war failed to support the Sakurakai soldiers.
- 1931: *October Incident* by Sakurakai; failed when the plot was discovered and the leaders were arrested.
- 1932: *League of Blood Incident* by radical nationalist civilians and young naval officers; assassinated the leader of Mitsui *zaibatsu* and a former finance minister.
- 1932: *15 May Incident* by League of Blood members and sympathizers; assassinated Prime Minister Inukai; attempted to kill other important officials.
- 1935, August: *Aizawa Incident* of August 1935; anti-Kōdōha General Nagata.
- 1936: *26 February Incident* by Kōdōha and other young officers; attempted to take control of the Emperor and have him abolish Japan's government; several high-ranking officials were killed; collapsed when the Emperor refused to support them.

As a result of turmoil within the army, the government increasingly turned to other army and naval officers. By turning to Tōseiha, the more radical elements could be opposed. The Tōseiha faction – now supported by the Emperor, the Privy Council, the cabinet, the Diet and the *zaibatsu*, mainly out of fear of other, more radical army factions – essentially took control of the government. This meant reorganization of the economy, suppression of political parties and dissent, expansion of military spending (see page 36) and war.

The government also worked to avoid any conflict with the Soviet Union. An indication of the strengthening of the military's political position is clear in the appointment of prime ministers from the army and navy. Between 1932 and December 1941, Japan had nine different men serve as prime ministers. Six of these were admirals or generals from the armed forces.

SOURCE X

Excerpt from *Emperor Hirohito and His Chief Aide-de-Camp: The Honjō Diary, 1933–36* by Honjō Shigeru, translated by Mikiso Hane, published by University of Tokyo Press, Tokyo, Japan, 1982, p. 173. Honjō was head of the Kwantung Army of Japan from 1931 to 1932 and later served as the military's liaison with Japan's Emperor until 1936. Mikiso Hane was an internationally renowned historian on Japanese history and was a professor at Knox College in the USA from 1961 to 1992.

March 2 [1936]: His Majesty [Emperor Hirohito] summoned me after 11:00 a.m. and said, 'Soon [genrō] Saionji will come to the capital, and a new cabinet must be chosen. It seems that the army's conditions concerning cabinet members continue to be rigid. It appears to be aggressive about policy matters too. Unless the military's wishes are taken into consideration, another incident like the recent [26 February] affair might break out again. For this reason, I would like to take the army's desires into careful consideration, but excessively radical changes would conflict with the state of the society as a whole. We must act with extreme caution. I, too, am pulled in two directions about this. The military may justifiably demand a strong national defense program, but it steps out of bounds when it moves into the area of national economy and calls for the distribution of wealth. When you confer with the high-ranking army officers you should keep this in mind.'

According to Source X, how did Emperor Hirohito attempt to limit military demands?

SOURCE Y

Excerpt from *The Age of Hirohito: In Search of Modern Japan* by Daikichi Irokawa, published by The Free Press, New York, 1995, pp. 8–9. The author is a professor at Tokyo Keizai University and has published books on Japanese history and culture in the nineteenth and twentieth centuries.

Because of such conditions at the lower levels of society, the military could take advantage of the unemployed, impoverished youth and the spiritually exhausted Japanese people to wage its aggressive adventures on the Asian continent. The move to expand the empire also appealed to the struggling financial community, which hoped new markets on the continent would end the Depression, and to an ambitious group of politicians who aspired to a stronger power base.

According to Source Y, why was the move by the military to expand Japan's Empire popular with the poor?

Instability: foreign affairs

Although there was supposedly a national government in China, the reality was that regional warlords ran practically independent states within China's boundaries. This, of course, prevented a single national policy when a foreign power threatened.

How did China's internal problems affect Japan's foreign affairs?

The Warlord Era

Between 1916 and 1928, China was in a state of civil war, as it was loosely divided into regions controlled by warlords. In southern China, there were seven major warlord groups, plus the Chinese Communist Party (CCP), based primarily in the cities. In northern China, there were three major groups that competed for power and territory. These groups were supported and opposed by a host of smaller warlords, battling on and off throughout these years. Eventually, the warlord Zhang Zoulin, based in Manchuria and Inner Mongolia, would become the most powerful of these groups.

Manchuria

Under Zhang Zoulin's rule, Manchuria declared independence in 1922 and was relatively isolated from the wars that consumed other parts of China. Zhang's army was also substantial, bringing peace to the region. Eventually, Zhang captured Beijing, the former capital of the Qing Dynasty, and other areas in northern China. He allowed Japan to continue developing railways, mills, mines and other businesses in Manchuria and in return Japan's government supported Zhang. Japan's **Kwantung Army** officers, many of whom advocated a Shōwa Restoration and were members of the Kōdōha faction, decided that the government's policy of allowing Zhang a large army and autonomy was wrong and assassinated Zhang in 1928. The army officers' motives were so popular with many in the military and civilian population that the government was unable and unwilling to punish the army's insubordination (see page 44).

(see page 44).

KEY TERM

🔑 **KEY TERM**

Kwantung Army Japan's most elite military unit before the Second World War, stationed in the Liaodong Peninsula, next to Manchuria.

Kuomintang China's main political group, also known as the Guomindang, or Nationalists.

? According to Source Z, what did the *zaibatsu* hope to do with an Asian empire?

SOURCE Z

Excerpt from *The Age of Hirohito: In Search of Modern Japan* by Daikichi Irokawa, published by The Free Press, New York City, USA, 1995, p. 13. The author is a professor at Tokyo Keizai University and has published books on Japanese history and culture in the nineteenth and twentieth centuries.

By cleverly making use of right-wing [Kōdōha] power in the military and political arenas but keeping a safe distance from the extreme rightists, a group of pragmatic military officers known as Tōseiha and government bureaucrats linked with the new and old zaibatsu then seeking to make the Asian continent their base of operations. This faction set out to free Japan from economic depression by pursuing a course of aggression.

To further their objectives, they assassinated Zhang Zuolin, and in the same year imprisoned several thousand communists and labor leaders.

Southern China and the end of the warlords

After years of war and division, the **Kuomintang** (KMT), or Nationalist, political party was able to unite various factions by increasing Chinese nationalism as the result of anti-Chinese discrimination by foreigners living and working in China. At this time the KMT announced that it supported the anti-foreign movement and, having made an earlier alliance with the CCP, now had enough strength to defeat rival warlords. From 1926 until 1928, the KMT conquered various warlords, broke its alliance with the CCP and attacked it. The Nationalists brought most of China under their control through a military campaign called the Northern Expedition, which took two-and-a-half years and involved over 1 million troops.

The Japanese Kwantung Army officers who assassinated Zhang hoped to weaken Manchuria's administration to such an extent that they would have to take control of the country to restore order. This would allow Japan to annex Manchuria outright, a policy not supported by their government. It had the opposite effect. Zhang's successor, his son, soon allied himself with the KMT and brought Manchuria officially back into a newly united China.

A newly united China
The results of the KMT's Northern Expedition included the following:

- destruction of railways, bridges and other important components of national infrastructure
- a famine in northwest China that killed between 3 million and 6 million people
- isolation of China from a powerful potential ally, the communist Soviet Union, by attacking the CCP, which was sponsored by the Soviets.

This basic unification meant that China could act as a single state. **Chiang Kai-shek** became the Director of the State Council, the equivalent to the position of president. China was strengthened by economic and political reorganization, although these were put into disarray by Japan's aggression in early 1930s (see pages 56 and 65). Additionally, the CCP survived the KMT's attempt to destroy it, creating conditions for further internal conflict.

KEY TERM

Chiang Kai-shek (1887–1975) Leading military and political ruler of China after 1925, dominating the Kuomintang political party.

Japan's foreign policy towards China up to 1931

> To what extent did Japan's policies towards China change by 1931?

Japan's foreign policy after the First World War through to 1927 was based on negotiation and working within the confines of international diplomacy. As such, Japan signed various treaties (see page 28) and worked to not antagonize the USA or China. Japan stationed some troops to protect its interests in Manchuria and in various port cities in China, but these had been agreed to by treaties, even if they were unpopular in Japan. This was known as the period of 'Shidehara Diplomacy', named after a Japanese Foreign Minister, Kijūrō Shidehara, who promoted the use of diplomacy instead of military actions.

In 1927, at the height of the Northern Expedition, this policy changed. Not only did the Japanese prefer a weak, divided China, they were alarmed at the rapid success of Chiang Kai-shek and the KMT. Troops were sent to occupy the Shantung Peninsula, where Japan had long interests and investments (see page 24). They were also there to support Zhang Zuolin, the soon-to-be-assassinated warlord of Manchuria. It was hoped that a large Japanese force on the Shantung Peninsula would prevent an invasion of Manchuria by the KMT. With Zhang's assassination, this no longer mattered.

The Positive Policy towards China was adopted by Japan's government in 1927. Essentially, this meant that Japan would treat Manchuria as a special case and not related to its other concerns in the rest of China. It also meant that Japan was no longer interested in the international community's input regarding Manchuria because it was felt that their policies aimed to keep Japan weak, and that foreign states simply could not comprehend Japan's needs and interests or its mission of leading Asia.

According to Source AA, what did the Kwantung Army and prime minister Tanaka disagree about?

SOURCE AA

Excerpt from *Emperor Hirohito and Shōwa Japan: A Political Biography* by Stephen S. Large, published by Routledge, New York, USA, 1992, pp. 35–6. Large is a historian whose books have concentrated on biographies of Japan's recent emperors and socialist politics in Japan in the early twentieth century.

The Emperor, Saionji and Shidehara were eager to prevent any further conflict in north China which might spill over into Japan's sphere of influence in south Manchuria. [Prime Minister] Tanaka, it must be said, fully agreed with this and accordingly urged Chang Tso-lin [Zhang Zuolin] to evacuate the region and retire to Manchuria, his original power base, lest [he] become embroiled in a military confrontation with Chiang Kai-shek's Nationalist [KMT] forces in north China. Tanaka believed that Chang's forces and Japanese interests could co-exist in Manchuria.

But this was not the view of the Kwantung Army, which pressed Tanaka to authorize at least the disarming of Chang's troops as he moved north. When Tanaka refused, Colonel Kōmoto Daisaku, a staff officer in the Kwantung Army, and several associates, plotted Chang's assassination which they would attribute to Chinese 'bandits'. They hoped that this course of action would stiffen the Japanese government's resolve to render Japan's position in Manchuria impregnable. In this, they were to be disappointed.

The Kwantung Army, Japan's elite armed forces, was stationed in the Liaodong Peninsula to safeguard Japan's installations and investments there as it bordered Korea, Japan's colony. After Zhang's assassination in 1928, this army was increased in size as it was realized that a united China might challenge Japan over aspects of Manchuria and the Liaodong Peninsula. The insubordinate officers and others who supported them were not replaced. They continued to believe that their policies and ideas regarding Manchuria were essential for Japan's long-term needs. Japan's government decided to replace the Kwantung Army's leadership to bring this military unit under government control. Hours before the new general was to take charge of the Kwantung Army, the Manchurian Crisis occurred.

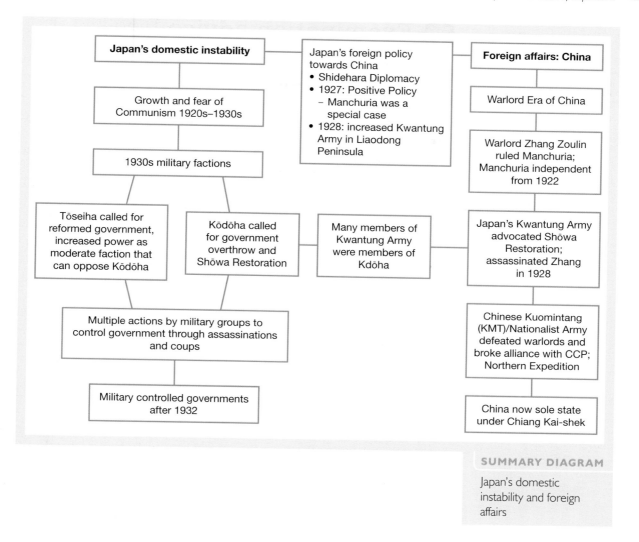

SUMMARY DIAGRAM

Japan's domestic instability and foreign affairs

Chapter summary

Causes of expansion

In the nineteenth century, Japan underwent mass industrialization and rapid modernization. By the early twentieth century it was a major military and political power in global affairs. The political system created by the Meiji Constitution was relatively stable initially, but with increasing economic problems, including rural poverty, the system became unworkable. By using the Meiji Constitution, the military had direct access to the Emperor and bypassed an increasingly weak civilian government that was unable to manage the country's crises. The military and their supporters believed that solutions for Japan's problems were not just military control over domestic politics, but also the creation of a larger empire at the expense of a weak China. The main focus of Japan's military and allied industrialists, the *zaibatsu*, was increasingly the Chinese province of Manchuria.

✓ Examination advice I

Remember that questions for Prescribed subject 3 will be numbered 9, 10, 11 and 12 in the Paper 1 exam.

Paper 1 Question 9: how to answer direct questions

Question 9 on the IB History Diploma examination is in two parts 9a and 9b. Each part involves reading comprehension and simply asks you to tell the examiner what the sources say. Each of the questions will ask only about one source. You will often see questions that ask you to convey the message or meaning of a source. This is asking you to explain what the source is saying.

Question 9 requires no prior knowledge, just the ability to read and understand sources. When you start your examination, you will receive five minutes of 'reading time' when you cannot actually touch your pen and start writing. Use the time wisely and read Question 9a to see which source it is asking about. Once you understand which source the question is about, read the source and then think of your response. When the five minutes are up, you may begin writing and you should be ready to answer the question immediately.

Question 9 is worth 5 marks out of the total of 24 for all of Paper 1. This means it is worth about twenty per cent of the overall mark. Answering Questions 9a and 9b should take five minutes or less of the actual examination time.

How to answer

In order to best answer the question, you first have to determine what the question is asking you about the source and what type of source it is. The vast majority of sources are fragments of speeches, quotes from various historians or historical figures, or any other type of written source. However, questions may also be asked about visual sources, such as photographs, charts, maps, cartoons and diagrams.

When you start your answer, it is good practice to use the wording in the question to help you focus your answer. For example:

Question	Begin your answer with:
According to Source *n*, what is the significance of the Washington Naval Treaty for Japan?	The significance of the Washington Naval Treaty, according to Source *n*, is …
What was the importance of the military in Japanese politics, according to Source *n*?	The importance of the military, according to Source *n*, was …
What were Emperor Hirohito's beliefs about the military's role in government, according to Source *n*?	According to Source *n*, the Emperor believed the military …

After starting your answer, understand that you should paraphrase what the original source stated. This means you should explain what the source says, but in your own words. Sometimes this is impossible because the words used in the source may be so specific that there is no other way to restate them. If this occurs, make sure you put quotation marks around the phrases which you are copying from the source.

The total number of marks available for Question 9 is 5. One part is worth 3 marks and the other 2 and this will be clearly indicated on the examination. If a question is worth 2 marks, try to have at least two specific points to your answer. If a question is worth 3 marks, have at least three points.

Example

This question uses Sources D (page 14) and I (page 21).

a) According to Source D, why was the Restoration needed in Japan? (3 marks)

b) What is the message conveyed in Source I? (2 marks)

It has just been announced that your reading time has begun on the IB History Paper 1 examination. Find the Paper 1 questions for the prescribed subject 'The move to global war' and read Question 9a. It asks you to explain what Source D indicates about the need for a 'Restoration'. You cannot touch your pen for several minutes, so go to Source D in the booklet and read it. Once you are allowed to pick up your pen and start writing, do so. Below is a good sample answer for the questions for 9a and 9b:

9a) According to Source D, the Restoration of the Emperor to full power was needed to change Japanese society. First, it would remove 'materialism', the desire to accumulate objects and wealth. Second, it would bring the people of Japan and the Emperor closer together. This would, third, allow Japan to become Asia's leader.

9b) The message conveyed in Source I is to indicate the bravery of Japan's troops while depicting the enemy Russians as either cowards or overwhelmed by Japan's expertly exploded bombs.

> Each answer repeats part of the question, using phrases such as 'According to Source D' and 'The message conveyed in Source I is.' This helps the answer focus on the question.

> Both sources are paraphrased in the answers.

> Both questions are answered in paragraph form and not bullet points.

Questions 9a and 9b are worth a combined 5 marks. Both answers indicate that the student read and understood what each source stated. Question 9a is worth 3 marks. The answer for 9a contains at least three different points to address the question. Question 9b is worth 2 marks. The answer has more than two points to answer the question. Mark: 5/5.

Examination practice I

The following are exam-style questions for you to practise, using sources from the chapter. Sources can be found on the following pages:

Source A: Page 10   Source Q: Page 32
Source E: Page 16   Source R: Page 33
Source H: Page 20   Source S: Page 34
Source L: Page 24   Source X: Page 41
Source O: Page 28   Source Y: Page 41

1 What, according to Source A, is the Emperor's relationship to the Diet, Japan's parliament?

2 What is the message of Source E?

3 What is the message of Source H?

4 According to Source L, why was Japan considered different from other modern states?

5 What, according to Source O, was the significance of the Washington Naval Conference?

6 How, according to Source Q, did the *zaibatsu* influence Japan's government?

7 What, according to Source R, was the effect of the Great Depression on peasants?

8 How, according to Source S, was Japan's silk production industry affected by the Great Depression?

9 What, according to Source X, concerned Emperor Hirohito with reference to the army?

10 Why, according to Source Y, were the military's policies appealing to many?

 # Examination advice II

Paper 1 Question 10: value and limitations based on origin, purpose and content

Remember that questions for Prescribed subject 3 will be numbered 9, 10, 11 and 12 in the Paper 1 exam.

Question 10 on the IB History Diploma examination requires to you to discuss the origin and purpose of one source and then to use that information to determine its potential value and limitations. The question always asks you to refer to the origin, purpose and the content provided to assess its value and limitations for historians. Some knowledge of the topic, value of types of sources or historians can be useful, although this is not required.

Question 10 is worth 4 marks out of the 24 total for Paper 1. This means it is worth seventeen per cent of your overall mark. Answering Question 10 should take approximately ten minutes of your examination time.

How to answer

Read Question 10 carefully. You will notice that it is asking you to analyse the value and limitations of a source for historians studying a particular event or action in history. These are to be determined by referencing the origin, purpose and content of the source. You should address Question 10 in a paragraph.

Structure will help you in answering the question. Incorporate the words origin, purpose, content, value and limitation into your answer:

- 'The origin of this source is …'
- 'the purpose of this source is …'
- 'the value of this source is …'
- 'the content of this source indicates …'
- 'a limitation of this source may be …'.

This keeps you focused on the task, making sure you cover all the required elements, but also helps the examiner understand your answers by providing a framework that they can follow.

It is important to remember that you are to use the origins, purpose and content to determine the value and limitations of the named source for historians studying something in particular.

Origin

The origin of a source is the author, the type of publication, the year it was published, and sometimes the country it originates from. If there is biographical information included as part of the source's introduction, this may also be used in addressing the source's origin. If only the author is stated, then the origin is simply the author or authors.

Purpose

The purpose of a source is usually indicated by the source's title, the type of source, the writer or speaker, if it is a speech, or the location of the source, such as in a newspaper, an academic book or a journal. Purposes can range from speeches (that try to convince certain groups or nations that what the speaker is saying is the truth), to documents that explain the history of a certain period. If a book's title is *The League of Nations' Mandates and Japan*, the purpose of this particular source is likely to be to explain the League of Nations and Japan's mandates after the First World War. If you are making a hypothesis regarding the purpose, use words such as 'perhaps', 'likely' or 'possibly' instead of stating your theory as a fact. The content may help determine the purpose.

Content

The content of a source, especially if the source is a speech, a cartoon or an official document of some sort, may help determine the purpose as well as any value or limitation. An official statement by a prime minister of Japan could potentially include important details for a historian studying Japan's economic crises during the 1920s, such as statistics, dates, locations and the names of officials.

The content of larger works by historians may be more difficult to use to determine the source's value and limitations. Historians tend to discuss historical events, emphasizing various pieces of evidence while ignoring or explaining away other details. Use the content to help explain the value and limitations of the source for historians, but do so with care. Use words like 'possibly' and 'perhaps' if you are not completely sure about your hypothesis.

Value

The value of a source flows naturally from the origins, purpose and content. For instance, imagine there is a book called *Japanese Militarism in the Late 1920s* that was written by an army official who served during that period. The value will be that the writer probably witnessed or participated in certain events, perhaps supporting or resisting various military factions working to control the government. This individual might have even met and spoken with other participants, including those who made important decisions. This would give the author first-hand knowledge regarding the establishment of a military-dominated government by 1931.

If the author wrote the book 70 years later, rather than the 1920s, it could be that this individual has access to records from that period. This would mean that the author might have a less emotional and more objective view of Japanese politics, economic crises and foreign policy, and therefore is better able to determine the long-term effect of decisions and actions of the period.

Your answer will have to be determined by the origin, purpose and content of the source you are asked to discuss. Do not state that primary sources have more value than secondary sources; this is not necessarily true.

Limitation

The limitation of a source is determined in much the same way that you determined the source's value. If the writer of *Japanese Militarism in the Late 1920s* is Japanese, the writer is likely to have more access to Japanese sources than a non-Japanese historian because of the language. Likewise, a Japanese historian is unlikely to have easy or any access to Chinese or other archives. This means that a Japanese historian's views might be limited or unbalanced as a result of this lack of access. Therefore, you can use the word 'possibly' in trying to determine the limitation of a source, unless the source gives you other information to clarify your theory.

There are other ways to determine possible limitations of a source:

- The title of the source may be of a limited nature or too broad for the topic.
- The date of publication, if given, may be limiting if it is too close to or far from the historical events.
- A source that is political in nature may be trying to advocate a certain view or policy instead of being objective.
- The content of the source may clearly indicate bias, such as advocating a specific view while possibly attacking another potential view of the historical event or individual.

Do not state that sources are limited because they are secondary sources; this may not always be true.

Visual images

Visual sources will have information explaining their origin; the content of a photograph is critically important as well. Remember that photographs can capture a single moment in time so that they can show exactly what happened, but they can also be staged to send a particular message. A photograph of smiling Manchurians standing with Japanese soldiers captures a moment when they were either genuinely happy or told to smile, perhaps not knowing even what they were smiling about. Cartoons, posters and even photographs often have a political message. The purpose of any of these could potentially be to convince the viewer of a certain point of view. Another purpose could be to make fun of a particular idea or person for some other reason. Further information on visual sources can be found on page 88.

Example

This question uses Source O (see page 28).

> With reference to its origins, purpose and content, analyse the value and limitations of Source O for historians studying Japanese militarism.
>
> (4 marks)

You will immediately turn to Source O and read that it is an excerpt from an autobiographical book by Ozaki Yukio. There is no need to plan an outline for this question because the structure of your answer is indicated by the question, so get started.

The *value* of Source O for historians studying militarism is that it is an account written by someone personally involved in the struggle to maintain Japan's constitutional government as indicated by the stated origin and purpose. As such, he would have potentially witnessed and/or participated in events regarding the rising power of Japan's military. The content of the source clearly indicates that Mr Ozaki was crucially important to events as he is held personally responsible and called names, again meaning that he worked against Japanese militarism personally, further indicating that this is indeed a valuable source for historians studying militarism in Japan.

A *limitation* of Source O for historians is that Mr Ozaki indicates in the purpose of the source that it will be about the fight to maintain Japan's constitutional government. As such, he is unlikely to view militarism and

> The terms origin, purpose, content, value, and limitation are used throughout.

> Use of words such as 'potentially', 'perhaps' and so forth indicate where hypotheses are being stated.

> There are two values and they are connected to the origin, purpose or content.

those who advocated it positively or objectively. The <u>content</u> supports this, in which his opponents are depicted as irrational. The <u>content</u> of the source implies that Mr Ozaki was not just present, but personally responsible for agreeing to naval limitations and responding to opposition; no others are given credit or mentioned. Again, Mr Ozaki's objectivity could perhaps be called into question by historians as it is highly unlikely that a single individual would have that responsibility or authority in Japan's government of that period.

There are two limitations and they refer to the origin, purpose or content.

Question 10 is worth 4 marks. The answer indicates that values and limitations have both been addressed using the origin, purpose and content of the source. There are at least two values and two limitations discussed with reference to the usefulness of the source for historians studying militarism. Mark: 4/4.

Examination practice II

The following are exam-style questions for you to practise, using sources from this chapter. Sources can be found on the following pages:

Source D: page 14

Source R: page 33

Source Q: page 32

Source X: page 41

Source Z: page 42

1 With reference to its origin, purpose and content, assess the value and limitations of Source D for historians studying the emergence of Japanese militarism.

2 With reference to its origin, purpose and content, assess the value and limitations of Source R for historians studying economic stresses in Japan in the early twentieth century.

3 With reference to its origin, purpose and content, assess the value and limitations of Source Q for historians studying the influence of the *zaibatsu* on Japan's government.

4 With reference to its origin, purpose and content, assess the value and limitations of Source X for historians studying the relationship between Japan's Emperor and the military.

5 With reference to its origin, purpose and content, assess the value and limitations of Source Z for historians studying the influence of Japan's military on foreign policy before the Second World War.

 Activities

1 In groups, using paragraphs of this chapter as sources, create questions in the style of question 9a and question 9b, assigning them either 2 or 3 marks. Use the paragraphs that focus on the Japanese government's struggle with the military and factions within the military. Vary your questions such as in the examples above. Try to create at least two different questions per paragraph. Exchange your questions with other groups, being sure to indicate the location of the paragraphs in the chapter, and give yourselves approximately five minutes to answer the two questions. Once questions have been answered, review the answers and assign marks. Be sure to indicate what was successful and appropriate and what might be improved.

2 Collaboratively create a timeline. One part of the timeline will indicate major economic events in Japan's history as indicated in this chapter. In another colour or in parallel, create a timeline that plots actions by Japan's military, including actions by rival military factions. Finally, in another colour or in parallel, create a timeline that deals with Japanese foreign policy events such as treaties or actions. What conclusions might one be able to draw based on evidence presented in the timelines? Which events were the most important and which led to military actions?

3 Create flashcards with important dates and personalities. For example, on one side of the card you will have the date 1902. On the other side of the card, you will have Anglo-Japanese Alliance. Do this with various dates and individuals mentioned throughout Chapter 1. You can use these for revision or to create a game for class in which student teams compete to answer the questions correctly for points.

4 Divide the class into two groups. Each group in class will create governmental and economic solutions for Japan's problems in the early twentieth century. Create a Venn diagram on the board, indicating the similarities and differences between the solutions proposed by each group. The class should discuss each solution, debating the merits and weaknesses of each.

CHAPTER 2

Japan's expansion and the international response

Rural poverty, the Great Depression, militarism, ultranationalism and other factors led to increasing calls for Japanese imperial expansion. The need for empire to solve its problems focused initially on Manchuria. Japan was geographically near Manchuria; it had absorbed even closer territories already, and had substantial investments along the South Manchurian Railway. Soon, expansion would involve all of China. War in China would lead directly to war with the USA in 1941, provoking the Second World War in the Pacific and Asia. You will need to consider the following questions in this chapter:

★ What were the main results of the Manchurian Crisis?

★ How did the Second Sino-Japanese War affect both China and Japan?

★ What Japanese actions led to war with the USA?

① The Manchurian Crisis

▶ **Key question:** *What were the main results of the Manchurian Crisis?*

Japan was heavily invested in Manchuria in the 1920s. Manchuria was over four times the size of Japan, had a low population and tremendous amounts of resources that Japan lacked or had in low quantities: cotton, vast forests and farm products, coal, iron, aluminium, magnesite, gold and lead, among others. Manchuria, or land of the Manchu people, a people with their own language and culture, was part of China and therefore had direct access to China's markets and massive population. Japan's military and some in its government saw Manchuria as a solution to many of its problems, for instance, as a place to relocate Japan's extremely poor rural farmers.

Japan was increasingly concerned about communism (see page 38). The Soviet Union shared a 3200-km (2000-mile) long border with Manchuria. Japan's military reasoned that taking control of Manchuria would make it less likely that the Soviet Union would foment communist unrest in the region. The border of any potential Soviet–Japanese conflict would be far removed from Japan's home islands if Manchuria was more tightly controlled.

Japan was also alarmed that their South Manchurian Railway, which justified their military presence, was rapidly being undermined. China had begun construction of rival railways that were starting to operate at full capacity. This would mean decreased revenues for Japan and increased ones for China's government. For these, and many other reasons, Japan's Kwantung Army, acted insubordinately – just as in 1928 (see page 42).

SOURCE A

Excerpt from *The Wars for Asia, 1911–1949* by S.C.M. Paine, published by Cambridge University Press, UK, 2012, pp. 14–15. Paine is a professor of strategy and policy at the US Naval War College and has written many books on modern Chinese history.

After the Russo-Japanese War (1904–5), when Japan had acquired the [South Manchurian] railway in lieu of a Russian indemnity, company investments increased more than fifty times between 1907 and 1930. Prior to Japan's invasion, it accounted for 72 percent of the region's foreign investments and Russia 24 percent. Great Britain, the next largest foreign investor, controlled just 1 percent. Industrial development in the rest of China lagged far behind Manchuria, which accounted for 90 percent of China's oil, 70 percent of its iron, 55 percent of its gold, and 33 percent of its trade. If Shanghai remained China's commercial center, by 1931 Manchuria had becomes its industrial center.

According to Source A, what was the economic importance of Manchuria?

Events leading to the Manchurian Crisis

Why was Japan able to conquer Manchuria with relative ease?

On 18 September 1931, a bomb exploded on the South Manchurian Railway outside the leading city of Manchuria, Mukden. This minor explosion, later known as the Mukden Incident, did not even prevent trains from using the railway, but had conveniently taken place near a garrison of Japanese soldiers protecting the South Manchurian Railway, operated by Japan (see page 41). Although many historians believe that Japanese troops, specifically Kwantung Army officers, placed the bomb, Japan blamed the explosion on Chinese troops.

SOURCE B

Excerpt from *The Manchurian Crisis and Japanese Society, 1931–33* by Sandra Wilson, published by Routledge, London, UK, 2002, p. 1. Wilson is a professor of Asian history at Murdoch University, Australia.

On the night of 18 September 1831, a minor explosion occurred on a section of the Japanese-owned South Manchurian Railway near Mukden (now Shenyang) in the north-east of China. Japanese troops, stationed in Manchuria since 1905 to protect the railway and its associated operations, moved swiftly and decisively to defend Japan's interests. Meanwhile their leaders loudly asserted to the world that Chinese soldiers were responsible for the explosion, which was branded as only the latest in a series of anti-Japanese 'outrages'. Actually, damage to the railway had been slight, and the 'incident' had in any case been perpetrated not by Chinese soldiers but by Japanese troops, as part of a wider plan to extend Japanese power in Manchuria.

According to Source J, what was the purpose of the explosion on 18 September 1931?

The Kwantung Army used the Mukden Incident as an excuse to occupy all of Manchuria. They were soon joined by a Japanese army based in Korea, and, after all areas along the South Manchurian Railway were under control, moved west and north. While the more heavily populated areas were occupied in about a week, the rest of Manchuria was progressively occupied over the next couple of months. By February 1932, only the southern province of Manchuria, Jehol, also known as Rehe, remained out of Japan's control. Although China had over 100,000 soldiers in the province and Japan had probably fewer than 25,000, there was relatively little fighting. Japan's army was better trained and better equipped. The Kuomintang (KMT) government of China led by Chiang Kai-shek (see page 43) ordered its troops not to resist the invasion.

According to Source C, why did Chiang order his military not to resist Japan's invasion?

SOURCE C

Excerpt from *War and Nationalism in China 1925–1945* by Hans J. Van De Ven, published by RoutledgeCurzon, London, UK, 2003, p. 151. Van de Ven is a professor of modern Chinese history at Cambridge University and Director of Oriental Studies at St Catherine's College at Cambridge, UK.

For any government to be shown to be weak cannot but damage its reputation and the refusal to stand up to an aggressor provides easy openings for its critics. It is less clear that realistically Chiang had any other option. The northern militarists, including Zhang Xueliang, would no doubt have pounced had Chiang begun an offensive. China's forces were also no match to the Japanese. In January 1932, Chiang Kaishek stated that 'China lacks real military power' and that if it declared war, 'within three days Japan would vanquish the coast areas and the Yangtze River basin.' He was probably right. In three weeks of fighting along the Great Wall between 6 and 21 March 1933, Nationalist units were badly mauled. In his diary, Chiang noted that 'it won't do to pretend that we are powerful. The urgent task is to stabilise the line of resistance against Japan and strengthen our defences in the north.'

Almost immediately, Japan created the illusion that they had only helped Manchuria achieve independence from chaotic China. It was presented to the world as an independent state. The new state of Manchukuo, 'Land of the Manchurians' in Japanese, was established and headed by the last Emperor of China, Puyi, a Manchu; he was soon made Emperor of Manchukuo, called the Kangde Emperor. The Imperial Army of Manchukuo was created, along with a comprehensive postal system, primary schools and even a national sports league, led by baseball and football (soccer). Japan sponsored Manchukuo in applying for Olympic membership, and Manchukuo applied to be a member of the League of Nations (see page 25). Both applications were denied, a clear indication that other countries considered Manchukuo's independence a sham and that the country was really just a puppet-state.

SOURCE D

Various postage stamps from the Manchukuo Empire.

What do the stamps in Source D indicate about Manchukuo?

Responses to the Manchurian Crisis

> **Why did no nation intervene militarily in the Manchurian Crisis?**

There were several responses to the Manchurian Crisis by world political and economic powers. While most countries responded to Japan's aggression negatively, little could be done to undo the results. This was partly the result of a crushing economic situation with the Great Depression (see page 34) which prevented any major military actions. Perhaps another reason was that by invading Manchuria, Japan created another border against the communism of the Soviet Union; communism was opposed and feared by most governments as it advocated complete destruction of existing economic, social and political systems. Many may have thought that Japan had saved Manchuria from a chaotic, corrupt Chinese government.

Response: League of Nations

As Japan completely occupied Manchuria, China appealed to the League of Nations (both China and Japan were League members). The League responded with great caution; this was the first major military conflict between League states. The League eventually formed the Lytton Commission in December 1931 to investigate the Mukden Incident and Japan's occupation. Once its report was completed and submitted to the League, the League would then decide what action to take. The Lytton Commission began to operate in late January 1932 when it first visited the Japanese government in Tokyo, finally making it to Manchuria in February.

The Lytton Commission's report was finally submitted to the League in October 1932, a full year after the invasion. The report admitted that before Japan invaded there was an inefficient and corrupt Chinese government in the province and that Japan had made major financial investments. It also explained the details of the invasion, the establishment of the state of

?

What images does Source E
show that imply mutual aid
and peace?

SOURCE E

'With Japanese, Chinese and Manchu working together, a Great Peace
can be brought to this world.' A 1930s propaganda poster used in China
and Manchukuo.

Manchukuo and the economics of Manchuria, China and Japan. The report
determined that the invasion was not, as Japan insisted, a result of wanting
to protect Manchurians from China's government; there was no obvious
support for the new state of Manchukuo by the Chinese population of the
province. Over 90 per cent of people in Manchuria were Chinese, not
Manchus. It recommended that Japan pull its forces back to the South
Manchurian Railway.

The League of Nations General Assembly voted on a motion in February
1933 to condemn Japan as an aggressor nation. Forty-two nations voted
against Japan, while Japan voted the sole vote for itself. Japan withdrew from
the League in March 1933, suffering no consequences as a result of its
departure.

SOURCE F

Cartoon by David Low for the *Evening Standard*, 24 November 1932, London, UK.

'Judge: "The court orders you to respect the law and sentences you to a good talking to."

Japan: "And I order the court to mind its own business and I sentence it to go and chase itself."'

According to Source F, what is the international reaction to Japan's actions in Manchuria?

Response: China

Chiang Kai-shek was forced to resign as premier of China's government in December 1931 by various political groups, including much of the KMT's leadership. This was done for several reasons, but primarily so that a united government composed of various groups could be formed to respond to the crisis. Chiang remained head of the military, however, and Wang Jingwei became premier. Chiang would be named premier again in 1935, replacing Wang, becoming the head of government again.

The lack of resistance by Chiang Kai-shek's armies certainly helped Japan achieve rapid victory with minimal losses of soldiers or weapons. Chiang, naturally, wished to retain Manchuria as a part of China as it was the richest region in terms of resources and industry, although he did realize that Japan's military was stronger and likely to win in a direct battle. Additionally, Chiang may have been more concerned with challenges to his own rule in the rest of China.

Japan's armies continued the conquest of outlying areas. Jehol was finally conquered in March 1933 and soon Japanese armies had moved into northern China, outside Manchukuo. On 31 May 1933, China's government signed the Tanggu Truce, essentially recognizing that Jehol and Manchuria were now under Japan's control and promising not to fight to remove Japan from these areas. This agreement also established a neutral zone between Japanese-controlled territory and that of China's government, although this would be violated repeatedly by Japan as it continued to enlarge territory under its control.

?
What messages are conveyed by Source G?

SOURCE G

Japanese soldiers planting Japan's flag on the Great Wall of China, 28 January 1933.

Chiang's attempts to destroy the Chinese Communist Party (CCP) had certainly reduced its strength (see page 42), but by the early 1930s, the CCP was again gaining power and the KMT continued to battle its forces. Chiang saw communism as a greater threat than Japan – and a more beatable enemy. Proving Japan's argument that by conquering Manchuria it was bringing stability to areas that had only known civil war for years, Chiang spent the majority of 1933 fighting a warlord in northern China for control of the region who advocated fighting Japan; Chiang defeated him.

Response: USA

The USA was not part of the League of Nations and was in a period of **semi-isolation**. This was partly the result of a US public that did not wish to become entangled in international machinations such as those that had led to the First World War. At the Paris Peace Conference in 1919 (see page 25), it seemed to many in the USA that Britain and France, as well as Japan, had enriched themselves by gaining more colonies in the form of mandates (see page 26). Most believed at the time that imperialism and territorial competition among European states had been one of the main causes of the First World War. There was also a large anti-war movement and a complete lack of political desire to increase taxation to pay for large numbers of ships and troops.

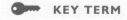

KEY TERM

Semi-isolation A policy of having limited involvement in international diplomacy.

The USA had always enforced an **Open Door Policy** with regard to China. With Japan's invasion of Manchuria, there was fear, rightly, that the Open Door Policy would be disrupted. The USA was primarily concerned with the economics of the invasion since it had no ability or desire to interfere militarily. It protested Japan's actions in Manchuria by formulating the **Stimson Doctrine**, named after the Secretary of State (Foreign Minister) Henry Stimson. Stimson also indicated that the USA continued to uphold the Open Door Policy. The Stimson Doctrine had no effect on the Manchurian Crisis. The US government decided not to place any restrictions on its trade with Japan or Manchuria.

Response: Soviet Union

The Soviet Union in late 1931 was in no condition to oppose any actions by Japan in Manchuria. The world's only communist state was in the midst of social and economic upheaval with the **collectivization** of agriculture and its campaign to industrialize. For various reasons, including government inefficiency and ignorance – but also as the result of resistance, extreme weather and lack of farming machinery – millions starved to death. The Soviet Union was too busy trying to stem the threat of outright revolt by its own starving people to intervene in Japan's invasion.

The Soviet Union owned and operated the Chinese Eastern Railway (CER) in Manchuria, having lost the South Manchurian Railway (see page 21). The Japanese informed the Soviets that they had no plans to interfere with the operation of the CER. In 1935, the Soviet Union, clearly unable to defend the railway in case of Japanese aggression or nationalization, sold the CER to the state of Manchukuo in a transaction negotiated solely by Japan.

Japan's government after the crisis

Japan's government had been unaware of the Kwantung Army's plan to conquer Manchuria, but knew that the army planned some further act of insubordination. The government replaced the overall commander just hours before the Mukden Incident and therefore was unable to prevent its implementation.

The government's main concern remained the army's disobedience. The army and government agreed that Manchuria should be dominated by Japan, but Japan did not wish to provoke the Great Powers (see page 43). The government ordered the arrest of the perpetrators of the Mukden Incident; the army refused and the government collapsed over its inability to have the military obey. The next prime minister attempted to assert his authority over the military. He survived two attempted assassinations after he began negotiating with Chiang Kai-shek to resolve the crisis, but during the 15 May Incident (see page 40), he was finally killed and replaced by a navy admiral. Thus, the direct effect of the Mukden Incident and the invasion of Manchuria was that government policy was now aligned with military policy.

<aside>
KEY TERM

Open Door Policy Policy advocated by the USA that called for all nations to have equal access to China's markets.

Stimson Doctrine This policy stated that the USA would not recognize international border changes that resulted from war.

Collectivization The Soviet Union's policy of ending privately owned and operated farms by consolidating farmers, farm animals and equipment in state-managed farms.
</aside>

Key debate

▶ *Key question:* *What was the significance of the Manchurian Crisis for the League of Nations?*

The League of Nations was established at the Paris Peace Conference and member states had pledged to defend each other in case of war (see page 25). Many historians have claimed that the road to the Second World War began in 1931 at Mukden and that profound weaknesses of the League were revealed. This initial failure, according to this argument, led to the Abyssinian Crisis (see page 119).

SOURCE H

According to Source H, what was the main result of the Manchurian Crisis?

Excerpt from 'Great powers paid price for "peace": history shows that the pacifist movement of the 1930s ultimately helped to usher in the horror of World War II by allowing rogue nations to rise to power unabated' by Stephen Goode, in *Insight on the News*, Vol. 19, 2003. Goode was senior writer for this conservative US news magazine, which ceased publication in 2008.

The League of Nations declined to recognize Manchukuo, but it also refused to place any sanctions on Japan's behavior, in part because neither Great Britain nor any other member nation was strong enough to enforce them. The United States had not joined the League of Nations, nor did it support sanctions. The result: Japan continued to occupy Manchukuo and to make war in China. And it removed itself from membership in the League.

The failure to put an end to Japanese aggression had ramifications beyond the Far East. Benito Mussolini, dictator in Italy since 1922, noted the failure of the League of Nations to say 'no' to Japan. In October 1935, Italy invaded Abyssinia …

While weaknesses were revealed, some historians state that the failure of the League of Nations to confront Japan actually demonstrated a new reality. This reality was that the Great Powers within the League of Nations, such as Britain, France, Italy and Japan, would not oppose each other's dealings with smaller states. These historians go further and state that smaller, less powerful states realized that they were now more vulnerable and would be expected to give in to the demands of more powerful nations.

SOURCE I

According to Source I, what did the Manchurian Crisis acknowledge in international diplomacy?

Excerpt from *The League of Nations: Its Life and Times 1920–1946* by F.S. Northedge, published by Holmes & Meier, London, 1986, p. 164. Northedge was a professor of international relations at the London School of Economics, UK, writing numerous books on the subject as well.

Britain and the other great Powers did not worry overmuch about the implications of the Manchurian affair for collective security. As always, they had more immediate questions to think about. In the result, collective security was dealt a blow from which it never fully recovered. The smaller countries were left to conclude that, if the League was to protect them, it would have to be when the great Powers were united against a common enemy, which happened to be victimising a small country. But it was as likely as not that the great Powers, so far from joining together to defend the small country, would join together to attack it, or to shut their eyes if one of them attacked it. Something like that had happened in the Corfu crisis in 1923, when Italy was sheltered by [being a member of the Conference of Ambassadors]. Japan profited in the same way in the Manchurian affair. Later in the 1930s the European dictators were shielded by sympathisers in the form of states which were supposed to be the very pillars of the League system. And what were the smaller states to do in such a situation? They could make their peace with one or other of the great Powers in good time, perhaps losing part of their territory in the process of accommodation. Or they could relax their links with the collective system in the hope of diverting from themselves the predatory attentions of great Powers. In either case, the solidity of the League system was bound to be affected as it prepared for the next great challenge. That challenge was not long in coming.

Other historians claim that the Manchurian Crisis actually strengthened the League by forcing it to set up committees and internal structures to deal with conflict between states, which had never been set up before because they had never been needed. A.J.P. Taylor makes this argument in *The Origins of the Second World War* and claims that historians only later gave significance, wrongly, to the Manchurian Crisis.

SOURCE J

Excerpt from *The Origins of the Second World War* by A.J.P. Taylor, published by Penguin Books, UK, 1991, p. 92. Taylor was a British historian who wrote many books on European history and lectured at many British universities.

According to Source J, what was the main result of the Manchurian Crisis?

The Commission did not reach a simple verdict. It found that most of the Japanese grievances were justified. Japan was not condemned as an aggressor, though she was condemned for resorting to force before all peaceful means of redress were exhausted. The Japanese withdrew in protest from the League of Nations. The Chinese reconciled themselves to the loss of a province which they had not controlled for some years; and in 1933 peace was restored between China and Japan. In later years the Manchurian affair assumed a mythical importance. It was treated as a milestone on the road to war, the first decisive betrayal of the League, especially by the British government. In reality, the League, under British leadership, had done what the British thought it was designed to do: it had limited a conflict and brought it, however unsatisfactorily, to an end. Moreover, the Manchurian affair, far from weakening the coercive powers of the League, actually brought them into existence. It was thanks to this affair that the League again on British prompting set up machinery, hitherto lacking, to organize economic sanctions. This machinery, to everyone's misfortune, made possible the League action over Abyssinia in 1935.

Debate about the significance of the Manchurian Crisis continues today. Did the failure of collective security in the Manchurian Crisis lead to the fall of the League? Did this crisis contribute to the origins of the Second World War? Was the League really prepared for another crisis between its member states? While these questions continue to be debated, it is important to understand that whatever the overall significance of the Manchurian Crisis may have been, the League clearly failed to protect China from Japan. This moved Asia closer to war since Japan invaded the rest of China in 1937, but it is still unclear whether this also moved Europe closer to the Second World War. Establishing internal structures within the League to deal with any future aggression by member states was important, but addressing the lack of political willpower and financial ability of the Great Powers (see Chapter 3) to intervene in conflicts was more complicated.

T O K

Historians continue to debate the significance of the Manchurian Crisis. Why does our society believe that the study of history is important? (History, Language and Reason)

SUMMARY DIAGRAM

The Manchurian Crisis

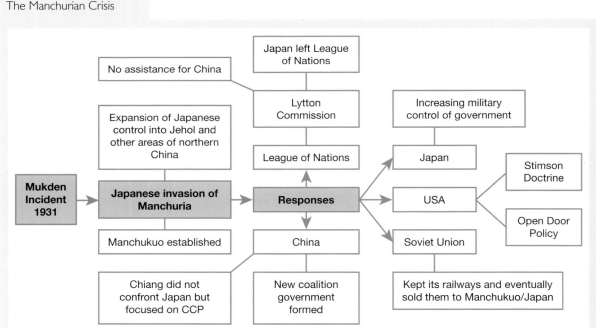

Second Sino-Japanese War 1937–45

▶ *Key question: How did the Second Sino-Japanese War affect both China and Japan?*

There was no real cessation of war after Japan's invasion of Manchuria. Japanese armies continued to operate, expanding Japan's control of northern China by 1937. In 1937, a larger war erupted with millions of troops and millions of deaths, primarily civilians.

Japan expands into China 1935–6

Japan formed the China Garrison Army to operate outside the borders of Manchuria. This army first occupied the eastern half of Charar Province by mid-1935. The China Garrison Army was then moved south into the neutral zone formed by the Tanggu Truce (see page 59). When two Chinese newspaper owners were assassinated for being pro-Japanese, the China Garrison Army demanded that China withdraw from Hebei Province or face an invasion. The Umezu–He Agreement of 10 June 1935 made this official and created a large demilitarized zone throughout much of northern China. A puppet government called the East Hebei Autonomous Council was formed to rule this region for Japan.

> **Why was there little resistance to Japanese expansion in northern China?**

> **Second London Naval Treaty 1935**
>
> By 1935, Japan's military controlled the government and had no interest in participating in treaties that limited Japan's ability to build war ships, such as those conferences in Washington and London (see pages 28 and 29). Britain and the USA continued to work to get other countries to limit their navies, partly as a result of the economic stress of the Great Depression (see page 34). Japan ended its involvement by withdrawing from the treaty meetings in January 1935. The end result was that no agreement could be made regarding limitations on ship numbers because of Japan's absence, but decisions were made on limitations of ship sizes for battleships, submarines and aircraft carriers, sizes of guns that various types of warships could carry and so forth. The only countries to sign were the USA, Britain and France.

Mengjiang

On 27 June 1935 in the Doihara Kenji–Qin Dechun Agreement, China agreed to remove all troops from the Manchukuo border, again, and from all Charar Province. China's military agreed because it remained more interested in destroying the CCP than in resisting Japan for the time being. The China Garrison Army copied the Kwantung Army's policy of creating a

Map of China in 1935–6, indicating areas under Japan's control by mid-1936.

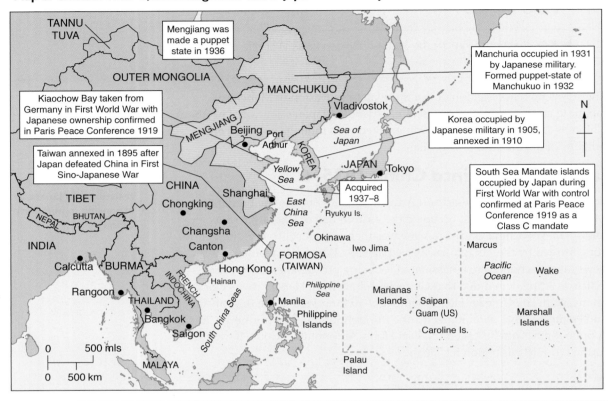

According to Source K, which provinces were under Japan's control by mid-1935?

puppet-state. In 1935, Demchugdongrob, a descendant of Genghis Khan, became the head of the government of Inner Mongolia. Fighting soon erupted between pro-China and pro-Japan factions throughout the region. In 1936, the new Mongol-led state was named Mengjiang, or Mongolland (Mengkukuo in Japanese).

By 1936, much of northern China was under Japan's control, either directly by its army or through its carefully managed puppet-states. China attempted to rule the demilitarized area through local councils, but this was ineffective; Japan could move troops through the region as it desired.

Second United Front

By the end of 1936, Chiang Kai-shek's policy of opposing the CCP, rather than Japan, was highly unpopular. Chiang held a meeting with his generals at Xian in December 1936. Alarmed at Chiang's obsession with communism, Zhang Xueliang (see Source C on page 56), the former warlord of Manchuria who now co-operated with the KMT, arrested Chiang. He forced Chiang to negotiate with the CCP to create a united anti-Japanese front. Chiang agreed after two weeks of pressure. This move proved very popular throughout China, and Japan understood that it might now face organized opposition to its conquests. The new alliance between the KMT and CCP was known as the Second United Front, with the first being the earlier alliance at the start of the Northern Expedition (see page 42). Both KMT and CCP forces fought together as the National Revolutionary Army.

China resists: the Marco Polo Bridge Incident 1937

In July 1937, Chinese and Japanese troops fought briefly at the Marco Polo Bridge, or Lugouqiao (Lugou Bridge), near Beijing, the former Qing Dynasty capital of China. Japan's government demanded an apology from China and Chiang Kai-shek's government refused. By the end of July, both Japan and China had sent large armies into northern China and fighting began. Beijing and most areas in northern China were rapidly occupied by Japanese armies. Unable to affect the war in the north, Chiang looked for a victory elsewhere, responding on 13 August by having bomber aircraft attack an area of Shanghai that was controlled by Japan. Japan and China were now at war.

SOURCE L

Excerpt from *Modern Japan: A History in Documents* by James L. Huffman, published by Oxford University Press, New York, USA, 2004, pp. 143–4. This is a section of a speech by Japan's Prime Minister Kanoe to the Diet regarding the Marco Polo Bridge Incident. Huffman is professor emeritus for east Asian history at Wittenberg University in the USA, authoring many works on modern Japanese history.

Since the outbreak of the affair in North China on July 7th, the fundamental policy of the Japanese Government toward China has been simply and purely to seek the reconsideration of the Chinese Government and the abandonment of its erroneous anti-Japanese policies …

The Chinese, however, not only fail to understand the true motives of the Government, but have increasingly aroused a spirit of contempt and have offered resistance toward Japan, taking advantage of the patience of our Government. Thus, by the outburst of uncontrolled national sentiment, the situation has fast been aggravated, spreading in scope to Central and South China. And now, our Government, which has been patient to the utmost, has acknowledged the impossibility of settling the incident passively and locally, and has been forced to deal a firm and decisive blow against the Chinese Government in an active and comprehensive manner.

According to Source L, what led to Japan's war with China?

KEY TERM

International Settlement
Area of Shanghai controlled by foreign governments where foreign-owned factories and other enterprises were located, and where many non-Chinese lived.

The Second Sino-Japanese War 1937–45

On 15 August, Japan formed the Shanghai Expeditionary Army with the intention of capturing China's largest city and economic centre: Shanghai. While Chinese troops attacked Japanese military installations in the **International Settlement**, Japan used bomber aircraft against Nanjing,

Why was Japan unable to defeat China's government and its military forces?

China's capital, nearly 400 km (250 miles) from Shanghai. Other cities were also attacked by air as the Shanghai Expeditionary Army began arriving by ship on 23 August. Meanwhile, Japanese armies moved from the north towards large cities farther south, using China's railways to travel rapidly and keep supplied.

SOURCE M

'East Asian Peace: Topple the Nanjing Government.' A propaganda poster depicting Chiang Kai-shek being hit by a Japanese soldier who holds ordinary people waving Japanese and Manchukuo flags, 1937.

? What imagery in Source M is used to depict Japan positively?

Shanghai

Hundreds of thousands of troops from both China and Japan battled in and around Shanghai for several months. Chinese troops were not as well equipped or trained as those of Japan, but they fought aggressively. Nevertheless, Japan prevailed, using its superior air and naval forces, along with its army. By the end of October 1937, Chinese forces were ordered to evacuate, thus giving Japan control of the mostly destroyed city. Chiang redeployed his troops to protect the route to Nanjing.

SOURCE N

Japanese soldiers breaking into a Chinese residence near Shanghai in 1937.

What is implied about the Second Sino-Japanese War through Source N?

Nanjing

Japan organized the Central China Area Army in November to move against Nanjing. Japanese forces quickly overwhelmed the Chinese troops sent to block their approach. On 16 November, Chiang Kai-shek ordered the government to relocate to the city of Wuhan, over 500 km (300 miles) west of Nanjing. By early December, Chiang had left Nanjing and a small army remained to defend the capital. The city was under siege by 9 December and captured on 13 December.

The Nanjing Massacre

Japan's Emperor Hirohito appointed Prince Asaka, his uncle, as head of the Central China Area Army just before the capture of Nanjing. Asaka was an ultranationalist and ordered that any Chinese captured be executed. As the Japanese army moved from Shanghai to Nanjing, troops executed captured Chinese soldiers, looted property of Chinese civilians, and raped women and children.

SOURCE O

? According to Source O, how will China resist Japan's invasion?

Excerpt from *The Collected Wartime Messages of Generalissimo Chiang Kai-Shek, 1937–1945*, Vol. 1, by the Chinese Ministry of Information, published by The John Day Company, 1946, p. 50. The Chinese Ministry of Information was a division of Chiang's government.

In face of the great crisis confronting us at this moment, there is no use in looking back with vain regrets. If we look ahead to the final outcome of the whole struggle, we may say that the present situation is definitely favourable to China. The basis of our confidence in China's ultimate success in prolonged resistance is not to be found in Nanking, nor in the big cities or municipalities, but in the villages, and in the widespread and unshaken determination of the people. Let our fellow-countrymen realize that there is no possible way of avoiding Japan's wanton aggression; let fathers inform their children and elder brothers encourage the younger ones; then, animated by general hatred of the enemy, our people will erect defences everywhere. Throughout the 4,000,000 square miles [10 million km²] of Chinese territory, strong fortifications, both visible and invisible, will be erected, and the enemy will receive a mortal blow.

SOURCE P

? Read Source P. How did Japanese soldiers treat Chinese prisoners?

Excerpt from *Japanese Terror in China* by H.J. Timperley, published by Modern Age Books, New York, USA, 1938, p. 19. Timperley was an Australian who lived in China, including Manchuria, from 1921. He was a correspondent for the British newspaper *Manchester Guardian* and an advisory editor to *Asia Magazine*; and contributed to *Foreign Affairs* and *Pacific Affairs*, two political journals.

Squads of men picked out by Japanese troops as former Chinese soldiers have been tied together and shot. These soldiers had discarded their arms and, in some cases, their military clothing. Thus far we have found no trace of prisoners in Japanese hands other than such squads, actually or apparently on the way to execution, save for men picked up anywhere to serve as temporary carriers of loot and equipment. From one building in the refugee zone, four hundred men were selected by the local police under compulsion from Japanese soldiers, and were marched off tied in batches of fifty between lines of riflemen and machine gunners. The explanation given to observers left no doubt as to their fate.

KEY TERM

Bayonet A type of knife that is attached to the end of a rifle for stabbing enemies when fighting at close range.

Once Nanjing was captured, these crimes multiplied. Tens of thousands of women and children were raped and usually murdered through mutilation afterwards. Probably hundreds of thousands of captured soldiers and civilians were killed. Many victims were tortured to death, but also burned, decapitated with swords, mutilated and used for **bayonet** practice. Japanese newspapers reported contests to determine which Japanese soldier could kill 100 captives with a sword first. Historians continue to debate the numbers of people killed during the Nanjing Massacre, but 300,000 is one possible figure. Many formerly indifferent foreigners were outraged at actions by Japanese soldiers, helping turn world public opinion against them.

Further Japanese conquests

Japan continued its conquest of China after the fall of Nanjing. Armies invaded southern and central areas of China. The main aim was to take control of railways, cities and ports. It was hoped that by severing supply lines, China's armies would collapse and Japan would achieve complete victory. In October 1938, the temporary capital of Wuhan was captured and most ports and railways along the coasts came under Japan's control. By mid-1939, Japan had conquered most of eastern China, where the bulk of its population and industries were located, yet a final victory was still elusive.

China's military was increasingly supplied by the Soviet Union (see page 74) and China changed its military strategies to fight superior Japanese armies (see page 78). China's government established itself at Chongqing in the far west. Japan attempted to bomb Chongqing into submission by aircraft, but this failed. Instead, Japan decided to concentrate on cutting supply lines to Chongqing, leading to conflicts with the USA by 1940 (see page 82).

SOURCE Q

Excerpt from *The Struggle for North China* by George E. Taylor, published by the Institute of Pacific Relations, New York, USA, 1940, pp. 78–9. Taylor was a professor of oriental studies at the University of Washington, USA.

The Japanese really had no plan for conducting a war and pacifying the country at the same time. Third-rate political generals with no more background than that of a military college were trying to meet first-rate political problems. They were divided and bewildered. A complete collapse of opposition was what they expected; in this they were disappointed … Conquest was rapid but incomplete. …

The Japanese have no political weapons to aid them. Not for them a political coup d'état, a well drilled party, and be-flagged streets to welcome the deliverer. Rather a puppet government of unreliable old men without popular support, and the task of subduing the resistance of the peasantry in every northern province.

According to Source Q, why did Japanese attempts to control China fail?

A rival Chinese-led government was created to manage areas of China under Japanese occupation. It was headed by Wang Jingwei, former head of China's pre-war government (see page 59). Wang served as president of the Republic of China, the government having the identical name of the independent government headed by Chiang Kai-shek. Its economy, education system and most other aspects were controlled by the Japanese military. With a population of 200 million, it was one of the largest countries in the world; its capital was Nanjing.

The impact of the war on Japan

Japan was not prepared for a long-term war. The First Sino-Japanese War, the Russo-Japanese War, actions in the First World War and the invasion of Manchuria were wars that were largely over in a few months, if not weeks.

While Japan had certainly expanded rapidly against China from 1931 to 1937, this was accomplished mostly through threats and limited military action. Entering the Second Sino-Japanese War, the Japanese military initially believed that the war would be largely over within three months.

Many leading generals and admirals believed that the war with China was too great a drain on resources and that meant that anti-Soviet defences were being critically weakened. To them, the Soviet Union was the greater threat as it bordered the industrial powerhouse of Manchukuo. Others believed that the Soviet Union was not a great threat and that the subjugation of China should be Japan's focus.

SOURCE R

According to Source R, how did Japan's military work to control the economy?

Excerpt from *A History of Shōwa Japan* by Takafusa Nakamura, published by University of Tokyo Press, Tokyo, Japan, 1998, p. 149. Takafusa Nakamura was a professor of economics at Tokyo University, Ochanomizu Women's University and Toyo Eiwa University, all in Japan.

The Law Relating to Temporary Export and Import Commodities regulated the processing, distribution, storage, and consumption of, as well as the production of, raw materials for, many items that were either exported or imported. This empowered the government through a range of ministerial ordinances and departmental directives to take complete control of many key industries. The government had already imposed restrictions on the use of steel and rubber, and on the mixing of staple fiber into cotton textiles for consumer products. The impact on the life of the people was immediate.

The Law for the Application of the Armament Industry Mobilization Law stipulated the means by which the army and navy could manage, utilize, and even expropriate factories ... It put all important supply industries under military control and provided for supervisors from the armed forces to be stationed at each key factory.

Millions of Japanese troops were deployed to China, absorbing many of those unemployed during the Great Depression. The military's war needs began to dictate economic and domestic policies (see page 36). Mass employment and shortage of consumer goods led to inflation and this led to the government instituting price controls. By the outbreak of the Second Sino-Japanese War, Japan's military controlled the government and soon political parties were banned.

How did the Second Sino-Japanese War affect Japan's relations with other states?

Responses to the Second Sino-Japanese War

Global responses to Japan's invasion of China were limited in many ways. Most countries had no intention of becoming involved in a war in China. Their primary concern was economic and this was directly related to their regional colonies.

Response: League of Nations

The League was consumed with European affairs in the late 1930s and also fully cognizant of how there was little they could do in regard to Japan or even China. This was also helped by anti-communist leanings in all member states except the Soviet Union, which joined in 1934. The governments of the League nations may have disliked Japan's actions, but they were fully aware of Japan's anti-communist stance and hoped that Japan would pressure the Soviet Union in Asia. The Soviets may have appreciated Japan being mired in China as it would reduce pressure against their border. Most League nations also saw China as a large, chaotic, corrupt nation that had only nominal control of its territory; it was not a nation any other country would be willing to fight another to maintain.

China did appeal to the League on 13 September 1937. The League referred the matter to the states that had signed the Nine-Power Treaty in Washington in 1922 since that treaty covered Pacific Ocean security matters (see page 29). The Nine-Power Treaty Conference met in Belgium in November and released a declaration that Japan and China should suspend hostilities and work with other countries to resolve the situation; they did not. The League simply remained uninvolved, uninterested and severely weakened as a result of the Abyssinian Crisis (see page 119).

SOURCE S

'Providing Aid to Refugees.' A postcard for the *Military Post* drawn by Matsunosuke Furushima, 7 July 1937. Matsunosuke was a Japanese artist who accompanied armies in China.

What message is conveyed by Source S?

Response: Soviet Union

The Soviet Union was largely pleased by Japan's invasion of China. Japan's pre-war pressure on Chiang Kai-shek's government ended Chiang's persecution of the CCP in late 1936 (see page 65). This opened the way for the Soviet Union to supply China's now-unified government with tanks, aircraft, ammunition and artillery. By late 1938, these allowed China to fight more effectively against Japan's armies. The Soviets were relieved that Japan's soldiers and industries were spending their energy and wealth against China. This essentially meant that they had little fear of a Japanese attack on their extremely long border with Manchukuo.

? According to Source T, why did the Soviet Union work to form the Second United Front?

SOURCE T

Excerpt from *The Wars for Asia, 1911–1949* by S.C.M. Paine, published by Cambridge University Press, UK, 2012, p. 103. Paine is a professor of strategy and policy at the US Naval War College, USA.

The Russians [Soviets] brokered the settlement that saved Chiang's life and created the Second United Front so that Chinese not Russian [sic] soldiers would die fighting Japan. … Chiang agreed to join the armed resistance against Japan, free his many political prisoners, end the encirclement campaigns against the communists, include all anti-Japanese parties both at home and abroad in the united front, and formulate a strategy to expel Japan from China …

The Russian strategy worked like a charm when the Japanese reacted viscerally with a full-scale invasion of China. By joining the Second United Front, the Nationalists acquired guilt by association. The Japanese saw spreading communism in China, their perennial nightmare, and were determined to stop it with their usual military solution of escalation.

The Soviets also took advantage of Japan's involvement in China, which also served to help Chiang's forces. In mid-1938, Japanese forces moved rapidly to capture Wuhan, China's temporary capital after the fall of Nanjing. The Soviets caused Japan to temporarily suspend its attack on Wuhan by provoking a conflict at Lake Khasan on the Soviet Union's border with Manchukuo. Fewer than 1000 soldiers were killed in total, but the Soviets clearly won, deploying at least 22,000 troops against less than 10,000 for Japan. Japan agreed to give the territory to the Soviet Union and resumed the attack on Wuhan. While Japan was able to capture Wuhan, the delay created by the conflict at Lake Khasan allowed the Soviets to ship large quantities of weapons to China's armies. These weapons allowed China's army to slow the Japanese invasion, allowing an orderly evacuation of civilians, factories and the army itself.

In May 1939, as Japan began moving west and deeper into China, the Soviet Union again moved to distract Japan and to enrich itself in the process. In May 1939, Soviet and Japanese forces battled at Nomonhan, Mongolia. Mongolia was a puppet-state managed by the Soviet Union and allowed the Soviets to deploy their troops along their border with Japanese-controlled

China. In September, 20,000 Japanese soldiers were killed, largely by Soviet tank forces, causing Japan to offer the Soviets a section of Chinese territory in return for an end to fighting; the Soviets accepted.

SOURCE U

'You take your foot off my hill top!' A cartoon by Sidney 'George' Strube from the *Daily Express*, 11 August 1938.

What is the message of Source U?

SOURCE V

Excerpt from *The Wars for Asia, 1911–1949* by S.C.M. Paine, published by Cambridge University Press, UK, 2012, pp. 144–5. Paine is a professor of strategy and policy at the US Naval War College, USA.

Russia [Soviet Union] agreed to loan China $50 million on 1 March [1938], and that same month the deliveries began arriving. Fourth-fifths of the money went to acquire airplanes. Between this 1 March loan and 13 June 1939, Russia extended three loans totalling $250 million, but actually delivering only $173 million. Military aid went mainly to Nationalist [KMT], not Communist [sic] forces. China repaid the loans in tea, wool, and tungsten. From 1937 to 1941 Russia sent 1,235 planes, 1,600 artillery pieces, more than 14,000 machine guns, 50,000 rifles, more than 300 advisers, more than 2,000 pilots, more than 3,000 engineers and technical experts, and thousands of drivers to deliver the goods. By the beginning of 1939, Russia had sent 5,000 military experts. Russian pilots flew from Nanjing, Wuhan, Chongqing, Chengdu, Lanzhou, Xi'an, and other places. More than 200 Russian pilots died in China. The Nationalists [KMT] relied on Russian planes until 1942, when U.S. generosity took over.

According to Source V, how did the Soviet Union support China against Japan?

The Soviet Union would continue to supply China's government with weapons, even when Chiang again turned against the CCP while still in the midst of war with Japan (see page 80). Over $173 million dollars were loaned to China's government and large quantities of military supplies provided until Germany invaded the Soviet Union in June 1941. At that point, shipments essentially ended as the Soviet Union fought for its very existence.

Response: USA

The primary policy of the USA was to preserve its Open Door Policy in the region, which would allow it to continue to sell its products to China. The US government wanted to demonstrate its displeasure with Japanese aggression, but not to the point where Japan would prevent US exports from reaching Asian markets. The USA also did not want Japan to move against its major regional colony: the Philippines. To this end, the US government's initial response was to prohibit the shipment of weapons or war supplies to either China or Japan in September 1937. Since Japan produced most of its own weapons, this only hurt China, the state that the USA wished to indirectly support. The USA was the world's largest producer of oil at the time and Japan relied on US oil imports to fuel its ships and industries. Oil and metals, both essential for Japan's war effort, were not prohibited and continued to be exported from the USA until sanctions were imposed in 1940.

A small US navy ship was sunk by Japanese aircraft in December 1937 as Japan moved against Nanjing (see page 69). This issue was quickly resolved when Japan stated that it was an accident and paid the USA for damages. Reports regarding the Nanjing Massacre (see page 69) widely circulated in the USA and around the world, perhaps helping the US government become slightly more involved in the conflict. In February 1938, the USA lent China $25 million and then remained relatively uninvolved in the conflict until 1940, when Japan began to move against territories outside China.

Response: Germany

Germany was in an awkward position with regard to the Second Sino-Japanese War. Germany supported Chiang Kai-shek's government because it was anti-communist. It also supplied China with many military advisors and did a great deal of business with China. By 1936, Germany supplied 80 per cent of all weapons used by China's army and China supplied Germany with tungsten, a crucial metal used to make tools and weapons. Although China benefited from Germany's support, it may be that Germany was more dependent on China's tungsten supplies for its growing military expansion (see page 144).

In 1936, Japan and Germany agreed to oppose communism in the Anti-Comintern Pact (see page 159). Germany hoped that this would mean increased pressure on the Soviet Union. Instead, Japan concentrated on expanding into China. With the outbreak of war by August 1937, the Soviets faced little pressure on their borders with Korea and Manchukuo. Attempting to be friendly to both Japan and China, both of which it needed,

Germany continued to supply China with about 60 per cent of its weapons until late 1938. Only then did Germany, under strong Japanese insistence, end military exports to China.

SOURCE W

Excerpt from *Japan Among the Great Powers: A Survey of Her International Relations* by Seiji Hishida, published by Longman, Green & Co., New York, USA, 1939, p. 349. The following passage regards Japan's rationale for the Anti-Comintern Pact of 1936. Seiji Hishida was a Japanese historian who received his doctorate from Columbia University in the USA, but lived and worked in Japan. He explains in the preface of this book that he feels compelled to explain Japan's views as they are misunderstood by Western nations.

At its Seventh Congress, held in the summer of 1935 at Moscow, the Comintern [Communist International] decided on a policy of organizing a united front with the Second International to oppose fascism and imperialism. At the same time, the Comintern made it clear that its future objectives were to be Japan, Germany and Poland, and that further support would be given to the Chinese communist armies in fighting Japan … In Manchoukuo [sic] the Comintern surreptitiously endeavoured through the Manchurian district committee of the Chinese Communist Party to organize cells, to win over and instigate bandits, and to direct raids by partisan [communist guerrilla] troops. …

… The fundamental object of this agreement [with Germany] was common defence against the destructive operations of the Comintern.

> Read Source W. Why did Japan agree to the Anti-Comintern Pact?

SOURCE X

Excerpt from *The Wars for Asia, 1911–1949* by S.C.M. Paine, published by Cambridge University Press, New York, USA, 2012, p. 144. Paine is a professor of strategy and policy at the US Naval War College, USA.

German leaders had deplored the 1937 escalation of the Second Sino-Japanese War in the belief that the conflict would disrupt commerce with China and German war plans that depended on numerous imported resources. The escalation ruined German plans to maintain cordial relations with both China and Japan and reduced Japan's military pressure on Russia that had kept Russian attentions divided. Japan deplored continuing German military aid to China. In the sixteen months following the escalation, Germany provided 60 percent of Chinese arms imports at a rate of sixty thousand tons per month that the Chinese used to take Japanese lives. Although Germany rejected Japanese requests for its support under the Anti-Comintern Pact, it reluctantly cut off its aid to the Nationalists to preserve working relations with Japan.

> According to Source X, why was Germany reluctant to end relations with China in support of Japan?

🔑 **KEY TERM**

Nazi–Soviet Pact More correctly known as the Molotov–Ribbentrop Pact. Germany and the Soviet Union agreed that neither country would attack the other or help other states attack the other. Additionally, there were economic aspects and secret sections that divided parts of central and eastern Europe into Soviet and German spheres of influence.

Germany contributed to Japan's overall policies in significant ways, primarily in its dealings with the Soviet Union. Japan's government was completely surprised that Germany and the Soviet Union agreed to the so-called **Nazi–Soviet Pact** in August 1939 (see page 175). Germany had made clear anti-communist and anti-Soviet statements and policies since 1933, with the rise of the Nazi Party. The new Non-Aggression Pact promised that neither Germany nor the Soviet Union would interfere with the plans and policies of the other. Yet Germany also agreed to supply the Soviets with weapons; the Soviets also agreed to provide Germany with raw materials and other products. This clearly violated the pact and greatly alarmed Japan. Japan desired an aggressive, anti-Soviet government near the Soviet Union in Europe so that the Soviets would be less likely to attack Japanese-held territories in its east.

As a result of Germany's agreement with the Soviet Union, the Japanese government collapsed and was replaced by one that worked to build better relations with the Soviets and strengthen its relationship with Germany and Italy. In September 1940, the **Tripartite Pact** created a formal alliance among Germany, Italy and Japan. Germany's conquering of France and the Netherlands by mid-1940 created opportunities to expand into French Indochina, which it promptly did (see page 82). In April 1941, Japan and the Soviet Union signed a neutrality agreement promising that neither would engage in war on the other. This helped contribute to Japan's policy of expanding its empire into French Indochina and the Dutch East Indies and moving against the USA (see page 85); it did not have to fear a Soviet attack.

Response: China

Chiang's Nationalist government adopted a new strategy after Wuhan was captured and the government had moved to Chongqing in the far west. This was to simply keep Japanese forces tied down as much as possible so that they committed more and more of their scarce resources to the war. It was hoped that eventually Japan would simply leave, being totally exhausted and unable to achieve an overall victory. Guerrilla fighters were a key part of this strategy, with up to a million operating in Japanese-controlled territory. These fighters assassinated Japanese officers, destroyed railway tracks, sabotaged factories, killed Chinese collaborators and detonated bombs in buildings occupied by Japanese people.

KEY TERM

Tripartite Pact An alliance involving initially Germany, Italy and Japan, coming into effect in September 1940 and eventually joined by Hungary, Romania, Slovakia, Bulgaria and Independent Croatia.

?

According to Source Y, how did Japan treat Chinese peasants?

SOURCE Y

Excerpt from *The Struggle for North China* by George E. Taylor, published by the Institute of Pacific Relations, New York, USA, 1940, p. 78. Taylor was a professor of oriental studies at the University of Washington, USA.

The peasantry was the only group large enough to make a social basis for Japanese rule. The method of dealing with the peasants, briefly speaking, has been one of terrorism. The Chinese people are no exception to the rule that most persons prefer peace to war, and if the Japanese could have made the conduct of the war bad enough and their reprisals too severe, it is possible that the peasants would not have rallied to the guerrillas. This would have been especially true where the guerrillas did not have sufficient time or leadership to train the population politically … The guerrillas came into this area in the spring of 1938 and began attacks on the railway of such seriousness that the Japanese were forced to reply immediately. The treatment of the peasantry, or such as they thought had aided the guerrillas, was very severe and most of the guerrillas were driven out.

Loss of support

While the guerrilla war continued, along with occasional regular army battles, Chiang Kai-shek worked to consolidate his power. He executed former warlords who had previously had some independence, and named himself president of various clubs and organizations based at Chongqing. While millions of Chinese had been made refugees and millions of others killed as a result of the war, Chiang remained in Chongqing and made little effort to alleviate their suffering or assist in any way. Chiang and his government were widely known as corrupt; officials demanded payments in order to even co-operate with the military. International financial aid to

SOURCE Z

'The dead end to the war against the Japanese.' A Japanese propaganda poster from autumn 1937 depicting Chiang Kai-shek being destroyed by Japan's military strength, as he burns in the red flames that symbolize communism. (This is a reference to the Second United Front.) Opposite Chiang Kai-shek, KMT officials flee Nanjing. North China, under Japan's control, is radiant with hope.

What message is meant to be conveyed by Source Z?

China often never made it to the military, but instead was distributed by Chiang to his supporters. The CCP used his complacency and corruption to depict the Nationalists as not particularly interested in China's people, only in their own security and wealth.

Some decisions by China's armies also caused a loss of support. In an effort to end a June 1938 advance by Japan's armies, Chiang ordered the destruction of dikes that kept the Yellow River from flooding a large part of China. This caused 70,000 square kilometres (27,000 square miles) to flood and kill almost a million Chinese people. As Chinese troops retreated, anything useful to the approaching Japanese armies was destroyed. This included food supplies, equipment and so forth, leading to millions dying of starvation. These actions and others by their own government destroyed any popularity the regime may have formerly held.

Collapse of Second United Front

The alliance between the CCP and the KMT was under great stress by mid-1939. Historians have noted that communists often executed KMT guerrilla fighters who also fought in Japanese-occupied territory. On several occasions there were small battles between communist and KMT army units. The official end of co-operation against Japan was in 1941, when the CCP's New Fourth Army was essentially destroyed by a much greater force, led by the KMT. This only helped the CCP in portraying Chiang and his forces as being more interested in fighting their own people, the Chinese, than Japan.

SOURCE AA

'The CCP–KMT United Front has crumbled.' A Japanese-sponsored propaganda poster depicting Stalin and Chiang Kai-shek burning in the red flames of communism as Chinese puppet-state officials shake hands.

According to Source AA, what will be the result of the collapse of the Second United Front?

Chiang's responses to Japan's invasion may have been occasionally successful or at least prevented outright defeat, but they also meant that his government was discredited. CCP guerrillas operating in the countryside worked to educate peasants about their form of communism, the corruption of the capitalist Nationalists, and their plans for post-war China, while following a strict code of conduct that treated peasants respectfully.

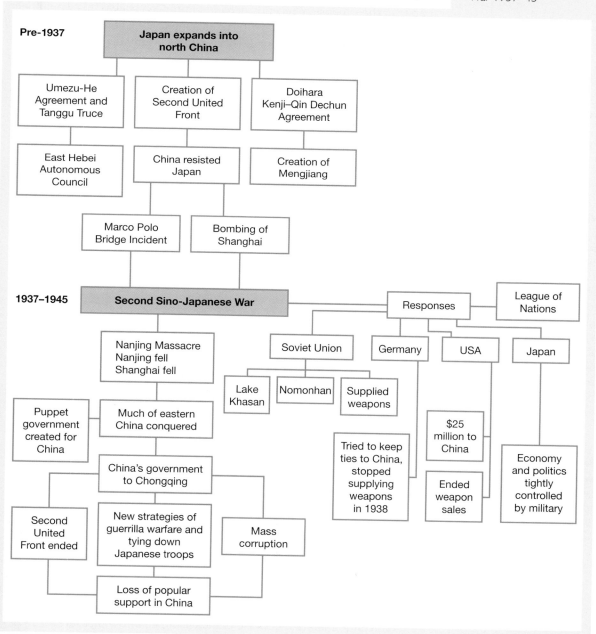

4 The route to Pearl Harbor

▶ **Key question:** *What Japanese actions led to war with the USA?*

Japan's army was the main protagonist in the Second Sino-Japanese War. Although Japan had not completed its victory against China, ultranationalists in Japan's government and military wanted to further increase the size of the empire at the expense of recently defeated European states. This would help Japan in China as it sought ways to cut all supplies to Chongqing, the base of Chiang and his Nationalist forces. These actions eventually provoked the USA to respond, leading directly to the outbreak of the Second World War in Asia and the Pacific.

French Indochina

What was the purpose of Japan's invasion of French Indochina?

Although Japan occupied China's ports, supplies continued to reach China's government at Chongqing. While some supplies were sent by the Soviets, the USA and Britain, through Burma and China's far western provinces, the largest conduit was through French Indochina, Laos and Cambodia. With France's defeat by Germany in 1940, its colonies were vulnerable. Japan requested permission from the French governor of Indochina to occupy its northern regions to cut supply lines to China. In exchange, Japan would allow the French government, now ruled by **Vichy France**, to remain in Indochina. This threat was clearly understood and permission was granted. Japan landed troops at Haiphong in French Indochina in September 1940 and soon built airbases.

KEY TERM

Vichy France The common label for the southern part of France that was not occupied by German troops between 1940 and 1942, with its administrative centre in the town of Vichy. While it was allowed a certain degree of autonomy over its internal affairs, and allowed to oversee France's colonial empire, it had no meaningful independence from German authorities.

SOURCE BB

Excerpt from *From the Marco Polo Bridge to Pearl Harbor: Japan's Entry into World War II* by David J. Lu, published by Public Affairs Press, Washington, DC, USA, 1961, p. 141. Lu was a former professor of East Asian studies at Bucknell University, USA.

Prior to the outbreak of war in Europe, Japan entertained no territorial designs towards French Indo-China. Its objectives were to gain French recognition of the state of war in China and of Japan's belligerent rights … Back in 1938, Japan repeatedly asked the French Indo-Chinese authorities to halt shipment of war materials to Chungking [sic] and had received no satisfaction. The War, Navy and Foreign Ministries [of Japan] advanced the idea of bombing the Yunnan railway which was built by French [investors], forcing a diplomatic settlement. But no concrete action was taken until the fall of 1939.

? According to Source BB, what was Japan's relationship with French Indochina prior to occupying part of it in 1940?

The USA's response was almost immediate. Three days after Japan's action, the USA prohibited the sale of scrap iron and steel to Japan. The USA was one of the main suppliers for metals to Japan for its industries. The USA also increased its financial assistance to China's government, but supply lines were difficult to maintain because of increasing Japanese pressure.

In July 1941, Japan occupied the rest of French Indochina. The USA immediately responded by:

- Freezing all Japanese assets in the USA and its territories, including bank deposits, stocks, bonds, ships and purchases that were waiting for shipment to Japan.
- Banning the sale of oil to Japan.
- Granting $240 million to China's government for military purchases.

Britain followed the USA and froze all Japanese assets throughout Britain and its empire. As the Netherlands ruled its colonial empire from London, since its own country had been overrun by German armies in 1940, it also froze Japan's assets in its territories. Both countries hoped that their response would warn Japan away from aggressive actions towards their possessions.

The oil embargo 1941

> How were Japan's foreign and military policies affected by the USA's ban on oil sales?

The ban on oil sales had the greatest effect on Japan and its policies. The USA was the largest supplier of oil to Japan, and without oil and its by-products, such as fuel for ships, aircraft and tanks, Japan's war against China would necessarily collapse. Japan had stored approximately 18 months' worth of fuel. This meant that in 18 months, Japan had to have another source of oil or their armies and industry would simply collapse. The largest nearby source of oil was the Netherlands' Dutch East Indies (Indonesia); Japan made plans for its occupation. Japan's government assumed that the USA would be provoked into war by a move to the Dutch East Indies, especially since the Philippines, a US colony, lay vulnerably between Japan and the Indies.

Japanese planning

Japan's Admiral Yamamoto developed a plan to attack the USA by defeating the US navy's Pacific fleet based at Pearl Harbor. Yamamoto hoped that the US government would be so surprised by Japan's action that it would choose not to fight Japan, allowing Japan time to absorb the Dutch East Indies into its growing empire and cut all supply lines to China. If the USA chose to fight, however, the loss of its navy would mean that it would take at least a year and probably longer for the USA to actually put any military stress on Japan. This would still give Japan plenty of time to defeat China, annex the Dutch East Indies and organize itself for war with the USA.

Another factor in Japan's planning for war with the USA was its support for the Soviet Union in its war against Germany. Japan's government was still primarily concerned about the military threat posed by the Soviet Union and the spread of communism. When Germany began an invasion of the Soviet Union in 1941, the USA responded with $1 billion of aid. Oil, food, trucks, tanks, ammunition and other goods were shipped from the USA to Soviet ports on the Pacific. In April, the Soviet Union and Japan had signed a neutrality pact (see page 78), preventing Japan from interfering with these shipments. Japan signed the pact so that it could finish its war against China and move against the Soviet Union at some later date; it did not want to have to have to fight a war with China and the Soviet Union simultaneously. US aid to the Soviets had the potential to save them from Germany's armies; Japan wanted the Soviets defeated, just not by their armies, at this point.

The Hull Note

The USA increased pressure on Japan on 26 November 1941. In the Hull Note, named after US Secretary of State Cordell Hull, the USA demanded that Japan:

- remove all its troops from Indochina and China, including Manchuria
- end its participation in the Tripartite Alliance
- repudiate the Republic of China that Japan had created, headed by Wang Jingwei.

Two weeks later, Japan attacked US and British forces all across the Pacific Ocean region.

SOURCE CC

? What is the message conveyed by Source CC?

'Death Takes a Holiday.' A cartoon published in the *Daily Mail*, 9 December 1941. The *Daily Mail* is a British newspaper published since 1896.

Pearl Harbor and the Pacific, December 1941

How effective were Japan's attacks on its targets on 7–8 December 1941?

On 7 December (8 December in Asia), a large-scale and highly organized series of attacks and invasions was launched by Japan against many targets. The most important of these was the attack on Pearl Harbor, the main US naval base in the US territory of Hawaii.

The attack on Pearl Harbor

A large Imperial Japanese Navy (IJN) fleet moved across the Pacific Ocean undetected by the USA in early December 1941. On 7 December, six Japanese aircraft carriers launched 353 aircraft of several types in two waves. These attacked US navy ships, airfields, aircraft and other facilities with torpedoes, bombs and machine-gun fire. The attack on the US fleet did the following:

- damaged four battleships and sank four others
- severely damaged or sank three cruisers, three destroyers and two other naval vessels
- destroyed 188 aircraft
- killed over 2400 people and injured 1200 others.

Japan's losses were minimal:

- twenty aircraft destroyed
- five small submarines sunk
- 65 men killed.

While Japan clearly won the battle, one of their main objectives remained unmet: to destroy all three US aircraft carriers. These were not present at Pearl Harbor as they were in training exercises elsewhere. Oil- and torpedo-storage facilities also survived the attack. The USA declared war on Japan the next day. This would eventually lead to Japan's defeat and surrender in August 1945.

SOURCE DD

Excerpt from *Modern Japan: A History in Documents* by James L. Huffman, published by Oxford University Press, New York, USA, 2004, pp. 148–9. Huffman is a professor emeritus for East Asian history at Wittenberg University, USA, authoring many works on modern Japanese history. The following is an excerpt from the declaration of war on the USA and Britain by Japan by Emperor Hirohito.

We [the Shōwa Emperor, Hirohito] hereby declare war on the United States of America and the British Empire. The men and officers of Our Army and Navy shall do their utmost in prosecuting the war. Our public servants of various departments shall perform faithfully and diligently their appointed tasks, and all other subjects of Ours shall pursue their respective duties; the entire nation with a united will shall mobilize their total strength so that nothing will miscarry in the attainment of our war aims.

According to Source DD, how will Japan conduct its war on Britain and the USA?

?

Attacks on other US territories

While Pearl Harbor was under massive attack, Japan moved against other US-held territories almost simultaneously:

- Japan attacked the Philippines by air on 8 December (7 December in the USA) and soon thousands of Japanese troops were landed to begin a large invasion of the islands.
- The island of Guam was a major junction point of undersea cables linking the USA and the Philippines, as well as other parts of Asia. It too was attacked on 8 December by aircraft, with Japanese forces landing within days to take control of the island.
- Wake Island held a US airbase. Japan attacked it by air on 8 December. The island was conquered in several weeks, giving Japan airfields that allowed it to control a large section of the Pacific Ocean.

SOURCE EE

Locations of Japanese military actions on 7/8 December 1941.

? According to Source EE, how many targets did Japan attack in December 1941?

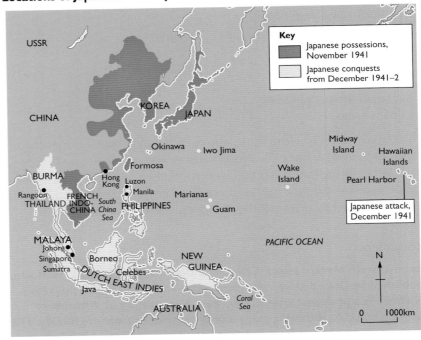

Attacks on British territories

As Pearl Harbor, Guam and Wake Island were under assault, Japan launched attacks against British territories in Asia. Japanese troops invaded Malaya (Malaysia) on 8 December and Japanese aircraft attacked British naval vessels in the area. All of Malaya and Singapore were captured by mid-February 1942. Japan also attacked Britain's great port in China, Hong Kong, on 8 December and conquered it by the end of December. Burma, a major British territory that also produced oil, was placed under immediate pressure when Thailand, an independent state, was invaded on 8 December from French Indochina. Thailand immediately surrendered and soon Burma was invaded by forces from Thailand and Japan, now allied.

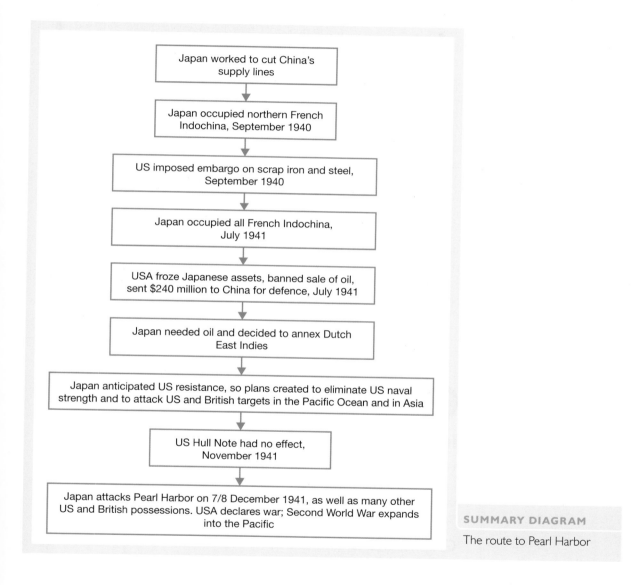

SUMMARY DIAGRAM

The route to Pearl Harbor

Chapter summary

Japan's expansion and the international response

Japan's chaotic and weak political system allowed the army to interfere with the state's foreign policy and ultimately dictate it. This led to the Manchurian Crisis, which was mainly caused by Japanese troops anxious to annex the Chinese province of Manchuria. While successfully invading Manchuria, the military increased control of the government in Japan and its economy. Pretending to liberate Manchurian people from China's rule, through the creation of the puppet-state of Manchukuo, did not convince the League of Nations that Japan only acted in the best interests of those that it conquered.

A slow-moving League eventually criticized Japan in the Lytton Report in 1932 but could do no more. As Japan's military took more control of the economy, it occupied more territories in China. In 1937, China and Japan entered a new phase as Japan launched a massive, two-pronged invasion of its neighbour. This, the Second Sino-Japanese War (1937–45), would see Japan conquer much of eastern China; the death of millions of Chinese through starvation and war; and the establishment of another Japanese puppet-state, the Republic of China. Japan was unable to end resistance to its rule or conquer western China, leading to attempts to cut off supply routes to the Nationalist government of Chiang Kai-shek in Chongqing. Japan invaded French Indochina and eventually controlled most of it, leading the USA to place an embargo on important industrial materials that Japan desperately required. Japan decided that the best course of action was to annex even more territory so that it would have an oil-producing region, the Dutch East Indies. Japan executed an attack on the main US naval base at Pearl Harbor in 1941, hoping to shock the USA into allowing the annexation of the Dutch East Indies or at least delay the US response. Instead, the USA declared war on Japan, eventually leading to the destruction of Japan's empire in the Second World War in the Pacific.

 Examination advice

Interpreting visual sources

Visual sources are often included on Paper 1 examinations and can be used in any of the questions. Visual sources include cartoons, maps, graphs, charts, tables, photographs, posters and potentially many other types of graphic art. Some visual sources are easier to understand than others.

Graphs, charts, and tables

Graphs, charts and tables usually convey very specific information such as economic data, how many people from a particular political party were in parliament or how many leaders a country had over a period of time. This visual source still needs interpreting, however.

Example: table

Look at Source T from Chapter 1 (page 35):

SOURCE T

Table indicating annual farm income in Japanese yen

Year	Owned land	Rented land
1926	1598	987
1927	1421	987
1928	1394	923
1929	1366	874
1930	837	579
1931	641	449
1932	703	538
1933	838	617
1934	837	612
1935	954	683

Indicates that the data covers the years 1926–35.

Indicates that those who rented always made less than those who owned land.

Indicates that the differences in financial terms between the groups was far less after 1930 than before.

States that there are two classes of farmers being reviewed here in terms of income: those with land and those without.

Source T conveys a tremendous amount of information, although it appears quite simple. After reading Chapter 1, you know that there was a problem for Japan's farmers in the 1920s and that these problems worsened as a result of the Great Depression. Knowledge from the chapter will be useful in understanding this table.

This table clearly indicates that farm incomes for both those who owned and those who rented began declining in 1927 from income levels of 1926. The most dramatic fall in income for both groups was in 1930, the first year of the Great Depression, although 1931 had the least income for both. The table also clearly indicates that the differences in income between the two groups became less through time. In 1927, those who owned land made 434 more yen than those who rented, but in 1931, the difference was only 192 yen; the difference in 1932 was only 165 yen. Farmers who owned land in 1926 made 40 per cent less income in 1935, the year with the highest income for farmers since 1929; renters made only 31 per cent less in the same period.

The data in this table shows that farmers suffered a tremendous loss of income in the decade between 1926 and 1935. Although those who owned land always had more yen than those who rented, it was those who owned land who suffered greater loss of yen over those ten years. This meant that there were fewer differences between owners and renters in terms of purchasing power. Using our knowledge from the chapter, one can understand why a change in governing structure and economic policy would generally appeal to farmers, who were obviously negatively affected by Japan's perpetual economic crisis.

Cartoons, posters, stamps, graphic art

Cartoons and posters can be very similar in terms of symbolism, message and intended effect. Either can be intended to make fun of something, criticize a person or an idea, try to get the viewer to agree with their point of view, or inform. They can be complex and should be treated very carefully and thoroughly.

Symbolism

First we need to consider symbolism. The chart below gives some of the more common symbols and their potential meanings. However, these are just some of the basics and you should know that the list is almost endless.

Symbol	Represents	Symbol	Represents
Red star, five points	USSR, communism	Hammer and sickle	USSR, communism
Bear	Russia, USSR	Justice	Scales, blind-folded woman
Bundle of sticks with axe on top, fasces	Italy, Roman Empire, Mussolini, fascism	Dragon	China
Workers' cap	USSR, communism	Money bags, fat men	Wealth
Swastika	Nazi Germany	Crown of leaves, winged goddess	Victory
Red flag	USSR, communism	Statue of Liberty (one arm holding torch, other holding tablet)	Democracy, USA
The colour red	Communism	Uncle Sam	USA
Outstretched arm salute	Nazi Germany	Olive branch, dove	Peace
Goddess of Freedom (two hands holding torch)	Freedom, democracy	Skull and crossed bones	Death
Red sun on white background	Japanese flag	Hourglass	Time
Turtle	Slow movement	Factory, smokestack	Industry
Chains	Oppression	Bulldog, eagle	War, possibly a nation such as Britain for bulldog or eagle for the USA
Bomb	Disaster, war, major tension	Woman or baby crying	Misery, death, destruction

Representations of people

Significant people like Hirohito, Chiang Kai-shek, Mussolini, Hitler, Chamberlain and others dealt with in this book appear in cartoons and other visual sources. Mussolini is always depicted as short, bald and aggressive. Hitler has his distinctive moustache and black hair. Cartoons from Europe and the USA very often have overt racist themes towards Asians and Africans that are rightly unacceptable now, so be aware of this. Cartoons in this and other chapters in the book will help you understand how individuals and groups typically appear in cartoons.

Captions

Captions are the labels that accompany visual sources. These are very important, often informing you of the date of creation, name of artist and perhaps country of origin. All of this information helps determine the message of the source. Often captions include a direct message which is easy to understand such as the message on the Japanese military-produced postcard that states 'Providing Aid to Refugees' (see page 73). It is clear from this caption that those who produced the postcard, probably to be mailed home to family in Japan, wanted people to believe that they were helping refugees in China. Read captions carefully.

Example: poster

Look at Source E (see page 58). The poster's Chinese text says 'Japan and China helping to promote world peace.' The message is clear that Japan and China should be seen as working together, and Manchuria is included for good measure. The caption is supported by an impressive amount of imagery. There are two white doves, symbols of peace, and each of the three individuals, perhaps children, is smiling and happy. We should note that each has a national costume: a Chinese girl and Manchurian boy in traditional outfits plus a Japanese boy in modern shorts and shirt, perhaps a child's version of a sailor suit. Three flags are present: the flag of Japanese-occupied China, the flag of Manchukuo and, of course, Japan's flag. Other symbols in the poster are a castle or fort that probably indicates the Great Wall of China and the red sun symbol of Japan that dominates the background of the entire poster.

You are aware from this chapter that Japan invaded Manchuria in 1931, occupied parts of northern China shortly afterwards and by 1937 began a massive invasion of the rest of the country, in parts of which it was able to establish a Republic of China puppet-state. It would seem that the wording on the poster contradicts what we know about history. While that may be true, it is still an important piece of evidence for us to consider. Who was the audience for this poster? What is the point of the message? When would this poster be produced? Why did the artist choose this particular imagery? These are the kind of questions you should consider when analysing posters and other visual sources.

Example: cartoon

Sidney 'George' Strube's 1938 cartoon regarding tensions between Japan and the Soviet Union (Source U, page 75) includes the caption 'You take your foot off my hill top!' You are aware, of course, that Japan and the Soviet Union fought over areas along their mutual borders during this period. The caption makes it clear that Japan claims a 'hill top' that is occupied by Soviet troops. By referring to the territory as a 'hill', the artist may be trying to convey the message that this is a petty dispute since a hill is usually small. The imagery of the cartoon is significant in that the artist indicates that Japan is likely to lose the argument over the hill. The Soviet Union is represented by a massive soldier's boot, complete with a spur containing the hammer and sickle symbol of the Soviet Union. Japan, on the other hand, is represented by a tiny soldier who is jumping on the Soviet boot's toe, unable to do more or believing it is more powerful than it really is.

Example: stamps

Source G from Chapter 3 (page 113) is a stamp from the era of Mussolini in Italy. The stamp says 'Pension Fund [for the] Black Shirts', the group that propelled Mussolini into power. Clearly, either the stamp wants people to contribute to the pension fund of Black Shirt members or the revenues generated from the stamp's sale will go into such a fund. The imagery on the stamp communicates that the government producing the stamp, the one established by the Black Shirts, is directly connected to ancient Rome. This imagery includes:

- Roman numerals that give the date 1923
- a Roman coin with important figures, perhaps a Roman emperor symbolizing Mussolini
- the word 'ROMA', which obviously stood for the city of Rome
- bundle of rods with an axe, the fasces, symbol of the Fascist Party that was once the Black Shirts.

The wording and imagery clearly state: support the Black Shirts because they have re-established the Roman Empire or the basis of a future one. The caption on the stamp is critically important in understanding this piece of evidence.

Photographs

Photographs are another visual source. Photographs can capture a specific moment. Sometimes photographs just record what the photographer saw at that particular moment, while many photographs, especially of political events, politicians and conferences, are ones in which everyone poses in a specific way for an intended effect.

Example: photographs

Source G (page 60) is a photograph of a group of Japanese soldiers standing on a wall in China and is captioned 'Japanese soldiers planting Japan's flag on the Great Wall of China.' Notice that:

- The soldiers are all facing the camera.
- Everyone has a weapon.
- Japan's flag is clearly visible.
- Everyone in the picture seems uninjured and there is no dead or wounded enemy present.

It is clear that this picture was staged. First, everyone is clearly visible, facing the camera, and the flag is not just present, but very visible. Second, the battle is clearly long over. While the wall is damaged, indicating that there was indeed fighting, we see no dead or wounded. In fact, the only people we can see on the wall are in the picture. Standing on top of a wall with enemy nearby would probably be very dangerous. Clearly, the enemy is not nearby and there are no threats to the safety of these men. Although it is staged, this, like all pieces of historical evidence, is important. Why would anyone want to take a picture of soldiers with a flag on the Great Wall of China? What do the clothing and weapons of the men indicate about the event that this is supposed to commemorate? What does the damage to the wall mean or what message does it convey?

How to answer

You may be asked to analyse one of the visual sources that appear on your Paper 1 examination in Question 9. The questions are usually very straightforward, asking you to indicate the message of the source.

> Remember that questions for Prescribed subject 3 will be numbered 9, 10, 11 and 12 in the Paper 1 exam.

Example 1

This question (in the style of question 9a) uses Source F (page 59).

What message is conveyed by Source F? (3 marks)

First, take note of any words. The caption clearly indicates that a judge disapproves of Japan's actions regarding a particular event, but the punishment is just words. Japan, according to the caption, rejects this and tells the court to mind its own business. The words 'Trial by Geneva' are at the bottom of the cartoon.

Next, notice symbolism:

- The League of Nations symbol is surrounded by doves representing peace.
- The judges, all European, are labelled: wisdom, sanity, decency, good faith, justice and honour.
- The Lytton Report, in the form of a huge book, is being read by other Europeans.
- A gun-toting Japanese man is alone to hear the verdict and is thumbing his nose, a gesture of contempt or ridicule, to the judges.
- Two spectators are talking to each other and not listening to the proceedings.

Lastly, write your answer to the question.

The type and origin of the source are stated in the opening of the answer.

Source F is a cartoon by David Low that was published in the 'Evening Standard' in November 1932. The message of the cartoon is that the League of Nations, represented by the judges and standing for various values such as sanity and good faith, has decided that Japan has acted wrongly. The Lytton Report located on the judge's table clearly indicates that this is about Japan's invasion of Manchuria. The caption indicates that although Japan did something wrong, the League of Nations either cannot or will not punish Japan for its actions.

Symbols, such as the doves and other details are clearly understood and used to support the answer.

The concluding sentence clearly states the message of the cartoon.

Japan is shown as a single individual, perhaps a statement about its diplomatic isolation. It is also shown with a gun indicating that this is a violent nation, in contrast to the unarmed individuals and the doves of peace located above the judges. The message of the cartoon is that the European-dominated League of Nations represents much good, but is unable to enforce its rules on member states, specifically Japan. The cartoon further indicates that Japan has little or no interest in the decisions of the League and will do whatever it wants, perhaps more violence as indicated by the weapons.

> The answer indicates that the question was understood. There are at least three points made about the cartoon. All points are clear, supported with evidence from the cartoon, and accurate. There is good use of analysis and deduction. Mark: 3/3.

Example 2

This question (in the style of question 9b) uses Source M (page 68).

What message is conveyed by Source M? (2 marks)

First, take note of any words. The caption states: 'East Asian Peace: Topple the Nanjing Government.'

Next, notice symbolism:

- The man in the blue uniform is being punched by the huge fist of a brown-clad soldier who has a Japanese sword.
- The man in the blue uniform holds a large knife or sword.
- The long arm of the Japanese soldier is holding people and animals.
- The held people are waving flags of Manchukuo and Japan.
- The Japanese red sun symbol positioned behind the people protected by the Japanese soldier.

Lastly, write your answer to the question.

Source M is a Japanese propaganda poster from 1937. The message of the poster is clear in its caption that asks people to get rid of the Nanjing-based Nationalist government in order to have peace. The Nationalist government, represented here by a likely depiction of Chiang Kai-shek with a sword, is violent and not peaceful. Japan, clearly the protector of people and peace, is represented by a soldier who is using only his arms and fist to protect Japanese, Manchurian and Chinese people from Chiang.

> The answer indicates which source is being analysed, the type of source and the date.

> The caption is discussed and integrated with a discussion of the imagery.

The prosperity of those being protected by Japan may be indicated by the inclusion of farm animals such as a pig as well as the large belly of the Japanese soldier who has plenty to eat. Chiang, in contrast, is thin.

> 'Likely' and 'may be' and other terminology is used when making hypotheses based on elements in the poster.

Finally, Chiang and the Nationalists are alone, with only one individual depicting them in the poster. Japan, however, is not alone. It has the support of many people representing many nationalities. The message is that Japan brings peace and prosperity while protecting people from aggressive Nationalists.

> All major elements depicted in the poster are discussed and analysed, including the soldiers, the civilians, flags and other imagery.

> The answer is summarized in the final sentence to make sure the meaning is clear.

> The answer indicates that the question was understood. There are at least two points made about the poster. All points are clear, supported with evidence from the poster, and accurate. There is good use of analysis and deduction. Mark: 2/2.

Examination practice

Using the examples given above, explain the message of each of the following sources:

Cartoons

Source H from Chapter 1 (page 20)

Source J from Chapter 1 (page 22)

Posters

Source S from Chapter 2 (page 73)

Source Z from Chapter 2 (page 79)

Photographs

Source N from Chapter 2 (page 69)

Source N from Chapter 3 (page 120)

Using the example of the analysis of the table given on page 85, explain the importance to historians of the following charts and tables:

Source V from Chapter 1 (see page 36)

Source A from Chapter 3 (see page 101)

The following are exam-style questions for you to practise, using sources from the chapter. Sources can be found on the page references given.

The questions also reflect the numbering style of the exam (there are no questions 1–8; questions for The move to global war begin at question 9).

PAPER 1 PRACTICE QUESTIONS FOR CASE STUDY 1 (USING SOURCES FROM CHAPTER 1)

See Chapters 3 and 4 for advice on answering questions 11 and 12.

Source V: page 36   Source Y: page 41

Source X: page 41   Source Z: page 42

9 **a)** What, according to Source Z, were the methods used by right-wing military groups to achieve their aims in Japan?   [3 marks]
   b) What message is conveyed by Source V?   [2 marks]

10 With reference to its origin, purpose and content, analyse the value and limitations of Source X for historians studying the influence of Japan's military in the government in the 1930s.   [4 marks]

11 Compare and contrast what Sources X and Y indicate about the strength of Japan's military in political affairs before 1941.   [6 marks]

12 Using the sources and your own knowledge, evaluate the relative strength of Japan's military in the government by 1941.   [9 marks]

PAPER 1 PRACTICE QUESTIONS FOR CASE STUDY 1 (USING SOURCES FROM CHAPTER 2)

See Chapters 3 and 4 for advice on answering questions 11 and 12.

Source O: page 70   Source Q: page 71

Source P: page 70   Source S: page 73

9 **a)** What, according to Source Q, were the problems for the Japanese military during the Second Sino-Japanese War?   [3 marks]
   b) What message is conveyed by Source S?   [2 marks]

10 With reference to its origin, purpose and content, analyse the value and limitations of Source P for historians studying the Second Sino-Japanese War.   [4 marks]

11 Compare and contrast what Sources O and S indicate about fighting during the Second Sino-Japanese War.   [6 marks]

12 Using the sources and your own knowledge, evaluate the success of Japan during the Second Sino-Japanese War.   [9 marks]

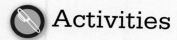 # Activities

1 Access the David Low cartoon archive that is hosted by the University of Kent at <u>www.cartoons.ac.uk</u>.
   - Each student in the class should select a cartoon to analyse, with no two students selecting the same one.
   - Each student should answer the question 'What message is conveyed by your selected cartoon?' and try and make at least three points.
   - Each student should present their analysis to another student for marking, along with the reference number to the cartoon. Students should mark each other out of three possible points.

2 One way to learn to analyse symbolism in cartoons is to create a bingo-like game where symbols are represented on a grid pattern. Each grid card should have symbols arranged in a different order from any of the others. Someone calls out the meaning of a symbol, keeping track of which meanings and symbols have been called out. As meanings are matched with symbols, students may cross out or otherwise mark the appropriate symbol. Once a line of symbols is complete, that individual is the winner of that round. Grid patterns can contain any number of symbols, with perhaps 5 across and 5 down being the easiest to work with.

3 As a class, debate which form of propaganda presented in this chapter is the most effective. Continue the debate regarding which forms of propaganda and political advertising are the most used and most effective today. Be sure to support your ideas with evidence.

Case Study 1: Timeline

1889	Meiji Constitution declared
1894	Japan occupies Korea
1894–5	First Sino-Japanese War
1895	Tripartite Intervention by Russia, Germany, France
1902	Anglo-Japanese Alliance
1904–5	Russo-Japanese War; Japan takes control of South Manchurian Railway
1914–18	First World War; Japan takes Shantung Peninsula; Japanese economy grows rapidly
1919–23	Japan's economy constricts causing hardship for farmers and workers
1921–2	Washington Naval Conference and treaties limit Japanese Navy
1923–7	Economic revival through rebuilding Tokyo earthquake damage
1925	Peace Protection Law allows arrest of communists and others who advocate government changes
1927	Bank failures, economy rapidly constricts
1928	Army faction assassinates warlord ruler of Manchuria; acts against government policy
1929	Great Depression constricts economy further
1930	London Naval Conference, limits Japanese navy
1931	**Mar:** Attempted coup against government by military **Sept:** Mukden Incident; invasion of Manchuria by Japan **Oct:** Failed coup against government by military **Dec:** Lytton Commission formed to investigate Manchurian Crisis for League of Nations
1932	**May:** Failed coup against government by military

	Oct: Lytton Commission recommends Japan withdraw from Manchurian conquests
1933	**Feb:** League of Nations condemns Japan as an aggressor state **Mar:** Japan leaves League of Nations; Chinese province of Jehol captured by Japan **May:** Tanggu Truce signed with China, recognizing Japanese conquests
1935	**June:** Umezu–He Agreement demilitarizes much of northern China, removing Chinese armies; Mengjiang or Mengkukuo formed by Japan
1936	**Feb:** Military faction attempts to seize Emperor and overthrow government; coup fails **Dec:** Second United Front formed between Chinese factions to oppose Japan
1937–1945	**Aug 1937–Aug 1945:** Second Sino-Japanese War
1938	**July:** Soviet–Japanese fighting along Manchukuo border
1939	**May:** Soviet–Japanese fighting in Mongolia; Soviets take territory to end fighting
1940	**Sep:** Japan begins occupation of parts of French Indochina; USA bans sale of scrap iron and steel to Japan
1941	**Jan:** Second United Front in China collapses **July:** All French Indochina occupied; USA bans sale of oil, seizes Japanese assets in the USA **Nov:** US Hull Note demands Japan withdraw from China and Indochina as well as Manchuria **Dec:** Japan attacks the USA at Pearl Harbor and other locations across Pacific Ocean region; British also attacked; USA declares war

Case Study 2

Italian and German expansion 1933–40

CHAPTER 3

Interwar conditions in Europe and Italian foreign policy 1933–6

In the 1930s, the Great Depression weakened the Great Powers economically, politically and militarily. It also caused Italy to seek new trading partners, and therefore more independence, and gave an opportunity to the Nazi Party to take control of Germany. The League of Nations' weakness was revealed in the Manchurian Crisis (see Chapter 2) and then confirmed by the Abyssinian Crisis (see page 119). During this period, Italy and Germany pursued foreign policies that challenged the Great Powers, the League of Nations and various treaties. Since no country implemented its foreign policy without considering the reactions and realities of other states, it is important to understand the context of renewed Italian and German initiatives. In this chapter, you will need to consider the following questions:

★ How were European states affected by the Great Depression?

★ How did Mussolini's Fascist Party affect Italian foreign policy?

★ What role did the Abyssinian Crisis have in destroying the League of Nations' credibility?

★ How did Italy's relationship with Germany change in 1939?

 # The economic and political effects of the Great Depression

> ▶ *Key question: How were European states affected by the Great Depression?*

 KEY TERM

Wall Street Crash A rapid decline of the US stock market, located on Wall Street in New York City, in October 1929, which led to an economic crisis throughout the world.

The Great Depression marked a turning point in interwar history. Not only did it weaken the economic and social stability of the world's major powers, but it also dealt a devastating blow to the League of Nations and international co-operation. Many historians have labelled it the third greatest catastrophe of the twentieth century, after the two world wars.

How did the Great Depression affect the economic policies of different countries?

Economic effects

Between 1929 and 1932, as a result of the **Wall Street Crash**, world trade declined by 70 per cent, leading to mass unemployment in most industrialized nations. The USA was at the time the world's largest economy and greatest importer of raw materials and manufactured goods. Yet by 1932, it suffered from 25 per cent unemployment, with only Germany faring worse with 26 per cent. The global banking industry was in crisis and loans were recalled as stocks lost value and industry shrank. US-based banks had lent to governments and corporations around the world, often through short-term loans. When these loans were recalled and not extended, many countries were immediately affected, especially Germany. Eventually, banks all over the world began to collapse, including 9000 in the USA alone during the 1930s.

Trade barriers

To keep money and investment within their own borders, most nations erected trade barriers by taxing imports, further hindering world trade and an economic recovery. As Germany was an exporting nation that relied on the US market, US trade barriers caused a 61 per cent decline in German industrial production overall. British international trade declined by 60 per cent and the USA saw its international trade retract by 70 per cent. Japan was also severely affected by US trade barriers (see page 34).

SOURCE A

The effect on unemployment and loss of trade of the Great Depression between 1929 and 1933. Statistics taken from *The Inter-War Crisis: 1919–1939*, second edition by R.J. Overy, published by Pearson Education, UK, 2007, p. 52, and *The European World: A History*, second edition by Jerome Blum *et al.*, published by Little Brown & Co., USA, 1970, p. 885. Overy is a modern history professor at King's College, University of London, UK. Blum was chairman of the history department of Princeton University, USA.

Great Depression 1929–1933

Country	USA	Britain	France	Germany
Estimated % of unemployed workers by 1933	25	23	5	26
% decline in wholesale prices	–32	–33	–34	–29
% change in exports	–69.5	–49.5	–63.1	–53.7
% change in industrial production	–36	–3.8	–19.5	–34.0

According to Source A, which nation was affected the most between 1929 and 1933 by the Great Depression?

Countries did not just erect trade barriers; they also turned to their colonies, if they had any, to protect their own industries. Britain turned to its empire, establishing a system of **imperial preference**. This placed large taxes on imports from outside the empire, stimulating industry in the more industrial areas, such as Britain, and allowing Australia and Canada, producers of agricultural products, to sell their products to Britain and India. By the mid-1930s over half of all British exports were to other parts of the British Empire, which at the time covered about a quarter of the world. The French imperial preference system was even more successful. The French Empire covered just over nine per cent of the globe and was a market for one-third of France's industrial production.

Vast countries such as the USA and the Soviet Union contained many of the resources needed for most types of industry and manufacturing. They could

 **KEY TERM**

Imperial preference
A system of commerce created by lowering import taxes between areas of an empire, while increasing taxes on imports from countries outside the empire.

turn inward during economic crises and reduce international trade. It was clear to smaller industrialized states that having an empire could provide raw materials, food, markets and lands to settle their surplus populations and would therefore help alleviate their economic crises.

How did the Great Depression affect the formation and policies of national governments differently?

Political effects

The Great Depression brought political crises to several countries, often leading to **coalition** governments that were often unstable. Other countries saw long-established governments voted out in preference for an alternative. Political parties and governments throughout the world feared violence and the spread of communist ideology, which seemed to go hand in hand to many observers.

The USA

The Republican Party fell from political power when they lost control of the presidency and both divisions of Congress (the US parliament) in elections at the end of 1932. Franklin Roosevelt, commonly known by his initials as FDR, won the presidency, leading the Democrats to victory. Democrats took control of both the House of Representatives and the Senate with huge majorities. Roosevelt was seemingly a man of action and inspiring speeches, who passed a barrage of laws and executive orders in the first 100 days of his presidency in 1933 with support from Congress:

- Banks were temporarily closed to give the government the opportunity to investigate their financial soundness.
- Taxes were raised.
- Government spending increased while government salaries were reduced.
- More trade barriers were erected.

KEY TERM

Coalition A government that includes multiple parties, often formed during times of national crisis.

Deficit spending When a government spends more money than it brings in through taxation, usually to stimulate a country's economy.

SOURCE B

Comparison of US national election results of 1930 and 1932.

Election year	President	House	Senate
1930	Republican with 58.2% of vote	Republicans 218 Democrats 216	Republicans 48 Democrats 47
1932	Democrat with 57.4% of vote	Democrats 313 Republicans 117	Democrats 59 Republicans 36

? According to Source B, how did the US federal government change between the 1930 and 1932 elections?

Roosevelt advocated a policy of **deficit spending**, while Republicans opposed this policy and continued to advocate a reduction in government power and in spending, and for the depression to run its natural course. However, Republican policies were unpopular because they had not alleviated the effects of the Great Depression from 1930 to 1932, so Roosevelt and his Democratic Party were able to dominate politics throughout the 1930s.

Roosevelt continued to support the US public's view that foreign wars and conflicts were not the concern of the USA. He put this succinctly in economic terms in a memo to his advisor Adolf Berle: 'Don't forget that I discovered that over ninety percent of all national deficits from 1921 to 1939 were caused by payments for past, present, and future wars.' The USA isolated itself from most European foreign affairs in the 1930s, primarily allowing Britain and France to take the lead in international diplomacy.

Britain

Britain's government was headed by the Labour Party until 1931. The government spent money to help the unemployed, but, as more and more people lost jobs, government tax revenue also decreased, leading them to attempt to borrow money from US banks. These banks were also stressed and therefore placed many conditions and guarantees on Britain that the government was unwilling to accept.

The Labour government entered into a coalition with other parties in August 1931, forming the National Government. While it was dominated by the Conservative Party, there were also ministers from the Liberal and Labour parties; the prime minister was from Labour. Many in the Labour Party, however, disagreed with the formation of the coalition government, so the party split into two unequal groups with the minority supporting the coalition. This National Government continued throughout the 1930s and brought a measure of economic stability by 1934; this was done partly through imperial preference (see page 101).

International impact of British economic policies

Historian P.M.H. Bell has argued that British trade barriers to countries outside the empire, specifically those in central and eastern Europe, caused many countries to economically gravitate towards Germany (see page 143). This helped Germany's economy and caused countries to form closer political relationships with Germany as well. Germany soon became as important as France and Britain in these economies, if not more so in some cases.

Affect on military programmes

All political parties had to compromise in various ways to make sure the National Government remained in power. The Labour Party, however, would not compromise on the issue of military spending. They believed that large numbers of weapons made war more likely and argued that the stockpiling of huge amounts of weaponry, ships and other tools of war had been one of the key causes of the First World War. This meant that Britain's military remained weak throughout the 1930s, preventing aggressive responses to any Italian and German challenges.

Economic stress also meant that Britain did not have the funds to invest in rearmament. Instead, it worked to limit armaments, specifically warships, through treaties signed in 1930 and 1935 (see pages 29 and 65).

? What were two results of the imperial preference system, according to Source C?

SOURCE C

Excerpt from *The Origins of the Second World War in Europe*, second edition by P.M.H. Bell, published by Pearson Education, UK, 1998, pp. 148–9. The book is currently in its third edition, published in 2007. Bell is an honorary senior fellow in the Department of History at the University of Liverpool, UK, and has published several books.

A Foreign Office [Ministry of Foreign Affairs] memorandum put to the Cabinet in December 1931 warned that a high protective tariff along with imperial preference would separate Britain from European affairs and diminish British influence on the Continent … In 1933 and 1934 the Foreign Office urged the importance of Britain providing a market for bacon, eggs, butter and timber for the Baltic states and Poland, which might otherwise come into the economic orbit of Berlin or Moscow. Similarly, it was argued that Britain should buy cereals and other farm produce from Hungary and Yugoslavia, to prevent them from becoming over-dependent on the German market. In both cases the government refused …

Rearmament programmes in the early 1930s were politically impossible, at a time when it was obvious that Italy and then Germany were starting to rebuild their military forces (see pages 116 and 144).

It is important to keep the coalition government, a product of the Great Depression, in mind when considering the Abyssinian Crisis (see page 119) and the remilitarization of the Rhineland (see page 156).

France

Whereas Britain had to import many raw materials and was almost completely dependent on imported food, France was essentially self-sufficient in food production. The French government established a very strict quota on imports of all kinds, including food. A very thorough system of imperial preference was created whereby France and its colonies formed an exclusive trade zone. Government wages were reduced by about twelve per cent and government spending was slashed. France did not suffer from mass unemployment as experienced in Britain, partly because large numbers of people were employed in agriculture and the huge French army used conscription to keep young men occupied. Foreign workers were sent back to their own countries. In 1935, France only had 500,000 unemployed. Although France seemed much more successful than Britain and the USA in fighting the effects of the Great Depression, its government was extremely unstable during this period.

As in Britain, France had a coalition government. A myriad of parties gathered together to form majorities in the parliament to pass a few pieces of agreed-upon legislation, before collapsing. This collapse would lead to new elections being called or new coalitions being formed to create some unity for another list of agreed items. In 1932, there were three different governments; four in 1933; two more in 1934; and then two in 1935: that is eleven governments in four years.

Germany

In the early years of the Great Depression, tax revenues were in decline and leaders believed that the economic downturn would be temporary at best. Some governments decided that reducing spending would be better than saddling people with debt, which they believed would make matters worse over the long term. Germany was one such country, at the time led by **Chancellor Brüning**. Germany kept its currency at a high exchange rate while other countries were devaluing theirs. This meant that many countries' products were cheaper than German-produced goods. Brüning also tried to reduce prices on consumer goods and keep the government's budget balanced. These policies failed to stimulate or protect Germany's economy, contributing to the unemployment of 6 million people by 1932. Economic conditions were so poor that Britain and France suspended indefinitely reparation payments from the **Treaty of Versailles** (see box) from Germany at the **Lausanne Conference** in 1932.

 **KEY TERM**

Chancellor A position equivalent to prime minister in most countries and the most powerful official in Germany.

Heinrich Brüning (1885–1970) Chancellor of Germany from 1930 to 1932.

Treaty of Versailles Treaty imposed on Germany in 1919 by the victors of the First World War, which included financial penalties, severe military reductions and loss of land.

Lausanne Conference A conference in 1932 between Britain, France and Germany that suspended Germany's First World War reparations as a result of the world economic crisis.

Paris Peace Treaties 1919–20

Starting in 1919, the victorious Allies of the First World War convened at the Paris Peace Conference to create and impose peace treaties on the defeated Central Powers. These treaties and countries were:

- Versailles for Germany
- St Germain-en-Laye for Austria
- Trianon for Hungary
- Neuilly for Bulgaria
- Sèvres for the Ottoman Empire.

The Treaty of Versailles:

- severely limited Germany's military to 100,000 troops, no artillery, aircraft or tanks
- limited Germany's navy to a few ships
- required war reparations to France for decades
- required Germany accept responsibility for causing the war
- removed all Germany's overseas colonies and sliced off large sections of the country, granting them to other states; Poland received the largest areas.

Parts of the Treaty of Versailles were moderated over time, such as the reparations, which were suspended during the Great Depression before Hitler came to power in 1933. Nevertheless, that Germany was surrounded by large militaries of hostile states, and hundreds of thousands of Germans now lived in Poland and other states, continued to remind the German people of their defeat at the end of the First World War and the imposition of what they considered to be an unjust peace.

National Socialism versus communism

As the traditional coalition parties were linked with economic failure, other parties such as the National Socialists in Germany and communist parties in Russia and globally grew in popularity, as they seemed to offer legitimate alternatives to an obviously broken system. The German Communist Party also benefited from the apparent success of the first Five Year Plan in the Soviet Union (see page 111).

The **National Socialists**, the Nazis, were more popular than the Communist Party, and most other parties, by 1932. Adolf Hitler, their leader, ran for president of Germany in 1932, losing to General **Paul von Hindenburg**, president since 1925, in both the first and second rounds. Hitler did, however, poll far ahead of the leader of the Communist Party, Ernst Thälmann, and became better known to the German people through speeches, propaganda posters, radio addresses and visits to their towns and villages; he took 13 million votes out of about 36 million cast in 1932.

Hitler was a nationalist and preached that a powerful Germany could prosper, take its place on the world stage and end the humiliation of Versailles. Hitler argued that the German economy was too dependent on other countries for raw materials and markets, and that meant that when other nations had economic problems, Germany had them also. He preached a need for *lebensraum*, or living space, in lands ruled or won by Germany in the First World War against Russia but taken away in the Treaty of Versailles (see page 105), roughly Poland and parts of Ukraine. He claimed that *lebensraum* would provide raw materials for industry, food and land for Germans to settle. Non-economic beliefs included a hatred of Jews, homosexuals and other minority groups, that women should stay at home and rear children, and that Germans were a master race, meant to rule over other nationalities.

Nazi Party beliefs appealed to more people than strict communist ideology. This was partly because communism opposed the concept of nationalism, preaching that working-class people around the world were the same. Communism also believed in the ending of all social classes, the confiscation of private property, and that religion was just a creation of people in power to control people not in power. The violence of the Bolshevik takeover of Russia in 1917 and the Russian Civil War from 1918 to 1921, as well as various revolts in the first years of the German Republic, made many nervous about communist government.

Industrialists and large landowners naturally opposed communism and poured money into the Nazi Party funds. This allowed more Nazi propaganda, paid staff workers, offices and the employment of tens of thousands of young men in armed gangs who often violently attacked opponents of the Nazis.

KEY TERM

National Socialists
Abbreviated name for the National Socialist German Workers' Party or Nazi Party, an ultranationalist group.

Paul von Hindenburg
(1847–1934) A highly decorated general and president of Germany from 1925 to 1934.

Lebensraum German for living space, loosely defined as parts of eastern Europe.

SOURCE D

Excerpt from *Hitler: A Study in Tyranny* by Alan Bullock, published by Harper & Row, New York, USA, 1962, p. 199. Bullock was a British historian who served as vice-chancellor of Oxford University, UK.

When Hitler sat down [from the speech,] the audience, whose reserve had long since thawed, rose and cheered him wildly. 'The effect upon the industrialists,' wrote Otto Dietrich [Nazi Party Press Chief], who was present, 'was great, and very evident during the next hard months of struggle.' … as a result of the impression Hitler made, large contributions from the resources of heavy industry flowed into the Nazi treasury. With an astuteness which matched that of his appeal to the Army, Hitler had won an important victory. As the Army officers saw in Hitler the man who promised to restore Germany's military power, so the industrialists came to see in him the man who would defend their interests against the threat of Communism and the claims of the trade unions, giving a free hand to private enterprise and economic exploitation …

According to Source D, which two groups supported Hitler's stance against communism?

SOURCE E

Excerpt from 'Why the German Republic Fell' by Bruno Heilig, published in *Why the German Republic Fell and Other Lessons of War and Peace Upholding True Democracy through Economic Freedom*, edited by Arthur Madsen, published by The Hogarth Press, London, UK, 1941. Heilig was a journalist for newspapers in Vienna, Budapest, Prague and Berlin who was arrested in Austria in 1938 for being Jewish. He was released from a concentration camp in 1939, emigrated to Britain, and served in the British Royal Air Force during the Second World War.

Was there a link between the economic and the political collapse? Emphatically, yes. For as unemployment grew, and with it poverty and the fear of poverty, so grew the influence of the Nazi Party, which was making its lavish promises to the frustrated and its violent appeal to the revenges of a populace aware of its wrongs but condemned to hear only a malignant and distorted explanation of them.

In the first year of the crisis the number of Nazi deputies to the Reichstag [parliament] rose from 8 to 107. A year later this figure was doubled. In the same time the Communists captured half of the votes of the German Social Democratic Party and the representation of the middle class practically speaking disappeared. In January 1933 Hitler was appointed Reichskanzler [Chancellor]; he attained power, as I said before, quite legally. All the forms of democracy were observed. It sounds paradoxical, but it was in fact absolutely logical.

How did Hitler and the Nazi Party come to power in Germany, according to Source E?

Hitler comes to power

While Hitler himself was not elected as president, the Nazi Party went from 2.6 per cent of the representatives in the **Reichstag** in 1928 to 37.3 per cent in July 1932, rising in direct correlation with the economic hardships of the Great Depression. There was another election in late 1932 as a stable government coalition could not be formed between the various political parties, none of which had a majority. In this election the Nazis lost seats, yet

 **KEY TERM**

Reichstag Germany's parliament.

still had more than any other individual party. In January 1933, in an attempt to stabilize the country politically, President von Hindenburg appointed Hitler as chancellor.

An election was called in March 1933 to see if the election returns would endorse and confirm the appointment: the Nazi Party won almost 44 per cent of the *Reichstag* seats. The election, it must be noted, was held with Hitler as chancellor. He had outlawed the Communist Party, which had been accused of burning down the *Reichstag*, the parliament building. Other parties had many of their candidates attacked and harassed by Nazis during their campaigns since Hitler intentionally withdrew their police protection for this purpose. Within a few days of the election, the Nazis combined with other nationalists and the Catholic Centre Party to form a parliamentary majority. The **Enabling Act** was immediately passed, which gave Hitler the power to pass laws and sign treaties for the next four years without consulting the *Reichstag*. The economic desperation in Germany was so great that a large number of its citizens, or at least their political representatives, were willing to forfeit their republican government to solve their economic problems.

KEY TERM

Enabling Act Officially the 'Gesetz zur Behebung der Not von Volk und Reich' or 'Law to Remedy the Distress of the People and the State', this act allowed the government to rule by decree instead of through parliament, including the implementation of laws that contradicted Germany's constitution.

What were the main factors affecting international diplomacy during the 1930s?

International diplomacy in the early 1930s

Foreign diplomacy in Europe in the 1930s was a complex system of alliances, treaties, pacts, expectations and commitments to the League of Nations. Since the Soviet Union was not involved directly with most European states, Britain and France, often under the guise of the League of Nations, essentially directed most European affairs. Italy joined them, although Italy had its own designs and desires (see page 115) that contradicted those of both France and Britain.

League of Nations

The League of Nations by 1933 included almost all European states, with the exception of the Soviet Union which would join the next year. The League, however, had been weakened by recent international events.

The Manchurian Crisis proved that the League's collective security policy was fundamentally flawed (see page 57). Governments were still responsible to their citizens and if a state's citizens objected to sending troops to distant lands to defend lofty goals of international peace, then that state would not send troops. In addition, the League was weak. The strongest states involved were Britain and France – and they were not particularly strong.

After the First World War, Britain owed huge sums to the USA, had lost trade to US industries and had severely reduced its military to save money. France maintained a massive army, but it was parked mostly on the border with Germany. Much of northern France had been destroyed by the war, and its reconstruction, plus the expense of the huge army, meant that France was financially unable to afford massive foreign undertakings. France's navy was limited too, since its main concern remained Germany; this required troops on the ground, not ships to transport troops or affect international disputes through use of a navy. The Great Depression reduced their strength even further. The two strongest League members were not equipped to enforce collective security, even if their citizens had wanted them to do so.

France

France worked without cessation to isolate Germany diplomatically and to enforce as much of the Treaty of Versailles (see page 105) as possible. In the early 1920s, France created an alliance of states on Germany's borders in eastern and central Europe that would come to its aid if it was attacked again by Germany. Foremost of these allies were Poland and Czechoslovakia, two states that were not on friendly terms with each other. Nevertheless, Polish and Czech armies, when coupled with the armies of France, meant that millions of soldiers were available to counter any German attack, or were ready to attack Germany, according to the Germans.

The French also worked to coerce Britain into a formal alliance, which they believed would guarantee their safety; Britain refused. France was aware that Italy desired some of its territories in France's southeast and the island of Corsica, but ignored this as Italy was weak. Instead, France, along with Britain, worked to include Italy in international diplomacy so that Germany would have no friendly states in Europe with which to closely co-operate.

Through the Treaty of Versailles, France and its allies forced Germany to reduce its military to 100,000 men, with no aircraft, no tanks, few ships and other restrictions, and were successful in doing so. This was to have been the first step towards general demobilization of large militaries in Europe. France, however, did not reduce its military and instead kept millions of men in the army. While France declared that these were only for defence, Germans were not so sure. In 1923, France had invaded part of Germany to punish it for not making war reparations. French refusal to disarm or even reduce the size of the army led to continued friction with Britain and Germany. France refused in part because conscription absorbed many of the country's unemployed (see page 104).

Governmental instability (see page 104) meant that foreign policy could be inconsistent in order to appease various political factions in France. Conservatives and national extremists, **fascists** in fact, were politically successful in the 1930s and supported Italy during the invasion of Abyssinia (see page 125). They were, however, opposed to the Soviet Union, which they saw as the ultimate threat to world peace because of its communism. These groups desired a large, active military in order to counteract the perceived threat. A large military would also protect them from Germany.

Socialist and communist parties also grew dramatically in France. These groups opposed the French fascists and conservatives as well as military build-up, believing that funds for the military would be better spent in social

 KEY TERM

Fascists Originally referring to Italy's ultranationalist Fascist Party, the term was eventually used to refer to most ultranationalist groups who advocated an end to or severe modification of republican forms of government in favour of authoritarian, nationalist single-party states.

welfare programmes. They supported the League of Nations and collective security as directed by the Soviet Union, which had recently joined the League (see page 152).

The most difficult year of the Great Depression for France was 1935, with rising unemployment and growing political unrest. France was unwilling to end its system of imperial preference, although this limited their economic ability to influence its allies in central and eastern Europe while German economic strength was starting to grow. In 1935, Germany announced its rearmament programme (see page 144) and Italy attacked Abyssinia (see page 119), neither of which France was able to effectively address, partly as a result of divided government and economic stress.

Britain

Britain's foreign policy was quite different from that of France. While France seemed to be obsessed with keeping Germany weak, Britain wanted Germany's economic rehabilitation. Britain was more concerned with the Soviet Union and its communist government than it was with Germany. Britain feared the spread of communist governments into Europe and Germany in particular. There had been several failed communist uprisings there after the First World War and in the early 1930s the Communist Party in Germany was becoming increasingly popular.

To resist the spread of communism and to help its own economy, Britain wanted Germany to return to normalcy in world affairs, but on British terms. This would allow Germany and Britain to develop stronger economic relations, which both countries desperately needed in the early years of the Great Depression. This meant that Britain believed that the Treaty of Versailles needed to be adjusted to reduce animosity towards it and the Western powers within Germany. Yet, Britain did not wish to act alone as it would disturb its relationship with France. While France developed alliances to encircle Germany, Britain refused to participate and through treaties continued to advocate arms reductions.

Germany

German foreign policy until 1933 was similar to German foreign policy after 1933 in terms of what it wanted. Germans first and foremost wanted the humiliation imposed on them in the Treaty of Versailles ended. War reparations were suspended by 1932 as a result of the Great Depression, removing one key issue. While Germany had pledged to respect its western borders with Belgium and France, it did not accept its borders in the east but had agreed that any territorial adjustments had to be through negotiation and not war. Much of Poland was created in 1919 from German territory and now Poland had millions of Germans living in it, most of whom wanted to live in Germany.

There were smaller areas that were also important to Germany that had been removed at the end of the First World War in the Treaty of Versailles.

SOURCE F

Map of Germany and surrounding areas after the First World War.

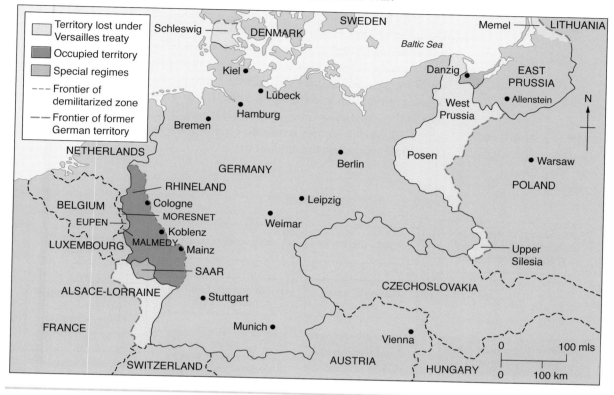

The region of Memel on the Baltic Sea had been placed under international administration, but was seized and annexed by Lithuania in 1923. The port city of Danzig on the Baltic Sea had a completely German population, but was under League of Nations' control and completely surrounded by Poland. The iron- and coal-rich Saar area that bordered France was also removed from Germany after the First World War; it was to be ruled by France until 1935, when there would be a vote to determine its future. While the Germans could not financially afford a large military in the early 1930s, it was humiliating that they had no way to defend themselves against anyone, especially Poland and France, both of which were hostile to Germany and had huge militaries.

Soviet Union

The Soviet Union was primarily concerned with its own development. **Stalin**, its leader, believed that the country needed economic and political reorganization if it was to survive. In the late 1920s, the Soviets began massive industrialization with the first Five Year Plan. This included the industrialization of agriculture, and the building of dams, railways, roads, factories and entire cities in central Asia. This reorganization of the economy

Which states benefited the most from Germany's losses of land after the First World War, according to Source F?

🔑 **KEY TERM**

Josef Stalin (1878–1953) Authoritarian leader of the Soviet Union by the late 1920s.

was chaotic and led to millions starving to death. By 1932, Stalin declared that the first Five Year Plan was a huge success, so a second one was begun.

The Soviets, busy with their own affairs and not particularly affected by the Great Depression, were relatively uninvolved in world diplomacy. They did not want any foreign entanglements, but certainly encouraged other communist groups such as those in Germany and France. By the mid-1930s, the Soviets perceived Nazi Germany as a threat, along with Italy and Japan, helping bring them into the League of Nations. They led world criticism of Italy in the Abyssinian Crisis and later during Italy's invasion of Albania (see page 131). Most countries remained wary of the Soviets and hesitated to co-operate with them throughout the 1930s.

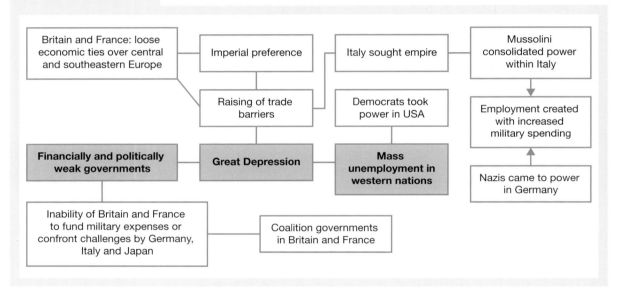

Mussolini and Fascist Italy

▶ **Key question:** How did Mussolini's Fascist Party affect Italian foreign policy?

Many states with republican forms of government became dictatorships between the First and Second World Wars and Italy was one of these. Benito Mussolini was named prime minister in 1922 and ruled the country as dictator until 1943. Mussolini's Fascist Party and its programme called for glory, war and empire. By the mid-1930s, as the height of the Great Depression, it made an effort to achieve these.

Mussolini and fascism

Fascism was a ruling philosophy of nationalism, which supported industrialists and (supposedly) workers, emphasized order and obedience to the state and enforced a single-party government. Mussolini came to embody this philosophy during his rule of Italy.

Mussolini

Although Italy had been one of the victors in the First World War, it was still weak, having struggled during the war. This was evident when Italy was not granted territories it had been promised in the Treaty of London in 1915, which brought Italy into the war against the Central Powers; France and Britain simply disregarded earlier promises, expecting Italy to comply.

Italy was already severely divided internally as the result of regional, economic and political issues before its entry into the First World War. Participation in the war meant even greater financial and social strain. Promises made to its 2 million soldiers, such as granting them farmland ownership, were not fulfilled and the government owed huge amounts to banks and industrialists that had been borrowed for the war effort.

Events such as riots, strikes, violence, a dysfunctional parliament, religious interference by the Catholic Church, the spread of communist ideology and more led to several turbulent years. Mussolini formed a gang that was financed by industrialists and bankers, as well as other conservatives. In time, this gang, called the Black Shirts, grew enormously in number and power. By 1922, Mussolini had admirers such as the king, industry leaders and the middle economic classes. He threatened to march on Rome and seize government. The king responded by naming him prime minister that year, a position he held until 1943. Soon Mussolini was simply called *Il Duce* or The Leader.

Mussolini's political party, the National Fascist Party, was soon the only political party allowed. Internal dissent was suppressed by:

- banning publications that opposed fascist views
- outlawing labour unions, replacing them with government-managed organizations
- resolving various long-term disputes with the Catholic Church
- the creation of youth groups to teach the young about fascist ideology
- violence against opponents.

Efforts were made to depict Mussolini's rule as a revival of the ancient Roman Empire. These efforts relied heavily on imagery and ancient symbolism, including the **fasces**, the use of Roman letters, new versions of Roman-inspired architecture, public sculpture and more.

> **How did Mussolini come to power and what views on international relations were advocated by fascism?**

What imagery in Source G attempts to connect the Black Shirts with ancient Rome?

SOURCE G

An Italian postage stamp from 1923 showing an ancient Roman coin and other symbols. The Latin words read: 'Pension Fund [for the] Black Shirts'.

KEY TERM

Fasces A bundle of bound rods that included an axe that was carried by guards of important Roman officials, which eventually represented government authority and power.

KEY TERM

Imperialism Policy or system of a state gaining control of foreign lands for reasons of trade, prestige or military advantage.

Indemnity A financial penalty.

Fascism

In terms of foreign policy, fascism advocated war and **imperialism**. Essentially, fascism held that the country should be prepared for war so that it could expand. Only through warfare could it become the great nation for which it was destined. While women were supposed to stay at home and produce strong, healthy children for Italy's future armies, men should be warriors for the state. Women were encouraged to have children; those with the most children received awards. Various youth groups were founded by the Fascist Party to learn about fascism, and learn to march and shoot.

SOURCE H

? Why, according to Source H, does Mussolini not believe in peace?

Excerpt from a speech by Benito Mussolini, quoted in *You Might Like Socialism: A Way of Life for Modern Man* by Corliss Lamont, published by Modern Age Books, New York, USA, 1939, p. 173. Lamont was a socialist, professor of philosophy at Columbia, Harvard and other universities, and Chairman of the National Council of American–Soviet Friendship.

War is to man what maternity [giving birth] is to a woman. From a philosophical and doctrinal viewpoint, I do not believe in perpetual peace.

How successful was Mussolini's foreign policy between 1922 and 1934?

Fascist foreign policy 1922–34

In terms of foreign policy, Italy was economically weak and therefore militarily weak. Italy's economy was dependent on Britain, France and the USA in the 1920s. While fascism advocated war and empire, there were clearly limits on what could be achieved without putting the country at financial risk. An embargo on fuel by the USA or Britain, for example, would severely restrict the economy. Reduction in food imports from France would cause food shortages in Italy and massive price increases. An unemployed, hungry population would possibly demand a change in government and remove Mussolini from power. Foreign policy had to be necessarily cautious.

Italy's foreign policy in the 1920s was primarily opportunist, taking advantage of small incidents to gain politically. In the 1920s, Italy responded to the assassination of military officers who were ostensibly mapping Albania's borders by shelling Greece's island of Corfu. Greece, far weaker than Italy, was coerced into offering an **indemnity** which Italy accepted. Yugoslavia, involved in a dispute with Italy over the city of Fiume, today's Rijeka, was also weak and simply handed the city over to Italy before it could be attacked. These foreign policy successes required little on the part of Italy.

SOURCE I

? According to Source I, why was Italy limited in terms of foreign policy in the 1920s?

Excerpt from *Italian Fascism, 1919–1945* by Philip Morgan, published by Macmillan, London, UK, 1995, p. 135.

But Mussolini's predilection was to make trouble wherever he could and disparage the forms of conventional diplomacy, using methods of internal political subversion as covert, undeclared warfare on countries he regarded as Italy's enemies. The point is not that Mussolini could be credited with a decade of good behaviour in foreign policy, but rather that the damage he could do in the 1920s was limited because of Italy's intrinsic economic and military weakness, and the lack of counterbalance to effective Anglo-French dominance in Europe which Italy could exploit.

Mussolini desired areas of southeastern France and the island of Corsica for Italy since their populations spoke dialects of Italian or closely related languages and not French. Since France was a far greater power than Italy, these desires were simply tabled for the future. France, working to isolate Germany, included Italy in its diplomatic efforts and was not concerned with Italy's weak military. While Italy needed France economically, there was little friction between the two states.

SOURCE J

Map of the Italian Empire in 1935.

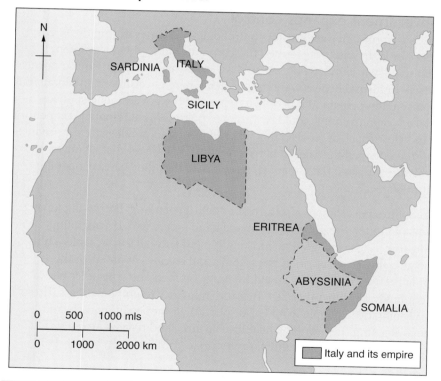

What does Source J indicate about Italy's empire in 1935? **?**

The creation of an Italian Empire was not Mussolini's idea; it had been Italian policy for decades. Before the First World War, Italy managed to wrest control of today's Libya from the **Ottoman Empire**. This territory had few people and few resources, and oil had yet to be discovered. This empire was more of a burden than an asset. Soon Italy added Eritrea and Italian Somaliland, part of today's Somalia. Again, these were poor territories that did not add to the glory or economy of Italy.

🔑 **KEY TERM**

Ottoman Empire Empire that once covered most of the Middle East, much of north Africa and the Balkan peninsula of Europe, with its capital at Istanbul.

How did the Great
Depression affect Italy
economically and
therefore in terms of
international
relations?

The Great Depression and Italy

The Great Depression (see page 100) severely affected Italy's economy. It had to export its manufactured goods to pay for food imports, fuel and raw materials for its industries. Britain, France and the USA, its main trade partners, erected trade barriers to protect their industries. So, to survive, Italy turned away from Western markets and traded more extensively with Yugoslavia, Austria, Hungary, Bulgaria and Romania. These countries mainly exported raw materials and food, allowing Italy to export manufactured goods to them in return.

This meant in terms of foreign policy that Italy had less fear of economic retaliation in response to its policies than it had before. So, in effect, the Great Depression gave Italy more freedom to operate its foreign policy than previously and more in line with its fascist governing philosophy.

Government expands control

Italy's government took greater control of its industries during the Great Depression. In what was termed the 'corporate state', the government attempted, with limited success, to have industries co-operate more closely with it. Industrial boards were established where government and industrial representatives, including people to represent the government-sponsored workers' organizations, could co-ordinate policy. This eliminated competition in industries such as steel so that all producers set a single price for products and then divided the market between them. This meant that all major industries survived the Great Depression and they did so by co-operating with the government.

Mussolini's government also turned to deficit spending. Borrowing large sums of money, the government made large orders with co-operating industries. These included military equipment such as trucks, tanks, ships and aircraft, as well as rifles, tyres, shells and engines. Workers in these industries would naturally spend their pay on food and consumer goods accordingly, causing other factories and industries to employ others. These newly employed people would also spend their money in markets and shops, keeping the economy healthy. The army and navy were both massively expanded, providing jobs for up to 1 million men by late 1935.

SOURCE K

According to Source K,
what helped Italy's economy
recover from the worst
effects of the Great
Depression?

Excerpt from *Italian Fascism, 1919–1945* by Philip Morgan, published by Macmillan, London, UK, 1995, p. 141.

The worst point of the Depression was 1932, when planning for an invasion [of Abyssinia] started. But the economy was beginning to recover during 1934. That recovery was certainly aided by the government's war-related commissions and contracts, which began to flow in late 1934 and early 1935, coinciding with and consequent on Mussolini's decision to invade … Preparation for war undoubtedly had an impact on employment, which by spring 1935 was down 250,000 [unemployed workers] on 1934. Some sectors benefited hugely from mobilisation, the war itself and colonial administration, obviously enough those supplying arms, clothing equipment, transportation and other logistical services for the war effort and the running of the empire.

Mussolini's Italy was better prepared for a more aggressive foreign policy as a result of the Great Depression. Not only was the country now less reliant on Western Europe and the USA economically, the government now had better control of industry and was in the midst of producing large amounts of military equipment. This meant that Mussolini's fascist goal for Italy could be realized, in terms of foreign policy. As a result of this new reality, Mussolini reorganized his government in 1933, granting himself the ministries of war, air and navy, while also serving as minister of the interior, minister of foreign affairs (until 1936) and prime minister.

SOURCE L

Excerpt from 'What is Fascism?' by Benito Mussolini, originally published in the *Italian Encyclopedia*, 1932, and republished in *Events that Formed the Modern World* by Frank W. Thackeray and John E. Findling, published by ABC-CLIO, Santa Barbara, California, USA, 2012, pp. 111–12. Thackeray and Findling are both professor emeriti of history at Indiana University Southeast, USA.

According to Source L, why is national expansion important?

For Fascism, the growth of empire, that is to say the expansion of the nation, is an essential manifestation of vitality, and its opposite a sign of decadence. Peoples which are rising, or rising again after a period of decadence, are always imperialist; and renunciation is a sign of decay and of death. Fascism is the doctrine best adapted to represent the tendencies and the aspirations of a people, like the people of Italy, who are rising again after many centuries of abasement and foreign servitude. But empire demands discipline, the coordination of all forces and a deeply felt sense of duty and sacrifice: this fact explains many aspects of the practical working of the regime, the character of many forces in the State, and the necessarily severe measures which must be taken against those who would oppose this spontaneous and inevitable movement of Italy in the twentieth century, and would oppose it by recalling the outworn ideology of the nineteenth century – repudiated wheresoever [sic] there has been the courage to undertake great experiments of social and political transformation; for never before has the nation stood more in need of authority, of direction and order.

Intimidation of Germany, July 1934

Germany offered the only European challenge to Italy's growing strength. After 1933, Germany was under the control of the Nazi Party (see page 106). Italy had worked with France and Britain to isolate Germany after the First World War and Austria was a buffer state between the two countries. Italy wanted to prevent any expansion of Germany into Austria or anywhere else for fear that it would replace Italy's interests in central and southeastern Europe, which had increased as a result of the Great Depression (see page 110). Italy wanted Austria to remain in its sphere of influence and to limit German influence in the entire region as much as possible.

In 1934, members of an Austrian version of the Nazi Party assassinated Engelbert Dollfuss, Austria's dictator. The plan was to overthrow the state and merge Austria and Germany. Mussolini immediately announced that Italian troops were heading to Italy's border with Austria. This was a clear threat to Germany that Italy would not allow Germany to absorb Austria and that Mussolini wanted it to remain independent. Germany had an extremely weak army and Hitler did not fully control his military at this point of his dictatorship (see page 142). A military challenge by Italy might cause Germany's military to oppose Hitler, something Hitler was not prepared for. Hitler's government did not intervene and the assassins and their co-conspirators were captured. Mussolini had demonstrated to his people and other states that Italy was now a significant military power.

Stresa Front 1935

In April 1935, the heads of government of Britain, France and Italy met in Stresa, Italy, to form a common diplomatic front against Germany. This was partly in response to Germany's earlier move to annex Austria and a result of Germany's announcement that it would begin rearmament (see page 144). All three countries condemned Germany's plans to rebuild its military and all agreed to work together.

Almost immediately, Britain and Germany signed a naval treaty (see page 154) without consulting either Italy or France, demonstrating that the Stresa Front countries were not as united as their public statements indicated. Italy and France felt betrayed by Britain and spoke about the possibility of mutual military co-operation in case of war. These talks went absolutely nowhere as a result of the Abyssinian Crisis.

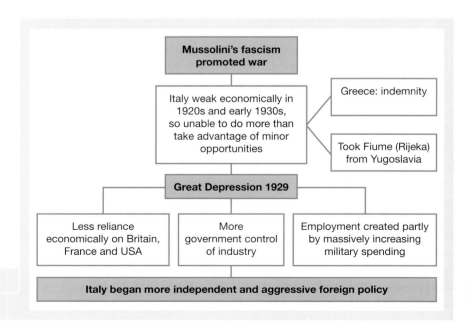

③ The Abyssinian Crisis

▶ *Key question: What role did the Abyssinian Crisis have in destroying the League of Nations' credibility?*

The Abyssinian Crisis was a key event during Mussolini's rule and Italian expansion. It had tremendous consequences for the League of Nations, Abyssinia, Italy, Britain, France, Germany and even central and eastern Europe. The crisis itself developed out of Mussolini's desire to have an empire at just about any cost.

SOURCE M

Speech by Benito Mussolini, 2 October 1933 regarding the invasion of Abyssinia, *Lend Me Your Ears: Great Speeches in History* by William Safire, published by W.W. Norton & Co., New York, USA, 2004, pp. 134–5. Safire wrote speeches for several US presidents and was a political columnist for the *New York Times* in the USA, a newspaper with one of the largest circulations in the world.

It is not only an army marching towards its goal, but it is forty-four million Italians marching in unity behind this army. Because the blackest of injustices is being attempted against them, that of taking from them their place in the sun. When in 1915 Italy threw in her fate with that of the Allies, how many cries of admiration, how many promises were heard? But after the common victory, which cost Italy six hundred thousand dead, four hundred thousand lost, one million wounded, when peace was being discussed around the table only the crumbs of a rich colonial booty were left for us to pick up. For thirteen years we have been patient while the circle tightened around us at the hands of those who wish to suffocate us.

> With reference to Source M's content, origin and purpose, what are some values and limitations of this source? **?**

The Italian Empire

> **What were the main reasons that Italy sought an empire?**

Mussolini wanted to create an empire in order to make Italy a Great Power, like France and Britain were perceived to be. There were economic reasons why empire was needed as well, but Mussolini did not emphasize these in his public statements. While Italy held Libya, Eritrea and part of Somalia, these territories were not particularly important and were somewhat of an embarrassment because of their poverty. As it stood, the Italian Empire was not impressive to Italians or anyone else.

When reviewing the world map for suitable territory to conquer in nearby Africa, there remained only Abyssinia (Ethiopia) and Liberia, a state formed by freed slaves in the nineteenth century and under the indirect supervision and sponsorship of the USA. Abyssinia was conveniently located beside the Italian colonies of Somaliland and Eritrea, and its borders were loosely defined, if at all. Mussolini was completely uninterested in its economic potential and also disregarded the state of the Italian economy, which was totally unprepared to finance a war for any purpose.

? What does Source N indicate about Italy's military in 1936?

Hundreds of aircraft have been lined up for Mussolini's inspection before they are sent to support Italy's invasion of Abyssinia in 1936.

SOURCE O

? What is the message conveyed in Source O?

'The Jap in the Vase.' A cartoon by Sidney 'George' Strube, the *Daily Express*, 29 November 1935. Strube was a British cartoonist who worked at the *Daily Express* from 1912 to 1948. The *Daily Express* is a British newspaper started in 1900.

The Wal-Wal Incident and war

In December 1934, a clash occurred between Italian and Abyssinian troops at the small oasis of Wal-Wal, 80 km (50 miles) on the Abyssinian side of the border with Italian Somaliland, leaving at least two Italian soldiers and over 100 Abyssinian troops dead. Italy demanded $100,000 and an official apology from the Abyssinian government. Abyssinia responded by appealing to the League of Nations, of which both Italy and Abyssinia were members. An arbitration committee was established and announced in September 1935 that the Wal-Wal Incident, as it became known, was minor and that neither country was at fault. Mussolini, however, had already directed the Italian army in December 1934 to prepare for the invasion of Abyssinia. Armies also prepared to invade from neighbouring Italian colonies. Britain and France were very aware of Italy's plans, but were unwilling to jeopardize their relationship with Italy, which they believed was important for opposing German foreign policies.

> **What was the significance of the Wal-Wal Incident for Italian foreign policy?**

SOURCE P

A group of soldiers in the Abyssinian army in 1936 carrying shields and rifles during the war with Abyssinia.

What does Source P indicate about the Abyssinian military?

October 1935 saw the long-expected invasion of Abyssinia. The relatively modern Italian forces annihilated the Abyssinian armies sent against them that used a variety of antique weapons. Aerial bombing by the Italians and the liberal use of poison gas over large areas led to the deaths of hundreds of thousands of men, women, children and livestock, poisoning water and destroying crops. The Emperor of Abyssinia, Haile Selassie, escaped to Britain while practically all organized opposition to the Italian occupation collapsed in the midst of the destruction in early 1936. Italian Somaliland, Eritrea and Abyssinia were then merged into one large colony: Italian East Africa. The capital of this new colony was Addis Ababa, Abyssinia's capital city, and the King of Italy was retitled as Emperor of Ethiopia.

According to Source Q,
what is the benefit of war?

Benito Mussolini quoted in *Social Darwinism in European and American Thought, 1860–1945: Nature as Model and Nature as Threat* by Mike Hawkins, published by Cambridge University Press, UK, 1997, p. 285. Hawkins is a sociology professor at Kingston University, UK.

… societies are formed, gain strength, and move forwards through conflict; the healthiest and most vital of them assert themselves against the weakest and less well adapted through conflict; the natural evolution of nations and races takes place through conflict … .

How significant were international responses to the Abyssinian Crisis for Italy?

Responses to the Abyssinian Crisis

Abyssinia

Over 750,000 people were killed in Abyssinia during the war. Inhabitants and livestock of whole villages were completely destroyed. Suffering in Abyssinia continued after the war officially was declared over. **Guerrilla attacks** on Italian forces were relatively minor, but continued throughout Italy's occupation of Abyssinia. There were no large-scale revolts, probably because of the lack of weapons and organization, but also because of the sheer violence of the Italian military's response. Mussolini ordered that prisoners be shot, that various villages be gassed where resistance had been discovered, and that priests and others suspected of complicity in armed resistance be executed without hesitation.

KEY TERM

Guerrilla attacks Military attacks by small groups, usually on a larger military force.

What is the value of Source R for historians studying the Abyssinian Crisis?

Telegrams from Mussolini to army commanders in Ethiopia, 1936, from *Mussolini Unleashed 1939–1941: Politics and Strategy in Fascist Italy's Last War* by MacGregor Knox, published by Cambridge University Press, UK, 1982, p. 4. Knox is an American professor of modern European history at the London School of Economics, UK.

Secret – 8 June 1936. To finish off rebels, as in case at Ancober, use gas. Mussolini

Secret – 8 July 1936. I repeat my authorization to initiate and systematically conduct policy of terror and extermination against rebels and populations in complicity with them. Without the law of ten eyes for one we cannot heal this wound in good time. Mussolini

21 February 1937. Agree that male population of Goggetti over 18 years of age is to be shot and village destroyed. Mussolini

Response: League of Nations

In October 1935, the League, led by Britain and France, condemned the Italian invasion of Abyssinia, voting for a gradually escalating programme of economic sanctions. Other than ignoring the issues outright, this was the least the League could do. The League placed no embargo on oil exports to Italy, which would have brought the Italian economy to a halt, and quickly. Backed by public opinion and a weak National Government, Britain did not threaten Italy with war or even consider it an option, so a divided French government did not either.

SOURCE S

'Santa Claus Comes to Mussolini.' Cartoon by David Low, *Evening Standard*, 13 December 1935. Low was a cartoonist from New Zealand who worked for many British newspapers from 1919 to 1953. The *Evening Standard* is a British newspaper published since 1827.

Who do you think the individuals are in the cartoon in Source S and why are they depicted as they are?

Britain refused to close the **Suez Canal** to Italian shipping on the grounds that this might lead to war in the Mediterranean. The lack of an oil embargo and use of the Suez Canal condemned Abyssinia to defeat and this was accomplished by May 1936. When the Emperor of Abyssinia, Haile Selassie, was allowed to speak at the League of Nations in the same month, Italy withdrew from the League in protest, much as Japan had done earlier (see page 58).

🔑 KEY TERM

Suez Canal Major canal linking the Mediterranean and Red Seas and therefore the Atlantic and Indian Oceans.

SOURCE T

Excerpt from a speech by Emperor Haile Selassie of Ethiopia to the League of Nations, 30 June 1936. *Haile Selassie I: Ethiopia's Lion of Judah* by Peter Schwab, published by Nelson-Hall, USA, 1979, pp. 168–70. Schwab is a professor of political science at the State University of New York, USA.

What is the message conveyed in Source T?

… The Ethiopian government never expected other governments to shed their soldiers' blood to defend the Covenant when their own immediate personal interests were not at stake. Ethiopian warriors asked only for means to defend themselves. On many occasions I have asked for financial assistance for the purchase of arms. That assistance has been constantly refused me. What, then, in practice, is the meaning of Article 16 and of collective security?

… Should it happen that a strong government finds it may, with impunity, destroy a weak people, then the hour strikes for that weak people to appeal to the League of Nations to give its judgment in all freedom. God and history will remember your judgment …

The consequences of the Abyssinian Crisis for the League of Nations

The Abyssinian Crisis revealed the League of Nations to be simply an extension of the foreign ministries of Britain and France. Collective security, at the core of the League of Nations' Covenant, failed in an effort by the governments of Britain and France to keep Italy as an ally against Germany while satisfying the demands of its citizens. Italy was actually driven closer to Germany by League actions. After the blatant failure of the League to address the destruction of a member state, it ceased to be an influential body. The crisis demonstrated that Britain and France would jettison key sections of the League's Covenant at will for their own interests, despite pledging to do otherwise. This meant that the League of Nations not only was impotent, but in terms of international security now had little reason to exist.

? What is the message conveyed in Source U about the League of Nations?

SOURCE U

Extract from *The Origins of the Second World War* by A.J.P. Taylor, published by Penguin Books, London, UK, 1961, pp. 127–8. First published in 1961 by Hamish Hamilton, this book has been most recently reprinted by Penguin Books in 2001. Taylor was a British historian who wrote many books on European history and was a lecturer at many British universities.

On 1 May the Emperor Haile Selassie left Abyssinia. A week later, Mussolini proclaimed the foundation of a new Roman empire.

This was the deathblow to the League as well as to Abyssinia. Fifty-two nations had combined to resist aggression; all they accomplished was that Haile Selassie lost all his country instead of only half. Incorrigible in impracticality, the League further offended Italy by allowing Haile Selassie a hearing at the Assembly; and then expelled him for the crime of taking the Covenant seriously. Japan and Germany had already left the League; Italy followed in December 1937. The League continued in existence only by averting its eyes from what was happening around it.

Response: Britain and France

Mussolini was convinced that neither Britain nor France would raise serious objections to the invasion and therefore the League of Nations, which they essentially controlled, would not interfere. In fact, in January 1935, Laval, the French foreign minister, had verbally promised Mussolini that France would not interfere with Italy's actions in Abyssinia; France's main concern was Germany. Britain's Foreign Office was desperate to avert the crisis either by offering Mussolini lands elsewhere or by helping to negotiate an arrangement which would give Italy effective control of Abyssinia without formally annexing it.

Why then could such a compromise not be negotiated? The scale and brutality of the Italian invasion confronted both the British and French governments with a considerable dilemma. The British government faced an

SOURCE V

Excerpt of a memo from Sir Robert Vansittart, permanent undersecretary of the British Foreign Office, to Sir Samuel Hoare, British Foreign Secretary, and Anthony Eden, Minister for League of Nations Affairs, 8 June 1935, quoted in *The Making of the Second World War* by Anthony Adamthwaite, published by Routledge, London, UK, 1992, p. 138. Adamthwaite is a history professor at the University of California, Berkeley, USA.

The position is as plain as a pikestaff. Italy will have to be bought off – let us use and face ugly words – in some form or other, or Abyssinia will eventually perish. That might in itself matter less, if it did not mean that the League would also perish (and that Italy would simultaneously perform another volte-face [change of policy] into the arms of Germany).

What are the origins, purpose, value and limitations of Source V?

election in November 1935 and was under intense pressure from the electorate to support the League and its policies. In an unofficial ballot in June 1935, organized by the League of Nations Union (formed in 1918 to win public support for the League), 10 million out of 11 million votes backed the use of economic sanctions, as opposed to military intervention, in a case of aggression. In France, public opinion was more divided, with socialists supporting the League and conservatives supporting Italy.

France believed that it needed Italy to help guarantee the borders of its central and eastern allies in the Little Entente (see page 144) against Germany, which Britain refused to do. Germany had recently announced rearmament and had the Saar region returned to it through a **plebiscite** (see page 154). These, coupled with Germany's rapidly expanding economy, reinforced British and French views that Germany, not remote eastern Africa, needed their attention.

KEY TERM

Plebiscite A national vote or referendum about one particular issue.

Britain and France, in addition to all the other pressures, did not want to militarily threaten Italy as this could lead to a war which they could not afford to fight. Again, in the midst of the Great Depression, no country wanted to have to rearm, much less rearm to defend a land far from home. As Mussolini was anti-communist, many people, especially in France, believed that Italy should be given free rein in Ethiopia (if not outright support) so that a united front could face a potentially aggressive Soviet Union in the future.

In December 1935, when Abyssinia was all but defeated, Laval and the British Foreign Minister, Samuel Hoare, produced a plan known as the Hoare–Laval Pact or Plan. This called for placing two-thirds of Abyssinia under Italy's control and giving what was left to an independent Abyssinia. This smaller state was a narrow strip of land, referred to as a corridor, to the sea. This land corridor would allow Abyssinia a seaport to build trade and a better economy for its people.

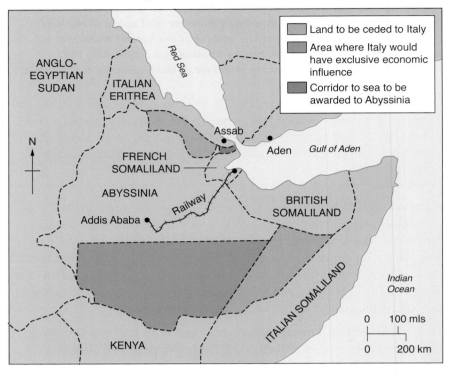

SOURCE W

The Hoare–Laval Plan (1935) for the partition of Abyssinia.

According to Source W, what were the most significant territorial changes proposed and who benefited?

There was a strong possibility that the Hoare–Laval Plan would have been acceptable to Mussolini, but it was leaked to the French press and an explosion of rage among the British public forced Hoare's resignation; the plan was dropped. *The Times*, a major British newspaper, ridiculed the idea of the corridor as a 'corridor of camels'. The sheer violence and aggression against Abyssinia, not to mention war being built on the flimsy excuse of the Wal-Wal Incident, meant that a compromise sought by various governments was destroyed by public opinion bent on not rewarding war and not wanting to be drawn into one. No one bothered to ask Abyssinia's government for its opinion on the Hoare–Laval Pact.

SOURCE X

What does Source X indicate about Italy's conquest of Abyssinia?

Excerpt from *The League of Nations: Its Life and Times, 1920–1946* by F.S. Northedge, published by Holmes & Meier, New York, USA, 1986, p. 243. Northedge was a professor of international relations at the London School of Economics, UK, writing numerous books on the subject as well.

The fact is that the British and French Governments never had any intention of using force against Italy to stop its advance in Abyssinia, or even of closing the Suez Canal, which would have locked Italian forces in East Africa in a trap. Nor had any other country, though all were ready to cheer Britain and France from the side-lines, had they gone into action. Laval even regarded an oil embargo as a form of military sanction since he considered that it would have military consequences, and he opposed it for that reason. It was equally evident that, for his part, Mussolini did not intend to be prevented from conquering his victim by anything short of superior force. The conquest of Abyssinia was too important in his foreign policy; he had invested too much money, too much of his own political future, in it … In these circumstances, what course remained for the chief League Powers except to try to reach a compromise settlement which might at least keep some part of Abyssinia outside the new Roman Empire [Mussolini's Italy]? The brutality and cynicism, the blatant deception, of the Hoare–Laval proposals might be deplored, but their logic was less easily condemned.

Response: USA

The USA worked diplomatically to encourage Mussolini not to invade Abyssinia, with no results. When the invasion began, the US government blocked the sale of weapons, ammunition and other war supplies to both Italy and Abyssinia through its **Neutrality Acts**; this only affected Abyssinia as Italy produced much of its own war materiel. Once Abyssinia was absorbed into the Italian Empire, the USA refused to recognize this annexation, in line with the Stimson Doctrine invoked against Japan (see page 61).

KEY TERM

Neutrality Acts A series of US government laws that generally imposed embargoes on the sale of weapons to states at war.

Response: Soviet Union

The Soviet Union in 1935 was in the midst of continuing economic reconstruction and social upheaval (see page 163). With mass industrialization and struggles to produce enough food, the Soviets were in no condition to exercise an aggressive foreign policy. Nevertheless, the Soviets issued a series of declarations that the independence of Abyssinia must be guaranteed by the League of Nations. When the issue of Abyssinia

SOURCE Y

Excerpt from *War and Peace in Soviet Diplomacy* by T.A. Taracouzio, published by Macmillan, New York, USA, 1940, p. 199. Taracouzio was a writer who produced several books on the Soviet Union and its diplomacy and wrote several articles for the US-based journal *Foreign Affairs*.

Nine days later he [Soviet Foreign Minister Litvinov] referred to these considerations as the real reason why the League should fulfil its purpose to the greatest degree possible [with regard to Italy's invasion of Abyssinia]. This defense of the League Covenant became the primary concern of the Soviets, and to that end the USSR was to be 'second to none in the legal discharge of assumed international obligations, more especially in the noble task of securing for all nations the blessing of peace, which mankind never valued or appreciated so much as it does now after the relatively recent orders.' This meant Soviet loyalty to Article 16 of the Covenant, whose provisions called for sanctions. The Soviets insisted on their application to the fullest extent.

According to Source Y, why did the Soviets insist on complete economic sanctions against Italy?

was debated at the League's Assembly, the Soviet representative harangued Italian representatives, condemning their statements regarding Abyssinia in the strongest of terms. Unable to affect the League's failure to impose collective security, the Soviets participated in the economic sanctions against Italy, imposing an embargo on all trade, unlike Britain and France.

Response: Italy

Italy was affected by the Abyssinian Crisis in many ways. Economically, Italy was further isolated from the markets and relative wealth of Western Europe and its trade with the USA was restricted. This certainly affected the economy, which was already weak. This encouraged Italy to continue expanding its economic ties with central and southeastern Europe, giving it more independence in its foreign policy (see page 116). Economic sanctions simply pushed Italy further from co-operative diplomatic relations.

? What is the message of Source Z?

(see page 116)

SOURCE Z

'International trick skating, practicing for the international event.' A cartoon by Sidney 'George' Strube for the *Daily Express*, 26 February 1937.

Italy was diplomatically isolated by its annexation of Abyssinia. It refused to participate in the London Naval Treaty conference that began in December 1935, although it had been part of the group that had initiated the naval treaty system in Washington in 1922 (see page 28). While this was partly a protest over economic sanctions by Britain and France, it was also because Italy wanted to build a larger fleet that could challenge France in the Mediterranean and perhaps even Britain eventually. As relations with Germany improved, Italy began to envision the possibility of Italy and Germany co-operating to create a joint navy capable of challenging Britain and France as well. The Stresa Front collapsed completely.

Italy left the League of Nations in May 1936, freeing it for other actions, much as Japan had done in 1933. Italy and Germany's new relationship was formalized in October 1936 with an agreement commonly known as the **Rome–Berlin Axis** (see page 159). This essentially outlined their mutual foreign policies and spheres of interest. Mussolini stated that he did not oppose German annexation of Austria, a key issue for Germany's Hitler.

KEY TERM

Rome–Berlin Axis Treaty of friendship between Germany and Italy in 1936, signalling an end to diplomatic co-operation between Italy and Britain and France.

SOURCE AA

Speech by Benito Mussolini in Milan, Italy, 1 November 1936, quoted in *The Causes of the Second World War* by Anthony Crozier, published by Blackwell Publishers, UK, 1997, p. 121. Crozier was a history lecturer at Queen Mary College, University of London, UK.

The Berlin conversations have resulted in an understanding between our two countries over certain problems which have been particularly acute. By these understandings … this Berlin–Rome line is … an axis around which can revolve all those European states with a will to collaboration and peace.

What, according to Source AA, was the purpose of the Berlin–Rome Axis?

Germany's economy was far greater than that of Italy, and with Germany's economic and military expansion in the late 1930s, Italy was soon reduced to a junior partner in their relationship. This meant that Germany, not Italy, determined the course of their mutual foreign policies and that in time, Italy's opinions were of little importance to Hitler and the German government.

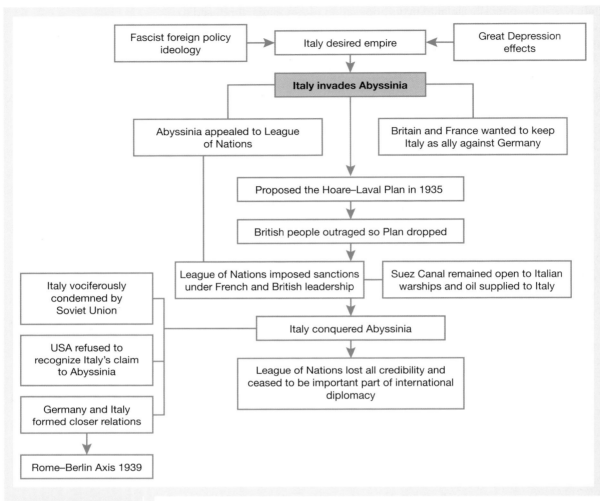

The Abyssinian Crisis

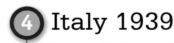 **Italy 1939**

> ▶ **Key question:** How did Italy's relationship with Germany change in 1939?

Between 1936 and 1939, Italy was deeply involved in Spain. Spain was in the midst of a massive civil war and Italy supported the conservative nationalist General Franco. Thousands of Italian troops and large quantities of weapons were sent in support of Franco's forces; Italy's navy assisted as well. Mussolini's hope was that France would become involved and that would allow Italy to seize Corsica and parts of southeastern France that Italy desired. This did not happen. Money, troops and supplies that Italy could not afford were wasted.

Perhaps as the result of this failure and the need for a foreign policy success, or in response to Germany's annexation of Austria and most of Czechoslovakia between 1938 and 1939 (see page 170), Italy decided to annex European territory as well.

Italy's interest in Albania

Albania was a small country with few people and great resources including forests, fields, metals and petroleum. It was also a relatively new state in European affairs, having been formed during the Balkan Wars in 1912 and 1913, just before the outbreak of the First World War. As a member of the Allies, Italy seized Albania in 1915 so that the Allies could use the port of Durrës, referred to in Italy as Durrazo, to supply the Kingdom of Serbia, another member of the Allies. This occupation was short lived and Albania was seized by the Austro-Hungarian Empire.

After the war, Italy worked to delineate Albania's ill-defined borders, working to prevent Greece from taking territory. This led to the assassination of an Italian military officer and a short military conflict between Greece and Italy (see page 114). Italy essentially assumed a protectorate over Albania, whether the Albanians desired it or not, and like Italy, Albania became less democratic in the 1920s. President Zogu, who had signed an alliance between Italy and Albania in 1926, worked to increase his power. He became King Zog I of Albania in 1928 by careful manipulation of a parliament which called for revisions to the constitution, allowing the formation of a **monarchy**, replacing the **republican** form of government.

> **What was the purpose behind Italy's annexation of Albania?**

 **KEY TERM**

Monarchy A government led by a king or queen.

Republic Form of government consisting of elected representatives of voters.

SOURCE BB

Excerpt from *The History of Albania from Its Origins to Present Day* by Stefanaq Pollo and Arben Puto, published by Routledge & Kegan Paul, London, UK, 1981, p. 206.

In June 1931 a new agreement was signed in Rome: Albania was granted a loan of 100 million gold francs, to be paid at the rate of 10 million a year. But these new funds only just covered the maintenance of [the government]. The country's economy and finance continued to flounder amid growing difficulties, which were made even worse by the effect of the world economic crisis [Great Depression]. A year later Zogu was unable to repay the first annuity on the loan … and Mussolini decided this was the moment to act: in exchange for putting off the payment again, he insisted on an Italian–Albanian trade agreement abolishing customs duty [tax on Italian imports].
… Zogu refused.

What does Source BB indicate about Albania?

Italy's growing control and war, 1931–9

Mussolini's attempt to gain further control of Albania's economy in 1931 (see Source BB above) made Zog more wary of Italy. In 1932 and 1933, Zog closed all schools operated by Italians and removed Italian military instructors and advisors. He hoped to demonstrate independence from Italy. Mussolini responded to these actions by suspending the previous loan of money granted to Albania in 1931. This led to a suspension of government projects throughout the country and unemployment in the cities.

King Zog's bankrupt government appealed to France for financial assistance. French demands on Albania were even greater than Italy's in many ways, calling for Albania to set aside large regions where France could settle its poor farmers. Zog ended discussions with France and returned to negotiating with Italy. Mussolini, in a show of force, landed military troops from Italy's navy in Durrës in June 1934, demanding that Zog allow Italian military instructors and advisors back into Albania's military and forbidding the country to join any alliances outside the one it already had with Italy. Italy also required Albania to end all trade restrictions with it and to allow the construction of an improved port at Durrës so that it could be used as a future naval base for Italy's navy.

In March 1939, Italy may have decided to demonstrate its strength and independence to its theoretical partner, Germany. Without informing Germany about its plans, Zog and his government were sent an ultimatum. Italy demanded that Albania allow Italian troops to be garrisoned in various parts of the country, that Albania grant lands to Italian colonists who would automatically become Albanian citizens and that Zog's government contain an Italian minister to represent Italy's interests. In short, Italy wanted almost complete control over the country. Zog responded by proposing a few, limited concessions to Italy which were rejected.

On 7 April, 30,000 soldiers, supported by aircraft, marines and ships, landed at Durrës and other ports. Albania's army and volunteer fighters were quickly overwhelmed and by 10 April, all Albania was occupied. Albania was annexed to Italy and Italy's king was now King of the Albanians, as well as Emperor of Ethiopia.

Responses to Italy annexing Albania

SOURCE CC

According to Source CC, what action did the League of Nations plan to take regarding Italy's invasion of Albania?

Excerpt from *King Zog of Albania: Europe's Self-made Muslim King* by Jason Tomes, published by New York University Press, New York, USA, 2004, p. 238. Tomes is a lecturer in British history at Boston University, USA.

... *[The] world accepted the seizure of Albania itself as a fait accompli [an accomplished fact]. They may not have rushed to recognise Victor Emmanuel's new title, but in most eyes, a land which had been virtually Italian was now really Italian, and that was that. When Zog asked the moribund League of Nations to protest at 'a state of things accomplished by blood and iron', Avenol, the Secretary-General, remarked: 'The reading of the letter constitutes the [only] action I intend to take.'*

International response

International responses to the invasion and annexation of Albania were limited:

- Britain and France were preoccupied with Germany's demands in Poland (see page 171) and therefore did not protest.
- Neighbouring states of Greece and Yugoslavia were afraid of Italian attack, but also hoped to gain slices of Albania, and therefore did not protest.
- The League of Nations had been proven ineffective earlier, so it ignored the situation in Albania.

Only the Soviet Union protested Italy's actions; its condemnation was only verbal, yet aggressive. It was also to no avail.

Second World War begins, 1939

In May 1939, Italy and Germany signed a formal military alliance commonly known as the **Pact of Steel**. In this agreement, both states pledged to support each other in the case of war. The agreement also called for mutual co-operation in economic areas and sharing of military aid, such as weapons. Verbally, Germany told Italy that any war would not be immediate so there was no need to be too concerned with war preparations.

Italy was clearly not prepared for war. Its economy, always weak compared to many other European states, was in very bad shape: the Great Depression, deficit spending for war preparations, the invasion of Abyssinia and huge military support to General Franco in Spain had depleted the government of funds. Its military was smaller as a result of the economy and its military supplies had been consumed in these conflicts. By the time the invasion of Albania occurred, one Italian government official stated that if Albania had organized a single fire-brigade, Italy's military would have been driven back into the sea. Italy was not remotely prepared for war.

Germany seems not to have taken the Pact of Steel very seriously. Some historians believe that the Pact was a means of making sure that Mussolini did not build relations with France and Britain so that Germany did not have to be concerned with its border with Italy, a border created by the annexation of Austria in 1938 (see page 159). Additionally, Italy and France shared a border, so the Pact could also serve to distract France from any military plans it may have had to attack Germany's western border. Whatever the reason, Germany did not assist Italy in any way with war preparations. It also did not inform Italy until August 1939 that a war might break out between Germany and Poland over Danzig (see page 176).

When Italy understood that war was imminent, the Italian government panicked. Mussolini stated clearly that Italy would not be ready for a large war for approximately three years. If Germany insisted on going to war, then it would need to supply Italy militarily. Italy handed over an enormous list of military needs, attempting to demonstrate to Germany how unready it was

> **What was Italy's response to the outbreak of war in Poland in September 1939?**

 **KEY TERM**

Pact of Steel More formally known as the 'Pact of Friendship and Alliance between Germany and Italy', the Pact publicly stated that the two countries supported and trusted each other; secret clauses stated that there would be a union of economic and military policies, although these were never enacted.

and its displeasure with Germany's probable war with Poland. Germany declined to supply Italy and instead granted Italy the right to remain in the alliance and not fight. Instead, Italy was to supply diplomatic and political support to Germany. Italy agreed readily, hoping that Germany's war with Poland would be limited in terms of time, involvement and impact on international diplomacy.

? According to Source DD, why did Italy try to deter Germany from war?

SOURCE DD

Excerpt from *Italian Fascism, 1919–1945* by Philip Morgan, published by Macmillan, London, UK, 1995, p. 170.

The new of German plans for immediate war put Mussolini in a corner. He was bound by the alliance to join Hitler in a war he had not anticipated would happen so soon, and which he knew Italy could not really fight. It was not only a matter of Italy's military and economic un-readiness to sustain a long war. Mussolini and [Foreign Minister] Ciano paraded this in front of the Germans, in order to get them to delay things or at least accept that the alliance could not be activated then. The other reason or pretext for prevarication was the need for more time to make the Axis popular in Italy and prepare the nation politically and psychologically for war.

? What is the message of Source EE?

SOURCE EE

A cartoon by Sidney 'George' Strube for the *Daily Express*, 30 October 1940, showing the rulers of Abyssinia and Ethiopia tied to the fasces, a symbol of the Fascist Party. Mussolini confronts a Greek man.

By June 1940, Germany had conquered Poland, Denmark, Norway, Belgium, the Netherlands, Luxembourg and most of France. France was all but defeated by 10 June when Italy declared war and began the invasion of France's southeast provinces and Corsica.

SUMMARY DIAGRAM

Italy 1939

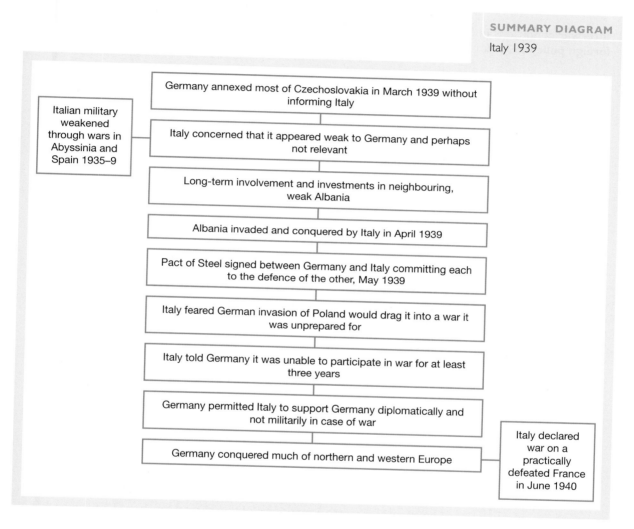

Germany annexed most of Czechoslovakia in March 1939 without informing Italy	
Italian military weakened through wars in Abyssinia and Spain 1935–9	Italy concerned that it appeared weak to Germany and perhaps not relevant

Long-term involvement and investments in neighbouring, weak Albania

Albania invaded and conquered by Italy in April 1939

Pact of Steel signed between Germany and Italy committing each to the defence of the other, May 1939

Italy feared German invasion of Poland would drag it into a war it was unprepared for

Italy told Germany it was unable to participate in war for at least three years

Germany permitted Italy to support Germany diplomatically and not militarily in case of war

Germany conquered much of northern and western Europe

Italy declared war on a practically defeated France in June 1940

Chapter summary

Interwar conditions in Europe and Italian foreign policy 1933–6

The Great Depression that began in 1929 affected countries throughout the world politically, economically and in terms of foreign policy. The Great Powers of Britain and France were unable to respond to international crises because of costs and divided governments. The economic crisis led to the rising popularity of communism in Germany, causing conservatives to increasingly turn to the Nazi Party, which took power in 1933. Italy became less dependent on Western states for its economic security and therefore able to exercise more independence in its foreign policy. French plans to contain Germany through close co-operation with Italy and Britain, symbolized by the Stresa Front, collapsed with Italy's invasion of Abyssinia. The Abyssinian Crisis led to Italy leaving the League of Nations, the impotence of that international peace organization, closer relations between Italy and Germany that would manifest themselves in the form of an alliance, the expansion of Germany to include Austria and Italy's annexation of Albania. By the outbreak of the Second World War in 1939, Italy was a much weakened state and dependent on its dominant partner, Germany.

✅ Examination advice

Paper 1 Question 11: Comparing and contrasting sources

Question 11 on the IB History Diploma examination requires you to compare and contrast two sources. This means you will discuss the similarities and differences between the two sources. The most commonly used form of the question will ask you to compare and contrast two sources and how they view a certain historical event, document or person. Usually the similarities and differences are fairly clear and the question can be easily answered in a few minutes. Question 11 requires no actual knowledge of history, just the ability to read and understand the sources. It is possible that one of the sources will have been used in Question 9 or 10. If this is the case, read/analyse the source again anyway.

Question 11 is worth 6 marks out of the 24 total for Paper 1. This means it is worth 25 per cent of the overall mark. Answering Question 11 should take approximately fifteen minutes of your examination time.

How to answer

You will obviously need to read Question 11 carefully. Determine which sources you need to read and what exactly you are being asked to compare and contrast. You will be asked to compare and contrast not just the two sources, but the two sources' views on something specific. Do not discuss the origins or purpose of the sources; focus only on the demands of the question. You should make notes on your paper from the source regarding the question's focus. Do this for both sources. There is no need to record or utilize any information which does not specifically address the question.

> Remember that questions for Prescribed subject 3 will be numbered 9, 10, 11 and 12 in the Paper 1 exam.

Once you have completed answering your question, you should draw a line through any notes so they will not be reviewed by the examiner.

When you start your answer, be sure to write a paragraph that explains how the sources *compare,* or are similar, on whatever is being asked in the question. Your second paragraph should be on how they *contrast* or how they are different. You should not treat each source separately, but integrate them in the same sentences as much as possible. Using quotes from the sources to strengthen your answer is an excellent idea and will help you obtain more marks, but do keep in mind that a good historian also knows when to paraphrase and summarize.

Remember, the total mark available for this question is 6. A general rule to follow would be to have at least three points of comparison and three for contrast. This is not always possible, so in certain circumstances it may be possible to have four compares, or contrasts, and two of the other. Again, this is a general rule and it is always best to make sure that all points are completely relevant and focused on the question. There may be minor similarities and differences between the sources. Do not let these take the place of the more significant points.

The example uses Sources U (page 124) and Y (page 127).

Example

> **Compare and contrast the views expressed in Sources U and Y regarding reactions to the Abyssinian Crisis in 1936.** (6 marks)

Immediately start making notes on Source U on your paper, perhaps organizing a chart to more easily compare and contrast the sources. Your notes may appear something like this:

Source U	Source Y
Focus: League response	Focus: Soviet response
• Allows Abyssinia Emperor to speak • This offends Italy • Italy leaves League in December 1937 • League ignores conflicts such as Spanish Civil War and Czech Crisis in 1938 • No reaction to outbreak of European war in September 1939 • Expelled Soviet Union in December 1939 for invading Poland • Never discusses German invasion of Western powers	• Soviet Union defends League Covenant • Sees itself as leader of defending the Covenant • Soviets support Article 16 about sanctions • Soviets apply sanctions against Italy completely
Compare: • Both sources indicate that the League was not effective • Both imply that the League was divided • Both discuss the Soviet Union's interaction with the League	Contrast: • One source about Soviet response, other about League response as a whole • Source Y doesn't discuss long-term effects, while Source U does • Source U indicates that the actions discussed in Source Y were ineffective

Your answer to this question could look like:

There is running comparison in both paragraphs, with both sources usually mentioned together in the same sentence.

Both Sources U and Y indicate that there were responses to the Abyssinian Crisis of 1936. Sources U and Y both relate that the Soviet Union was important for the League, although in different ways. Both sources imply that the League was divided in how to respond to the Crisis, with Source Y indicating that only the Soviet Union was applying sanctions to the fullest extent of all member states since they were going to be 'second to none' and with Source U stating that the Abyssinian Emperor was allowed to speak and then expelled from the Assembly.

There is an appropriate use of a quotation as supporting evidence.

Comparisons and contrasts have been separated into two paragraphs.

Sources U and Y contrast significantly. Source Y clearly focuses on the Soviet Union's response to the Abyssinian Crisis, whereas Source U is a more general overview of the League's reactions to the Crisis with no focus on any particular country within the League. Source Y does not review the Abyssinian Crisis's effect on the League as a whole, however Source U is almost exclusively about the effects over the following few years. Source U demonstrates that the sanctions mentioned in Source Y were ineffective since Italy simply removed itself from the League and independence was not restored to Abyssinia. Finally, Source Y states the Soviets were defenders of the League, while Source U states that this defence only went so far since the Soviets were expelled from the League in December 1939 for invading Poland.

The comparisons and contrasts are the most significant ones. Minor points have not been used, keeping the paragraphs focused and strong.

There is an appropriate use of language, especially in connecting sources or points. Examples of words that help build linkage include 'both', 'whereas', 'while' and 'however'.

The answer indicates that the question was understood. There are two strong comparisons and four contrasts between the two sources. There is running comparison and contrast in each paragraph, with both sources often treated in the same sentence. An appropriate quotation is used from one of the sources to reinforce the answer. The answer addresses all criteria. Mark: 6/6.

Examination practice

The following are exam-style questions for you to practise, using sources from the chapter. Sources can be found on the page references given.

The questions also reflect the numbering style of the exam (there are no questions 1–8; questions for The move to global war begin at question 9).

PAPER 1 PRACTICE FOR QUESTION 11 FOR CASE STUDY 2 (USING CHAPTER 3 SOURCES)

Source D: page 107
Source E: page 107
Source I: page 114

Source K: page 116
Source U: page 124
Source X: page 126

1 Compare and contrast the views expressed in Sources D and E about the effects of economics on the rise of the Nazi Party in Germany.

2 Compare and contrast the views expressed in Sources I and K regarding the importance of economics for Italy's foreign policy under Mussolini.

3 Compare and contrast the views expressed in Sources U and X concerning the international response to Italy's invasion of Abyssinia.

PAPER 1 PRACTICE FOR QUESTION 11 FOR CASE STUDY 1 (USING CHAPTER 2 SOURCES)

Source H: page 62
Source I: page 62
Source L: page 67

Source O: page 70
Source T: page 74
Source V: page 75

1 Compare and contrast the views expressed in Sources H and I regarding the significance of the Manchurian Crisis for the League of Nations.

2 Compare and contrast the views expressed in Sources L and O concerning Japan's invasion of China in 1937.

3 Compare and contrast the views expressed in Sources T and V regarding Soviet involvement in the Second Sino-Japanese War.

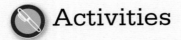

Activities

1 Compare and contrast the cartoons presented in this chapter in terms of their point of view and message regarding the Abyssinian Crisis. Remember to study imagery, symbols and the captions to understand the entire message, intended audience, point of view and so forth.

2 Create Paper 1 Question 10 questions using sources in this chapter in groups. Exchange questions with other groups in your class and in a timed exercise, respond to these questions. Discuss your answers and repeat the exercise as needed.

3 Watch the speech of Emperor Haile Selassie to the League of Nations in 1936 on YouTube or through some other media. What are the reactions of the audience? What was the purpose of the speech and why was it ineffectual? Was the speech actually ineffectual in the long term?

4 As a class, compare and contrast the Manchurian and Abyssinian Crises. Perhaps in the form of a chart or Venn diagram, review which nations were involved, short- and long-term responses of the League, effects on the League of each crisis and more. Debate which of the crises had the greater effect on the League, whether positive or negative.

CHAPTER 4

German foreign policy 1933–40

The Nazi Party was firmly in power in Germany by 1933. It immediately began to change Germany's political and economic systems. These changes allowed the start of massive rearmament, a direct challenge to restrictions placed in the Treaty of Versailles that ended the First World War. The results of these changes allowed further challenges to other post-war settlements and to international diplomacy. You will need to consider the following questions throughout this chapter:

★ Which domestic policies allowed a more forceful German foreign policy in the late 1930s?
★ How successful was Germany's foreign policy between 1933 and 1935?
★ How successful was Germany in achieving its foreign policy aims between 1936 and 1939?
★ Why did a multinational war erupt in Europe on 3 September 1939?

1 Hitler and Nazi Germany 1933–8

▶ *Key question: Which domestic policies allowed a more forceful German foreign policy in the late 1930s?*

In 1933, Adolf Hitler became Chancellor of Germany and was soon the head of a single-party state (see page 107). That said, it took Hitler several years, until 1938, to achieve total control of the state. As his authority increased, foreign policy grew more aggressive. This was also the result of an ever-strengthening economy that allowed not only rearmament but also economic power over much of central and eastern Europe, at the expense of Britain and France.

Hitler and the consolidation of power 1933–8

The Nazi Party moved swiftly to consolidate its power after taking control of the government in the midst of the Great Depression (see page 100). First, there was a merger between the Nazi Party and the government through *Gleichschaltung,* a policy meaning 'making the same' in German. This resulted in:

- all other political parties other than the Nazi Party being abolished
- all labour unions being abolished
- all governing councils and governors being replaced by Nazi Party-appointed officials
- all police forces being merged with the *Schutzstaffel,* a Nazi paramilitary organization known more commonly as the **SS**.

> What were the main stages in Hitler's consolidation of power within Germany?

KEY TERM

SS An acronym for *Schutzstaffel,* a Nazi paramilitary group that later functioned as the state police and operated a large part of the German economy.

While the German state and Nazi Party merged, Hitler consolidated his own power by having party rivals executed in 1934. Until that point, there had been internal debate and dissension about the nature and direction of the party and therefore the state; there was no debate after that.

The only institution beyond Hitler's total control was the German army, which was managed by the conservative nobility. Army officers saw Hitler, an Austrian who had only attained the low rank of corporal in the First World War, as a foreigner and a politician who could not be trusted. Hitler finally took control of the army in 1938 by replacing the top commanders. By 1938, there were no institutions that Hitler and the Nazi Party did not control within Germany.

At each stage of the consolidation of power within Germany, Hitler's foreign policy increasingly challenged the post-war settlements of the First World War (see page 105).

To what extent did Germany's economy improve between 1933 and 1939?

Nazi Germany's economy 1933–9

With the new Nazi government, new policies to deal with the Great Depression were generated. From October 1933, Germany would as far as possible trade only with countries that would purchase German goods of equal value to what Germany imported from that country. If Romania, for example, wanted Germany to purchase its oil or wheat, then Romania had to purchase an equivalent amount of German industrial goods, such as cameras or automobiles.

The 'New Plan'

In 1934 this new economic policy, now called the 'New Plan', was expanded on by the German Minister of Economics, Hjalmar Schacht. This new programme gave the German government much more control over the economy, dictating what could and could not be imported.

? What is the message conveyed by Source A?

SOURCE A

Excerpt from *The Origins of the Second World War in Europe*, second edition by P.M.H. Bell, published by Pearson Education, London, UK, 1998, p. 158. The book is currently in its third edition, published in 2007. Bell is an honorary senior fellow in the Department of History at the University of Liverpool, UK, and has published several books.

… he [Schacht] introduced his 'New Plan' for German foreign trade, based on the principles of buying nothing that could not be paid for by foreign exchange earned by German exports, and of making imports conform to national needs as decided by the government. All imports were subject to licences, which were used to differentiate between essential and non-essential items, with raw materials and food classified as essential. Whenever possible, imports were to be bought only from the countries which were willing to accept German goods in return; and any foreign exchange involved was to be paid into a clearing account, and not used freely by the exporting country.

By exchanging goods of equal value and purchasing only essential materials, plus exporting increasing amounts of manufactured goods to states that mainly produced raw materials, Germany's economy recovered more rapidly than any other European state during the Great Depression.

Schacht's plan meant that Germany:

- imported 284 million marks (Germany's currency) worth of materials and products more than it exported in 1934
- exported 111 million marks more than it imported in 1935
- exported 550 million marks more than it imported in 1936.

The success of the New Plan meant cheaper food prices in Germany, as food was now mainly imported from central and eastern Europe, and more money to purchase raw materials that could be used for rearmament (see page 144). Massively increased trade with central and eastern European states meant that their economies also benefited, and they became more dependent on Germany for their prosperity and economic stability. The effect of Germany's increasing economic and therefore political sway was compounded by British and French policies of imperial preference (see pages 101 and 104).

The Four Year Plan 1936–9

The New Plan was clearly successful in reducing unemployment and strengthening Germany's economy by 1936. Schacht was pressured to allow the purchase and use of more raw materials such as iron and coal to produce armaments such as aircraft, tanks, guns and ammunition. As the purchase of these raw materials consumed critically important foreign currencies and gold, for products that were not useful as export items (unlike consumer goods such as pots, pans and textiles), Schacht resisted. He believed that this policy of major military spending would wreck Germany's improving economy.

In September 1936, the government announced a Four Year Plan for the country's economy and that it would be led by Hermann Goering. Schacht remained minister of economics, but with steadily eroding authority; he resigned as minister in November 1937. The Four Year Plan aimed to:

- increase agricultural production
- achieve self-sufficiency in the production of raw materials
- continue strict government regulation of imports and exports
- increase military production at the expense of consumer production.

Historians such as Richard Overy state that it is clear that the Four Year Plan was enacted to prepare Germany for some eventual war, probably at some point in the 1940s. The plan indicates that Germany's government believed it was vulnerable to blockades and **embargoes** of raw materials, hence the call to increase its own agricultural and raw material production. As part of this preparation, new emphasis was placed on creating substitutes for

 **KEY TERM**

Embargo A restriction on the import of specific items or from a specific country.

KEY TERM

Synthetic oil Oil produced from non-crude oil sources such as coal by-products and fish oils.

Synthetic rubber Rubber made from petroleum by-products instead of tree sap.

Why did Germany rearm after 1935?

? According to Source B, which states on Germany's borders were not allied with France?

products such as rubber that Germany could never produce naturally; **synthetic oil** and **synthetic rubber** factories were given a priority in terms of construction.

What the Four Year Plan meant was that Germany was able to rapidly increase its production of military equipment. It also meant that there were far fewer goods for consumers to purchase, although wages increased and unemployment continued to drop. This led to inflation as prices rose for the increasingly smaller quantity of consumer goods available. Several historians have indicated that political pressure from workers and the economy generally was one of the major factors pushing Germany to war in 1939.

Rearmament

Germany was disarmed after the First World War as a first step towards general disarmament in Europe (see pages 105 and 145).

Vulnerability after 1919

While Germany was disarmed, its neighbours certainly did not follow. Poland, Germany's eastern neighbour, had up to 300,000 active soldiers and 700,000 in reserves. France had almost identical numbers on Germany's western border, and was determined to prevent another German invasion. In 1921, France and Poland formed an alliance which called for each to support the other in case either was attacked. France also created the Little Entente in 1920 and 1921, which included the promise of help from Czechoslovakia, Romania and Yugoslavia. These two alliances had the ability to field millions of troops against Germany.

SOURCE B

A map of Europe in 1925 indicating states allied to France.

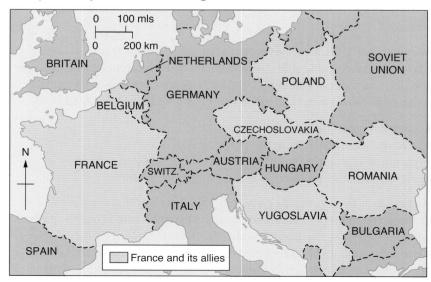

German vulnerability was clearly demonstrated in 1923. Germany was required by a provision of the Treaty of Versailles to repay France and Belgium for damages from the First World War. In 1922, Germany announced that it was unable to continue payments. France and Belgium invaded Germany in January 1923, occupying the Ruhr region, which was a major industrial centre. Although the occupation, which led to diplomatic, political and economic crises for all involved, ended by 1925, the event clearly indicated Germany's vulnerability to invasion. France and its allies argued that Germany had a larger population than any other state in Europe except the Soviet Union and with its industry it could rapidly rearm; maintaining large military forces was required for the long-term security of France and its allies.

Many in Germany were also concerned about communism and the growing strength of the Soviet Union, which helped propel the Nazi Party into power. The Soviet Union was the largest state in the world and by 1932 had completed its first Five Year Plan, which helped it industrialize on a massive scale. With the launching of the second Five Year Plan, many in Germany felt a need to prepare for the country's defence in case of an invasion; only Poland lay between the Soviet Union and Germany.

World Disarmament Conference 1932

After many years of research and reports, the League of Nations' **World Disarmament Conference** met in Geneva, Switzerland, in 1932. There were immediately calls for participating nations, including France, Britain and Germany, to reduce the size of their armies and amount of military equipment.

France simply refused to co-operate with disarmament talks unless Britain and the USA agreed to guarantee its security through an alliance; both countries refused. As talks continued into 1933, Germany declared that if France would not limit its military, then it would be forced to arm itself for defence. Germany withdrew from the conference when it became clear that France would not disarm, and withdrew from the League of Nations shortly afterwards. It was clear to many in Germany that rearmament was necessary for national security.

Rearmament begins

Although Germany had already produced some weaponry beyond what was allowed in the Treaty of Versailles, it announced massive rearmament in March 1935. Rearmament included:

- the introduction of conscription
- construction of 2500 aircraft of various types
- expansion of the navy (see page 154)
- mass production of guns of all types, tanks and artillery.

By 1936, Germany had the ability to produce 5000 aircraft annually and by 1939 it had an army of 700,000 with 3 million more in reserves. The rapidity

KEY TERM

World Disarmament Conference Conference held by the League of Nations which began in 1932, the aim of which was to reduce military sizes and weapons as a way to prevent future war.

of Germany's rearmament essentially validated France's belief that Germany had the ability to become a major military power quickly.

According to Source C, what was the main aim of Germany's military when rearmament began in 1935?

SOURCE C

Excerpt from 'The Nazi Economy – Was It Geared to War?' by Richard Overy, published in *History Review*, No. 31, September 1998. *History Review* was a major journal devoted to publishing authoritative articles by modern historians; it ended in 2012. Overy is a prominent historian and a history professor at Exeter University, UK.

… *The armed forces themselves were anxious to rebuild German military power cautiously, step-by-step, so that they could control its pace and character themselves. The first priority here was to rebuild the infrastructure of military life – barracks, airfields, training schools – that had been shut down or destroyed during the period of enforced disarmament. The first air force production programmes were largely devoted to building trainer aircraft. Between 1934 and 1938 some 58 per cent of aircraft production was made up of trainer aircraft and only 18 per cent of combat planes. Tank production was slow to get going and the programme for naval shipbuilding laid down in March 1934 had achieved little before the late 1930s. Remilitarisation on any scale took time to achieve because Germany began in 1933 from a very low base.*

While many historians now question the quality and equipment of Germany's new army, rearmament was accomplished during the Great Depression (see page 100), when most countries worked to do the opposite, that is, control spending and reduce imports. German rearmament appeared as some miracle to most observers, not least because much of it was achieved using imported materials and because it led to practically zero unemployment.

International response to rearmament, April 1935

Germany's announced rearmament caused multiple reactions, especially in Europe.

Stresa Front, April 1935

Almost immediately, the leaders of Britain, France and Italy met in Stresa, Italy, in April 1935 to respond to Germany's clear violation of the Treaty of Versailles. All the countries condemned Germany's plans to rebuild its military and promised to work together. This initiative is often called the Stresa Front and amounted to little. Each of these countries had differing goals (see pages 151 and 157 for examples) and had little ability to act militarily against Germany as a result of the Great Depression.

Hitler immediately assured these states of Germany's peaceful intentions. Germany proposed non-aggression pacts with its neighbours, similar to that agreed with Poland in 1934 (see page 151). Hitler also promised to observe the Locarno treaties (see textbox), in which Germany recognized the borders of neighbouring western states as permanent. Finally, he also stated that Germany would accept limitations on armaments if other countries limited their war capabilities as well.

> **Locarno Treaties 1925**
>
> Germany, Britain and France agreed in a series of treaties at the Locarno Conference to:
>
> - Recognize as permanent the borders between Germany, France and Belgium as established after the First World War.
> - Continue demilitarization of the Rhineland area between France and Belgium.
> - Adjust Germany's borders with Poland and Czechoslovakia, but only through negotiation, not war.

SOURCE D

Excerpt from *Chronicle of a Downfall: Germany 1929–1939* by Leopold Schwarzschild, published most recently by I.B. Tauris, London, UK, 2010, p. 126. Schwarzschild was a German historian admired by British politician Winston Churchill. He wrote from the USA in exile from Europe after 1940.

Mussolini felt as threatened as France by German rearmament, and even ordered partial mobilisation … France also reacted by reopening negotiations on a treaty with Moscow, with the result that a treaty of mutual assistance against Germany was signed on 2 May 1935. Two weeks later the Soviet Union and Czechoslovakia concluded a similar agreement, which continued the dismantling of the structures set up by the League of Nations and initiated by Hitler with the Polish non-aggression pact of January 1934.

According to Source D, what were international reactions to Germany's announced rearmament? **?**

France's response

Since Poland's non-aggression agreement with Germany in 1934, France no longer saw Poland as a reliable ally. France sought a stronger ally and since Britain refused any form of alliance, France turned to the Soviet Union. In May 1935, France and the Soviet Union established the Franco-Soviet Treaty of Mutual Assistance. This treaty stated that both would work through the League of Nations to ensure peace in Europe and each would come to the assistance of the other in case of attack by a third country. Many conservatives in France feared communism more than Nazi Germany and through political pressure managed to ensure that no military discussions or plans were made between the Soviet Union and France, rendering the agreement powerless.

France was already the strongest military power in Europe, and perhaps the world, in the early 1930s. Throughout the 1930s it increased military spending substantially. Initially, it built a massive series of fortifications, tank barriers, trenches, barbed wire and walls was known as the Maginot Line, which stretched primarily along the border between Germany and France.

Britain's response

The British government had followed a strict policy of limited military spending since the end of the First World War. There was little political support for rearmament as that would increase taxation, and with the onset of the Great Depression there was even less interest in building large military forces. German rearmament, however, alarmed many throughout the country and the government responded. The government realized that it would only be able to negotiate from a position of military strength. It was also understood that it would take many years before that strength was at a point where Britain could defend itself and strike Germany if required.

Rearmament began on a large scale. This consisted of not only mass production of aircraft, artillery and warships, but also expanding industrial capacity. The government focused on building the infrastructure necessary for large-scale war production, such as increased railway lines, shipbuilding facilities, factories, power plants and more. Spending on rearmament increased over 600 per cent between 1935 and 1939. It was projected that Britain would be at its strongest in relation to Germany in the autumn of 1939.

SOURCE E

Excerpt from *British War Economy* by W.K. Hancock and M.M. Gowing, published by His Majesty's Stationery Office (HMSO), London, UK, 1949, p. 68. Hancock was a professor of economic history at Oxford University. Gowing was a British historian who is best known for her works on the Second World War and on scientific history. HMSO was an official government printer until it merged with other government bodies in the UK to form the National Archives. Estimated total annual military expenditure by the British government between 1935 and 1939 in millions of British pounds.

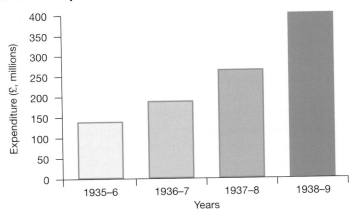

According to Source E, in which year did military spending in Britain increase the most from the previous year?

Germany's domestic, economic decisions to implement the Four Year Plan and rearm itself on a grand scale in the early 1930s had a major impact on the Western Great Powers, causing some of them to rearm as well. It also affected Germany's foreign policy in that this became increasingly aggressive as its economic power grew.

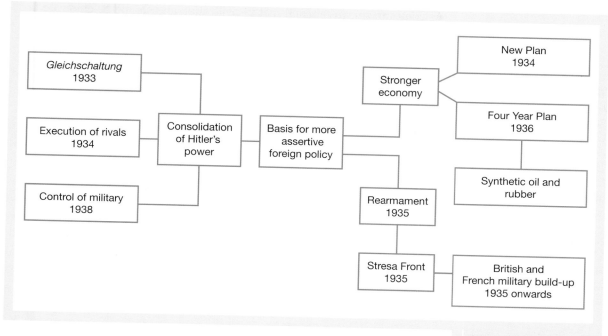

SUMMARY DIAGRAM

Hitler and Nazi Germany
1933–8

② Germany's foreign policy: 1933–5

▶ **Key question:** *How successful was Germany's foreign policy between 1933 and 1935?*

Germany's economic, political and military weakness before 1935 meant that foreign policy was carefully considered. Germany's economy was fragile, but recovering (see above), and, politically, Hitler was still consolidating power over the government, his party and the military. With a small military before 1935, Germany was not a threat to any significant European state. In addition, Italy, France and Britain, acting as the world's Great Powers, worked against Germany, restricting its ability to significantly affect world affairs.

Nazism and foreign policy

Nazism, primarily based on the beliefs and writings of Hitler, included many points, some of which changed through time. Many of these thoughts were not new and were either borrowed or expanded on by the Nazis. These beliefs included:

- The Treaty of Versailles must be completely undone.
- All Germans should live in an expanded Germany: **pan-Germanism**.

KEY TERM

Pan-Germanism An idea from the early nineteenth century that all German-language speakers should live in the same country.

What were the main beliefs in Nazism that may have influenced foreign policy?

KEY TERM

Treaty of Brest-Litovsk
A treaty signed between Russia (soon to be the Soviet Union) and Germany and Austria-Hungary in early 1918 in which Russia left the First World War, turning over huge territories to Germany and Austria-Hungary that would include today's countries of Poland, Ukraine, Lithuania, Latvia, Estonia and Finland, containing one-third of Russia's population and farmland and half its industry.

? According to Source F, why did Hitler oppose democratic governments?

- Communism was a real threat to civilization and should be eradicated.
- Germany must have *lebensraum,* or living space (see page 106), in eastern Europe for more food and land for settling.
- Non-Germans were inferior racially to Germans, who were born to conquer and rule others (although certain Germans were also 'undesirable' or were labelled as non-German, such as disabled people, homosexuals and Jews).
- Democratic states were fundamentally weak and greedy.

All German governments since 1919 had wanted to undo the Treaty of Versailles and regain territory lost to Poland; the Locarno Treaties (see page 147) are a great example of how previous governments worked diplomatically to regain losses from the First World War. The idea that all Germans should live in Germany came from the nineteenth century. Previous German governments also feared communism and had suppressed communist uprisings. Living space was also an old idea. During the First World War, Germany defeated Russia and gained control of much of eastern Europe in the **Treaty of Brest-Litovsk** in March 1918. This treaty was later reversed by the nations that defeated Germany in the same year.

SOURCE F

Excerpt from *Hitler: Diagnosis of a Destructive Prophet* by Fritz Redlich, published by Oxford University Press, Oxford, UK, 1999, p. 103. Redlich was a prominent psychiatrist who was dean of the Yale University School of Medicine, USA, and author of works on the medical and psychological state of Hitler.

It was the complete denial of the rule of the majority, which Hitler considered the rule of the stupid and incapable masses and their representatives. According to Hitler, the ideas of democracy and equality were promoted by Jews in order to destroy a nation. 'There must be no majority decisions,' he said … 'surely, every man will have advisors by his side, but the decisions will be made by one man.'

Racism was also not a new concept, but the Nazis made it state policy. Laws institutionalized racism in Germany, for example, with Jewish Germans now denied citizenship.

Most importantly, Hitler indeed believed that Western democracies, such as France and Britain, were fundamentally weak. This weakness was the result of the very nature of democracy in which political parties had to compromise and listen to their public to be elected. This was a contrast to Germany and Italy, both of which were ruled by dictators who had little need to pacify the public or various interests. They saw their system as stronger in that they could act quickly and decisively, based on a single philosophy or overall goal.

The Polish–German Non-Aggression Pact, January 1934

Why did the Polish–German Non-Aggression Pact have major support in both Poland and Germany?

Poland was far more powerful in military terms than Germany in 1934. It was also allied to France (see page 144) and was fully aware that Germany desired to regain territories granted to Poland in the Treaty of Versailles. Poland felt that with its large army and its alliance with France, it had nothing to fear from Germany. Poland also did not want to be drawn into a conflict with Germany in support of France; its main focus was the Soviet Union. This led to an agreement between Germany and Poland.

In January 1934, in the Polish–German Non-Aggression Pact, each state guaranteed that it would not attack the other for a period of ten years. It also led to:

- recognition by Germany of Poland's borders
- better diplomatic relations to discuss disputes
- increased trade between the two states.

For Germany, this treaty meant that it did not need to fear Polish military intervention, even when rearmament programmes began (see page 144). In addition, it clearly weakened the alliance between France and Poland in that France could no longer assume that its partner was inherently hostile to Germany, which had been a threat to both states up to that point. More trade between Poland and Germany benefited both states; Poland was a source of food and metals that the German economy desperately needed (see page 143).

Poland's primary enemy was the Soviet Union, with which it had fought a successful war that ended in 1920, effectively doubling the size of Poland. In the 1920s and 1930s, Poland continued to work against the Soviet Union by encouraging revolts and independence movements there, all unsuccessful. The second Five Year Plan of the Soviet Union (see page 111) was already in progress and the future industrial, and therefore military, might of the Soviet

SOURCE G

Excerpt of a memo from State Secretary B.W. von Bülow to German Chancellor Hitler, August 1934, quoted in *Documents on Nazism 1919–1945* by Jeremy Noakes and Geoffrey Pridham, published by University of Exeter Press, UK, 1995, p. 662. Noakes is a professor of history at the University of Exeter, UK. Pridham is a senior research fellow in politics at the University of Bristol, UK.

In judging the situation we should never overlook the fact that no kind of rearmament in the next few years could give us military security. Even apart from our isolation, we shall for a long time yet be hopelessly inferior to France in the military sphere. A particularly dangerous period will be 1934–5 on account of the reorganization of the Reichswehr [German army].

What is the message conveyed in Source G? **?**

Union needed to be observed and potentially opposed if Polish independence was threatened. The treaty with Germany allowed Poland to deploy its armies in the east of the country, where any Soviet invasion would naturally occur.

International response: France

While the British response to the Pact was muted, France was outraged. The alliance between France and Poland had clearly been weakened, but France had also been reminded that Poland would pursue whatever policy was in its own interest without consulting France or regarding France's needs. There was little that France could do, but one result may have been to draw France somewhat closer to the Soviet Union (see page 147), which was now ending its isolation in response to the Pact as well.

International response: Soviet Union

The Soviet Union initially worked with Nazi Germany, although the German Communist Party had been abolished and most of its members imprisoned and many executed in the Nazi state. The reasons for abandoning German communists were pragmatic. In 1922, Germany and the Soviet Union signed the **Rapallo Treaty**, which established diplomatic relations between the states and allowed trade and diplomatic co-operation. Shortly afterwards, the states started to co-operate militarily on a limited scale, such as weapons development and testing. While Germany needed Soviet supplies such as wheat and metals, the Soviets, in the midst of mass industrialization, needed German machinery and tools. The Soviets worked to maintain relations with Germany throughout 1933.

Co-operation between the two states collapsed with the Polish–German Non-Aggression Pact. Poland and the Soviet Union had no diplomatic relations and considered each other as their main enemy. The Pact meant that the Polish military could concentrate on its border with the Soviet Union and perhaps even attack it in the future. The earlier co-operation between Germany and the Soviet Union meant that there had always been a possibility of an alliance between the two to oppose Poland and perhaps seize territories that both believed belonged to them (see pages 111 and 151). It was now feared that Germany and Poland might even create an alliance to seize parts of the Soviet Union together.

The Soviet reaction to the Pact was to join the League of Nations in 1934. It had previously condemned the League as simply a tool for Britain and France to maintain their empires and as a means of promoting the business interests of capitalist countries. It now sought to support the concept of collective security, although this idea had already been damaged by the Manchurian Crisis (see page 54). In addition, Stalin ordered Comintern (see page 159) to alter its language and mission. Instead of advocating revolution, it now promoted peace, democracy and anti-fascist governments. Communist groups were ordered to co-operate with non-fascist political

KEY TERM

Rapallo Treaty Treaty signed in 1922 by the Soviet Union and Germany in which each renounced all claims against the other, recognized the other diplomatically and agreed to co-operate economically.

parties in order to oppose fascist groups and governments; this happened in Spain, France and other countries almost immediately. The Soviet response to Japanese, German and Italian anti-communist dictatorships was to build positive relations with other countries, most of which distrusted the Soviets and opposed communism, leading to limited success.

Austria 1934

A goal of many in Austria and Germany after the First World War was to unite the two countries. This was a step towards creating a larger Germany, a goal of many nationalists since the nineteenth century so that there would be one state for all Germans. Perhaps more importantly for Hitler, Austria was his original homeland, not Germany. By merging the two states, he would be, in a sense, more German. Fortunately for Hitler, Austria was a politically divided, weak state that had recently experienced severe fighting between **paramilitaries** representing different political factions. Many in Austria may have desired the stability that the Nazi Party had brought to Germany through *Gleichschaltung* (see page 141). An Austrian branch of the Nazi Party had been active until it was banned in 1933.

In June 1934, Hitler met Mussolini and tried to convince him that Austria should become a German **satellite state**. Italy was a major political and military power and shared a long border with Austria. When Mussolini rejected this idea, which contradicted his own plans for central and eastern Europe (see page 117), Hitler gave the Austrian Nazis strong, unofficial encouragement to stage a coup a month later. During the failed coup, Austria's head of state, Chancellor Engelbert Dolfuss, was assassinated.

Mussolini was determined to keep Austria as a buffer state between Italy and Germany. He may have also been eager to demonstrate to Britain and France that Italy was a powerful and important ally. He immediately mobilized troops on the Italian–Austrian frontier and forced Hitler to speak against the coup, which then promptly failed. Hitler was unable and unwilling to risk military intervention in Austria, not least because he did not have complete control of the army (see page 142). Any military action against Austria might also cause other states to intervene, since the merging of Austria and Germany was in the Treaty of St Germain-en-Laye (see page 105).

The failed annexation of Austria was a setback for Hitler, but it is impossible to know the general reaction to this in Germany; the state controlled all media, and opposition parties that might have protested had been banned by *Gleichschaltung*. What was clear, however, is that Germany was weak in 1934 and unable to affect international affairs to its liking. Germany's efforts to take over Austria, however, meant that relations between Germany and Italy were strained at best; Italy was determined to co-operate with Britain and France to keep Germany weak and under control.

> **What factors prevented Germany successfully supporting a coup in Austria in 1934?**

KEY TERM

Paramilitaries Military units that operate outside official control of a government.

Satellite state A state that is closely associated with another and is unable to act independently in many areas such as in economic or foreign policies.

Saar Plebiscite 1935

> **What was the importance of the Saar Plebiscite for Germany?**

The Saar was an iron- and coal-rich region of Germany that bordered France. It was placed under the administration of the League of Nations after the First World War and France was allowed to operate and prosper from its coalmines. This was done to compensate France for coalmines destroyed by Germany in northern France during the war.

The League of Nations held a plebiscite in the Saar in January 1935 in which residents of the Saar could vote to rejoin Germany, remain under League administration or merge with France. Over 90 per cent of voters indicated that they wished to rejoin Germany. This vote was celebrated in Germany and Hitler seems to have believed that it indicated support for his policies and government.

SOURCE H

Excerpt from *Germany, 1871–1945: A Concise History* by Raffael Scheck, published by Berg, New York, USA, 2008, p. 174. Scheck is an associate professor of history at Colby College, Maine, USA.

One success that had more to do with the legacy of the peace treaty than Hitler's foreign policy was the return of the Saar district to Germany. The Treaty of Versailles had separated it from Germany for fifteen years. A popular vote should then decide its future. The population of the Saar district, having never consented to French rule, voted overwhelmingly for return to Germany in January 1935. This both reflected and increased Hitler's popularity among Germans. In March 1935, Hitler felt safe enough to reintroduce general conscription. This blatant violation of the peace treaty did not provoke a punitive French attack, but it prompted France and Britain to form a closer alignment with each other and with Italy. At a conference in the Italian town of Stresa in April, the three powers condemned Germany's step and emphasized that treaties were sacrosanct. This so-called Stresa Front was too little to impress Hitler, however, much as Mussolini's alignment with France and Britain displeased him.

> **?** What was the importance of the Saar Plebiscite, according to Source H?

Anglo-German Naval Treaty, June 1935

> **What was the effect of the Anglo-German Naval Treaty on international diplomacy?**

While Mussolini continued to build up forces to invade Abyssinia (see page 119), both Germany and Britain had been as busy as France in breaking up the unity of Stresa (see page 118) by concluding the Anglo-German Naval Treaty in June 1935. This completely contradicted the declarations at Stresa made just two months before.

Britain believed that it had achieved a diplomatic victory because the treaty would limit the German navy to only 35 per cent of the size of the British navy while Britain began massive rearmament (see page 148). In the British view of the treaty, Germany would always have a small fleet that could never challenge the British for control of the seas militarily or threaten their merchant fleet. This had the added advantage of tying down Germany by allowing it to use its limited resources and expensive raw material imports on ships that would never be able to challenge Britain's substantial navy.

The Anglo-German Naval Treaty must be seen in the context of British diplomacy, which worked to treat Germany as a state with legitimate concerns (see page 110) yet limit its overall power so that it could not challenge Britain.

SOURCE I

Excerpt of a letter from British Foreign Secretary Sir John Simon to King George V of the United Kingdom, February 1935, quoted in *Sir Gerald Fitzmaurice and the World Crisis: A Legal Adviser in the Foreign Office 1930–1945* by Anthony Carty, published by Springer, USA, 2000, p. 179. Carty is a law professor at the University of Aberdeen, UK.

The practical choice is between a Germany which continues to rearm without any regulation or agreement and a Germany which, through getting a recognition of its rights and some modification of the Peace Treaties, enters into the comity [community] of nations and contributes, in this and other ways, to European stability.

> According to Source I, what was the value of Britain making agreements with Germany? **?**

Italy and France, however, believed that German rearmament had been encouraged and the Treaty of Versailles had been violated with British consent. This brought France and Italy temporarily closer together and in mid-1935 there were talks about mutual military co-operation in case of war with Germany. The Stresa Front was severely damaged as a result of the diplomacy of France and Britain, but collapsed completely with the Italian invasion of Abyssinia and economic sanctions placed on Italy (see page 122).

SUMMARY DIAGRAM

Germany's foreign policy 1933–5

▶ **Key question:** *How successful was Germany in achieving its foreign policy aims between 1936 and 1939?*

With rising economic and military strength, Hitler was able to conduct a more assertive foreign policy. It helped that Britain was sympathetic to many German demands, especially that Germans should live in Germany. In addition, Britain and France were often divided on how to respond to Germany's actions, and few states were willing to work diplomatically with the Soviet Union for any purpose, much less the isolation of Germany. Finally, Italy's relationship with Britain and France was permanently damaged by the Abyssinian Crisis (see page 119), preventing a united front against Nazi Germany while giving Germany the chance to gain a diplomatic partner.

> **Why, despite the Locarno treaties, was there no effective opposition to Germany's remilitarization of the Rhineland?**

→ ## Remilitarization of the Rhineland, March 1936

The Rhineland was a large strip of German territory that bordered Belgium, France and Luxembourg. This zone was demilitarized at the end of the First World War to create a buffer between Germany and its western neighbours so that if there was a future war, France and Belgium would be warned far ahead of time. Germany saw the demilitarized zone as a vulnerability since France could potentially invade Germany with no resistance until French armies were deep inside the country. Being unable to control its territory was also a national humiliation.

It seems that there were plans by Germany to potentially reoccupy the Rhineland in 1937, but the favourable diplomatic situation created by the Abyssinian Crisis persuaded Hitler to act in March 1936. In December 1935, the German army was ordered to start planning for this reoccupation. Meanwhile, German diplomats began to make a legal justification for such action by arguing that the Franco-Soviet Treaty of Mutual Assistance was contrary to the Locarno treaties (see page 147) and therefore allowed German to alter the agreements as well.

SOURCE J

? **According to Source J, what made the reoccupation of the Rhineland by Germany possible?**

Excerpt from *The Origins of the Second World War* by A.J.P. Taylor, Penguin Books, London, UK, 1961, pp. 129–30. First published in 1961 by Hamish Hamilton, this book has been most recently reprinted by Penguin Books in 2001. Taylor was a British historian who wrote many books on European history and was a lecturer at many British universities.

Hitler's excuse was the French government's ratification of the Franco-Soviet pact on 27 February 1936. This, he claimed, had destroyed the assumptions of Locarno; not much of an argument, but a useful appeal no doubt to anti-

Bolshevik feeling in Great Britain and France. The actual move on 7 March was a staggering example of Hitler's strong nerve. Germany had literally no forces available for war. The trained men of the old Reichswehr [German army] were now dispersed as instructors among the new mass army; and this new army was not yet ready. Hitler assured his protesting generals that he would withdraw his token force at the first sign of French action; but he was unshakably confident that no action would follow.

The reoccupation of the Rhineland did not take the French by surprise. They had been brooding on it apprehensively ever since the beginning of the Abyssinian affair.

Crucial to the success of Hitler's plan was the attitude of Italy. Mussolini was isolated from Britain and France because of Italy's invasion of Abyssinia and this assured Hitler that Mussolini would not co-operate with the British and French in opposing the remilitarization of the Rhineland.

German troops entered the Rhineland on 7 March 1936. To reassure France that they did not intend to violate the Franco-German frontier, they were initially few in number and lightly equipped.

International response: France and Britain

France did not move to intervene, partly because the French border had not been violated and there was little support in either France or Britain for preventing Germany from controlling its own territory. The French army had planned only for defensive war against future German aggression with the assumption that Germany would attack along its shared border, not through the demilitarized Rhineland; there were no military plans for opposing Germany anywhere other than at the French border. The French government refused to fight Germany alone and Britain made it clear that it was unwilling to go to war over the Rhineland. Military spending, however, was increased.

The British government did reassure France that in the event of an unprovoked German attack on French territory, it would send troops to France. British public opinion was convinced that Hitler was merely walking into 'his own back garden'. In fact, the British government was pleased at the reoccupation of the Rhineland because it removed a major German grievance against Britain and France and meant that France could no longer threaten Germany with invasion. Britain hoped that Germany would now be more co-operative; many in Britain saw Germany as a bulwark against communism (see page 108).

The remilitarization of the Rhineland was a triumph for Hitler, and, as an internal French foreign ministry memorandum of 12 March 1936 stressed (see Source L below), there was a feeling in Europe that Germany was now the centre of European power. It was clear that the Treaty of Versailles was no longer being followed or would not be altered further. Germany was emerging as an economic and military power.

SOURCE K

'Delicate Process.' A cartoon by British cartoonist David Low depicting the British government balancing on a fence with Hitler on one side, and the leaders of France, Italy and the Soviet Union on the other, published in the *Evening Standard* newspaper on 10 April 1935.

? According to Source K, what was Britain's foreign policy in 1935?

SOURCE L

? What is the origin and purpose of Source L?

Excerpt from a memorandum for the foreign minister from René Massigli, Deputy Political Director of the French Foreign Ministry, 12 March 1936, quoted in *The Foreign Policy of France from 1914 to 1945* by J. Néré, published by Routledge, London, UK, 2002, p. 337. Massigli was a senior French diplomat who was secretary-general of the Conference of Ambassadors from 1920 to 1931 and by 1937 political director in the French foreign ministry. Néré is a historian of modern French history.

A German success would likewise not fail to encourage elements which, in Yugoslavia, look towards Berlin … In Rumania this will be a victory of the elements of the Right which have been stirred up by Hitlerite propaganda. All that will remain for Czechoslovakia is to come to terms with Germany. Austria does not conceal her anxiety. 'Next time it will be our turn' … Turkey, who has increasingly close economic relations with Germany, but who politically remains in the Franco-British axis, can be induced to modify her line. The Scandinavian countries … are alarmed.

What was the main advantage for Germany of creating a relationship, even if just on paper, with Italy and Japan in 1936?

Germany ends diplomatic isolation, 1936

The invasion of Abyssinia led to severely strained relations between Italy and its former diplomatic partners: Britain and France. Italy and Germany, both isolated diplomatically, now began a closer diplomatic relationship to end this state of affairs and challenge British and French domination of international affairs. Germany was clearly an anti-communist state, leading to further opportunities to end its isolation from international affairs.

The Rome–Berlin Axis, October 1936

In October 1936, a new diplomatic relationship between Germany and Italy was announced. This became known as the Rome–Berlin Axis, indicating the desire or dream of this new diplomatic alignment that world affairs be determined by the governments of Italy and Germany, not London and Paris, the capitals of Britain and France. This was a clear announcement that Britain and France were no longer to be the states that determined international affairs and events and that Italy and Germany were instead to replace them in importance.

What, according to Source M, was the purpose of the Berlin–Rome Axis?

SOURCE M

Speech by Benito Mussolini in Milan, Italy, 1 November 1936, quoted in *The Causes of the Second World War* by Anthony Crozier, published by Blackwell Publishers, UK, 1997, p. 121. Crozier was a history lecturer at Queen Mary College, University of London, UK.

The Berlin conversations have resulted in an understanding between our two countries over certain problems which have been particularly acute. By these understandings … this Berlin–Rome line is … an axis around which can revolve all those European states with a will to collaboration and peace.

The Anti-Comintern Pact, November 1936

Hitler's government agreed with Japan in November 1936 to oppose the Soviet-sponsored organization Communist International. This organization was responsible for supporting communist groups around the world, which included groups in Spain that were fighting German-sponsored Nationalists (see page 160) and the Chinese Communist Party that fought Japan in China (see page 67). The agreement did not specifically mention co-operative work against the Soviet Union, but this was clearly implied. The Pact was primarily symbolic for both Japan and Germany in that it was a declaration that neither was diplomatically isolated and that they would co-operate in future international diplomacy. Being against communism was something most world governments could claim, so it was also a cause which most governments would not oppose or become alarmed about. Italy joined the Pact in November 1937.

Anschluss, March 1938

What was the international reaction to Germany's annexation of Austria?

After the failed attempt to take control over Austria in 1934, Germany boycotted Austrian goods and raw materials. This severely weakened Austria's economy, which had already been extremely strained by the Great Depression.

Nevertheless, Hitler's government wanted Austria to merge with Germany. Austria had hundreds of factories, large government reserves of gold, workers for factories and natural resources such as iron and magnesium. Italy, the state that had opposed Germany's first attempt to annex Austria in 1934 (see page 117), indicated as early as January 1936 that there would be

Spanish Civil War 1936–9

In 1936, the Spanish army essentially revolted against the elected government. The Nationalists (the army, supporters of the Catholic Church and other conservatives) fought the Republicans (a group that included socialists, republicans, anti-church groups and communists). Germany and Italy supported the Nationalists, while the Soviets backed the Republicans. Britain and France supported neither side and insisted on an arms embargo. Germany and Italy agreed to the embargo, but continued to support and even fight for the Nationalists.

As the Republicans were gradually destroyed, the Soviets grew more convinced that Britain and France believed in their own security far more than they did in collective security (even though Spain belonged to the League of Nations). Further, the Soviets understood that Britain and France opposed communism more than fascism and so they could not be reliable partners to oppose the policies of fascist states.

Germany primarily provided supplies to Nationalist forces, although German-piloted aircraft did participate in some of the battles of the war. Germany's primary desire was to prolong the Spanish Civil War since Spain lay along France's southern border. Germany hoped that France might eventually become involved in the conflict, which would mean a reduction of military forces along their shared border, and perhaps a diplomatic weakening of France generally. Historian A.J.P. Taylor went so far as to say that Hitler was disappointed when the Spanish Civil War ended with a Nationalist victory in 1939, since that ended the possibility of France becoming mired in the conflict.

no future objections to *Anschluss*, the German word for connection or annexation that came to represent the merger of Germany and Austria; this concession allowed the Rome–Berlin Axis to form that same year (see page 159). By 1938, Germany was in a much stronger economic and military position to effect any merging of these states.

Austria worked to prevent annexation by trying to negotiate with Germany. In February 1938, Hitler demanded that the Austrian government appoint an Austrian Nazi Party member, Arthur Seyss-Inquart, as minister of public security; this ministry was in charge of all police. In addition, all jailed Nazi Party members had to be released. Austria complied, only to have Hitler publicly denounce Austrian independence, stating that millions of Germans were suppressed by being separated from Germany.

Austria's Chancellor Kurt Schuschnigg decided to undermine Germany's argument that Austrians wanted to merge with Germany. A plebiscite was scheduled for 13 March in which voters would decide whether the two states should join. Schuschnigg had led a single-party state up to this point and in order to gain support for Austrian independence allowed the formation of labour unions and opposition political parties. He also increased the voting age to 24 as he felt younger people were more likely to support unification with Germany and to sympathize with the Nazi Party generally.

SOURCE N

Excerpt from *Modern Germany Reconsidered, 1870–1945* by Gordon Martel, published by Routledge, New York, USA, 1992, p. 185. Martel is a professor emeritus in the Department of History at the University of Northern British Columbia, Canada.

Moreover, as Hitler came to understand, neither the French nor the British were willing to fight to maintain the provisions of the peace settlement of 1919 [Paris Peace Conference] that violated the nationality principle to Germany's disadvantage. This British government in particular signaled as much to Hitler in November 1937 when [Foreign Minister] Lord Halifax, visiting Hitler, referred to Danzig, Austria and Czechoslovakia as 'questions which fall into the category of possible alterations in the European order', and added that Britain's interest was 'to see that any alterations should come through the course of peaceful evolution'. And, indeed, the new British Prime Minister, Neville Chamberlain, had decided to accept the realization of Germany's goals through negotiation in an attempt to avoid war. The French government had also written off Austria and was weakening in its commitment to Czechoslovakia – partly, though not exclusively, because of Chamberlain's attitude.

According to Source N, what was British policy towards Germany in November 1937?

SOURCE O

'One People, One Empire, One Leader.' A German propaganda poster showing German and Austria as one country, with a symbol of the Nazi Party and depiction of Hitler in the centre, 13 March 1938.

What may be one reason Hitler is depicted in the centre of Source O?

Hitler's government announced in Germany that riots had broken out against Schuschnigg's government and that there was a need for German forces to enter Austria to restore order. Schuschnigg was commanded to turn over all authority to Austrian Nazi Party officials or face an invasion on 11 March. Schuschnigg resigned as chancellor to prevent bloodshed and was replaced by Seyss-Inquart. Seyss-Inquart immediately sent a message to Germany's government, asking for Germany's military to restore public order, although there was no disorder in Austria.

On 12 March, German forces entered the country and on 13 March, Austria was officially annexed to Germany in violation of the Treaty of St Germain-en-Laye. An April plebiscite confirmed the annexation, with over 99 per cent of voters approving. Since German troops had been invited to enter Austria by its legal government and the voters had apparently approved the merger of the two states, the practically defunct League of Nations did not react.

International response: Britain and France

The international response to *Anschluss* was muted, primarily because France was more concerned with Spain (see page 160). Britain's Prime Minister Neville Chamberlain noted in a speech that British officials had indicated their displeasure over Germany's action to the German government. He also stated that there was next to nothing Britain or any other country could have done to prevent the annexation.

Many in Britain and France continued to believe that a strengthened Germany would be useful in any future conflict against what they perceived as the real threat: communism and therefore the Soviet Union. Additionally, few could see the point of preventing Germans living in Germany even if this came through expansion. Britain and France could have done little militarily since there were no plans of any type and neither had sufficient military might to force any changes; Germany was surely aware of this.

Appeasement

The policy of working with Germany to ease various conditions of the Treaty of Versailles, as well as allowing it to absorb German areas such as Austria, is known primarily as appeasement. Appeasement is often seen as giving Hitler the impression that Britain and France were eager to allow him to do whatever he wanted in central and eastern Europe so that they could avoid war. Some historians continue to hold that this has some truth. Most modern historians see the policy of appeasement as much more complex and based on diplomatic strategies from earlier periods. The British government in the late 1930s saw appeasement as normal diplomacy. It believed that negotiating made a lot more sense than threatening Germany militarily, especially since Britain did not have the military capability to attack Germany until 1939.

In addition, many saw most of Germany's demands as reasonable, right up until 1 September 1939. Why should Germans not live in Germany? Why not renegotiate borders that were artificially, in some cases, created only in 1919? While the British government may have seen these demands as reasonable, there may be some truth in the claims that Hitler viewed Britain and France as weak as a result of negotiating. Hitler, however, believed long before that these states were fundamentally weak simply because they were democratic.

International response: Soviet Union

The Soviet Union could also only protest as its government was in disarray. A series of **purges** began within the Soviet government in 1934. These intensified so that in the period 1937–8 at least 700,000 people were executed and approximately 1,500,000 were imprisoned. Many people in the ministry of foreign affairs had been killed in the purge, including many ambassadors, heads of departments, secretaries and deputy ministers. What this meant was that experts on various foreign issues were now mostly dead, along with those who had worked to build relations with France and Britain to oppose Germany's foreign policy.

Although France and the Soviet Union had signed an agreement in 1935 to mutually assist each other (see page 147), this agreement had meant little; no military talks ever occurred, which meant that any use of force against Germany was unlikely or even impossible. France was also divided by weak coalition governments (see page 104) and many in France were completely opposed to communism (see page 109). The British government was clearly reticent about working with the Soviet Union as they were more sympathetic to Germany. Part of this sympathy was based on a fear of communism generally and the Soviet Union in particular. The purges shocked many in both Britain and France and reminded them of what they viewed as the destructive, dangerous nature of communism. The purges helped ensure that neither Britain nor France would work with the Soviets to oppose Germany.

Sudeten Crisis, October 1938

With Germany's annexation of Austria, there was renewed agitation by Germans in Czechoslovakia to be included in an expanding, prosperous Germany. Over 3 million Germans lived in Czechoslovakia and the main German political party, the **Sudeten German Party**, demanded autonomy for the Sudeten area of Czechoslovakia, where most of the Germans lived. Excited about *Anschluss*, many saw an opportunity for the Sudetenland to join Germany in a way similar to what had happened in Austria.

Konrad Henlein, head of the Sudeten German Party, met Hitler in Berlin at the end of March 1938. A week later he presented a list of demands called the Karlsbad Programme. The main aim of the demands was German autonomy within Czechoslovakia. While the Czechoslovak government of President Edvard Beneš was willing to give Sudeten Germans more rights, it was not willing to allow self-government; this was seen as practical independence. The world, after witnessing the recent annexation of Austria,

> **KEY TERM**
>
> **Purge** The removal of people, through loss of work, imprisonment or execution, who were deemed a threat by Soviet government authorities.
>
> **Sudeten German Party** A German political party in Czechoslovakia in the 1930s that was closely allied to and adopted many of the ideals of the Nazi Party of Germany.

> To what extent was the Sudeten Crisis resolved for the benefit of Germany, Britain and France?

understood clearly that Germany was using Henlein's party as a tool to take control of the Sudeten.

The Sudeten was critically important for Czechoslovakia's advanced economy as it was a source of metals and other mined products. In addition, bordering Germany, the Sudeten was the location of the main defences against an invasion from Germany. If the government were to lose control over the Sudeten, the country would be defenceless in the face of invasion. To demonstrate its determination not to lose control of its territory, the country's military was partially mobilized for war at the end of May, when it seemed Germany might attack. No attack occurred, but Czechoslovakia had demonstrated that, unlike Austria, it was willing to fight.

International response

Unlike the earlier issue with Austria, foreign states were involved with the Sudeten Crisis from the start. Czechoslovakia had alliances with France and the Soviet Union. Only a minority of its population was German, unlike Austria. Again unlike Austria, Czechoslovakia had a modern, well-equipped military and its industrial capacity was important. If the country's industries and mineral resources were added to those of Germany, it would only expand its already impressive economy and allow further, faster rearmament. Understanding the international response is critically important to overall understanding of the outcome of the Sudeten Crisis.

France

France had a military alliance with Czechoslovakia and therefore was alarmed at the possibility of war. Its eastern European alliances (see page 144) had been created by the French government to apply pressure on Germany so there would be no future attack on France. France had never planned for the alliance to mean that they might have to defend a state in central Europe. There was no possibility of France intervening militarily as it was engaged in developing the defensive Maginot Line (see page 147) and producing weapons; France was not ready for a confrontation. France reached out to Britain to help resolve the crisis.

Soviet Union

Meanwhile, the Soviet Union and Czechoslovakia had had a mutual defence treaty since 1935. This was aligned with the mutual assistance treaty between France and the Soviet Union. If France moved to fulfil its military obligations to Czechoslovakia as part of the Little Entente treaties signed in 1921, then the Soviets, in support of France, would also help Czechoslovakia if it were attack.

The Soviets pledged to support Czechoslovakia if France would move militarily to prevent an attack on the country by Germany. This gesture was mostly a hollow one since the French government did not intend on going to war over Czechoslovakia, nor did it want to co-operate with the communist Soviet state. In addition, with the purges in the Soviet military (see page 163) and the fact that a powerful Poland stood between the Soviet Union and Germany, France was aware that Soviet pledges were essentially meaningless.

Britain

As with the Rhineland and Austria, many in Britain believed that there was little reason for Germans not to live in Germany. Germans, like other minority populations in Czechoslovakia, were certainly discriminated against and so there was some sympathy with German demands. Britain, like France, was simply not willing to go to war over the borders of any central or eastern European state. In the midst of substantial rearmament, Britain, even if willing, was not yet in a position where pressure could be applied to Germany.

Massive pressure, however, was placed on the government of Czechoslovakia to agree to the demands of Henlein and his party in the hope that this would indeed prevent an outbreak of war.

A continuing crisis

In July, France informed Czechoslovakia's government that France would not go to war to prevent the loss of the Sudeten. Britain sent a minister, Lord Runciman, to demand that the government comply with as many of the Sudeten German demands as possible. While the Czechoslovak government considered how to respond, Germany mobilized 750,000 troops to conduct manoeuvres on their mutual border in an attempt to force more concessions. Finally, in early September, Czechoslovakia's government gave in to most Sudeten demands.

This did not resolve the situation as Henlein was under orders from Hitler to prevent any overall agreement. It was critical that no resolution be found so that the Sudeten would have to be occupied by Germany's military in order to quell disturbances, as had happened in Austria. Therefore a crisis was created when two prominent members of the Sudeten German Party were arrested during violent demonstrations. Falsely claiming that Czechoslovakia had committed various atrocities against Germans in the country, Henlein ended all talks with the government. Hitler soon announced that Czechoslovakia should be broken up as a state and that there were plans to exterminate all the Germans living in the country.

On 13 September, British Prime Minister Neville Chamberlain flew to Germany to discuss the Sudeten Crisis directly with Hitler. He hoped that a reasonable solution could be found to the crisis so that war could be averted. After the meeting he returned to Britain to meet French Prime Minister Édouard Daladier. Both Chamberlain and Daladier agreed that areas of Czechoslovakia that held populations that were more than 50 per cent German should be ceded to Germany. This was initially rejected by Czechoslovakia, but by 21 September the Czech government had decided that this was the only way to avoid war.

According to Source P, what type of help is Britain offering Czechoslovakia?

SOURCE P

'Hozda [*sic*]: What! No passport? No paper? Nothing to declare? Runciman: Only this olive-branch – made in Birmingham [UK] – slightly used.' A cartoon captioned 'Wonderful Visit' by British cartoonist David Low depicting Czechoslovakian leaders Hácha (Hozda here) and Beneš, Henlein and Lord Runciman, published in the *Evening Standard* newspaper on 29 July 1938.

Almost immediately, Hitler made new demands. Areas of Czechoslovakia that held large Hungarian and Polish populations should be given to Hungary and Poland. He also stated that German troops should immediately occupy the Sudeten. Britain and France rejected these new demands and the countries began to prepare for war.

Hitler realized that he may have overstepped the mark; he did not desire war with Britain and France, not to mention Czechoslovakia. Yet, he did not back down as he believed that Britain and France would eventually capitulate; he ordered the army to prepare to invade the Sudeten, finally settling on 1 October for this to occur.

Munich Agreement, 30 September 1938

Mussolini was also alarmed as Italy was Germany's ally and might be dragged into a conflict for which it was clearly not prepared. Mussolini called for a meeting between the leaders of Italy, Germany, Britain and France. This was held in Munich, Germany, on 28 September; Czechoslovakia was not invited to attend, nor was the Soviet Union. An agreement was reached in the early hours of the next morning. The Munich Agreement stated, among other things:

- Germany was to receive the Sudeten from Czechoslovakia.
- German troops would occupy the Sudeten in stages between 1 and 10 October.
- Plebiscites would be held to determine in which country residents wished to be citizens.
- German troops were to be released from Czechoslovakian military service.
- An international commission would resolve disputed areas.

Czechoslovakia was bluntly informed by Britain and France that if it did not implement the Munich Agreement, it would fight Germany alone. Czechoslovakia complied.

SOURCE Q

Excerpt from *Hitler's Generals*, edited by Correlli Barnett, published by Grove Press, New York, USA, 1989, p. 6. Barnett is a military and economic historian and former professor at Cambridge University, UK.

By means of his 'shop-window' rearmament and his well tuned rantings about the terrors that would ensue if Germany were not accorded her just deserts, Hitler achieved his greatest diplomatic triumph at Munich in 1938, when Chamberlain persuaded France to abandon her ally Czechoslovakia, and the two democracies handed him the Sudetenland, which happened to contain the powerful Czech frontier defences. The Munich Agreement radically altered the strategic balance of Europe in Hitler's favour, opening the way to his final occupation of Czechoslovakia in March 1939, which in turn uncovered the southern flank of his next victim, Poland. But Munich marked not only Hitler's triumph over Chamberlain and Daladier, but also over the leadership of the German Army.

According to Source Q, what was the significance of the Munich Agreement?

Results of the Sudeten Crisis

Also on 30 September, Chamberlain succeeded in obtaining Hitler's agreement to what is known as the Anglo-German Declaration. This was a statement that Germany and Britain would not go to war to resolve problems. Instead, each state pledged to consult the other over issues that might lead to conflict and to resolve those through dialogue.

France

The French public was predominately in favour of the Munich Agreement and large crowds greeted Daladier, since war had been avoided. Yet, France was weakened by the Sudeten Crisis. Czechoslovakia, one of its main allies, had been sacrificed for France's own safety and this sacrifice could only strengthen Germany in the long term. France had proven to the Soviets that the mutual assistance guarantee had little value and could not be relied on if Germany attacked the Soviet Union. France had aligned its policies with those of Britain during the crisis although Britain continued to refuse to agree to a permanent military alliance; this would soon change (see page 172), but France for the time being assumed that no alliance would be forthcoming. In short, an isolated France had no choice but to follow where

Britain led diplomatically. France's government was well aware of its increased insecurity and increased military spending by 300 per cent in November 1938. In addition, France and Germany signed the Franco-German Declaration in December 1938, pledging to peace and respecting each other's borders (see Source X on page 180).

According to Source R, how will Germany and France resolve any foreign policy problems that develop between them?

SOURCE R

Excerpt from the Franco-German Declaration of 6 December 1938, located at The Avalon Project: Documents in Law, History and Diplomacy, which is sponsored by Yale Law School in New Haven, Connecticut, USA.

Acting in the name and by order of their respective Governments, [ministers] agreed on the following points at their meeting in Paris on December 6, 1938:

1. The French Government and the German Government fully share the conviction that pacific and neighbourly relations between France and Germany constitute one of the essential elements of the consolidation of the situation in Europe and of the preservation of general peace. Consequently both Governments will endeavour [work] with all their might to assure the development of the relations between their countries in this direction.

2. Both Governments agree that no question of a territorial nature remains in suspense [unresolved] between their countries and solemnly recognize as permanent the frontier between their countries as it is actually drawn.

3. Both Governments are resolved, without prejudice to their special relations with third Powers, to remain in contact on all questions of importance to both their countries and to have recourse to mutual consultation in case any complications arising out of these questions should threaten to lead to international difficulties.

Britain

The British public was also enthusiastic about avoiding war and proud of its government's role in resolving the crisis. Britain had negotiated what seemed to be a permanent settlement and had accomplished this while not fully rearmed and without any significant allies. Britain was aware, however, that France was now quite isolated and might work to reach some agreement with Germany to save itself from a future conflict. Furthermore, Germany had come close to using its military to force a resolution to the crisis, and so British rearmament continued, now at an accelerated pace.

Soviet Union

The Soviet Union had been ignored, neglected and dismissed throughout the entire crisis. More than ever, the Soviet government realized that Britain and France were willing to accommodate fascist states such as Italy and Germany (and Spain after May 1939). The main fear was that Britain and France would not oppose Germany if that state attempted a major attack on the Soviet Union; they might even join with Germany in that event. It certainly did not escape the Soviets that their military was in a terrible state as a result of recent purges (see page 163).

The Soviet Union was aware of its isolation, faced with Japan in the east (see page 39) and an ever-strengthening Germany in the west.

Germany

It is clear that Hitler was relieved that war with France and Britain had not erupted over the Sudeten Crisis. He had gambled that Britain and France would back down and they did. He had been, it seems, prepared for a short war with Czechoslovakia if necessary. After the annexation of the Sudeten, his military experts inspected Czechoslovakia's fortification systems and decided that it was fortunate that war had not occurred because victory might not have been achieved swiftly, or perhaps at all, as the defences were quite formidable.

SOURCE S

'We thank our leader.' A postcard celebrating annexation of the Sudeten with Germany, depicting Henlein and Hitler, December 1938.

What message about Germany is conveyed by Source S?

Hitler's popularity soared in Germany as a result of the annexation of the Sudeten and because war was avoided. This popularity saved him from a plot by military officers to assassinate him and end Nazi government; the plotters feared public reaction as he was now proclaimed a great hero. Meanwhile, Czechoslovakia was dismantled rapidly:

- 2 October: Poland seized Těšin (Teschen in German and Cieszyn in Polish) with approval from Germany.
- 6 October: Slovakia, which occupied most of the eastern areas of the country, was granted autonomy.
- 2 November: Hungary received a large strip of southern Czechoslovakia, mostly from the autonomous Slovakia.

- 20 November: Germany was granted rights to construct a highway across its territory to link eastern parts of Germany with Vienna.

On 14 March 1939, Czechoslovakian President Emil Hácha was summoned to meet Hitler in Berlin. He was told that either Czechoslovakia would be invaded by Germany immediately or he could agree, as the country's leader, to becoming a part of Germany with some autonomy over its own affairs. He signed over the country's independence to prevent a futile war and Slovakia was declared an independent country allied to Germany. Territories that had been taken from Germany, such as Memel, which Lithuania had seized in 1923, were now returned. The Munich Agreement, with all its hopes for peace, was completely undone in only six months.

SUMMARY DIAGRAM

Germany's foreign policy 1936–9

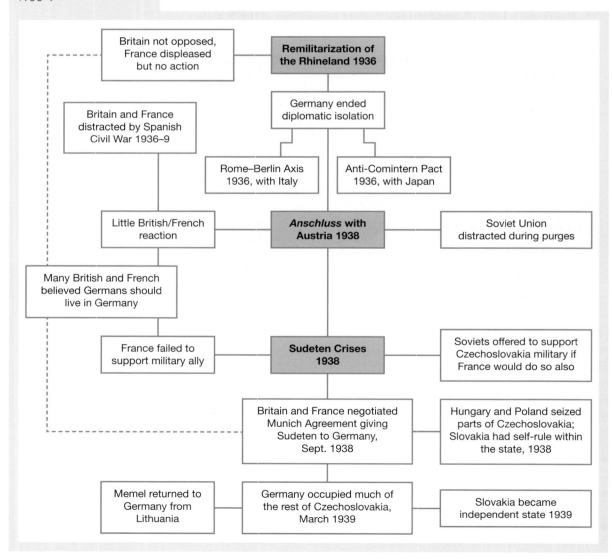

The final crises and outbreak of war 1939

▶ *Key question:* Why did a multinational war erupt in Europe on 3 September 1939?

Poland was created at the end of the First World War and included large parts of what had been Germany. Importantly, the port city of Danzig, with an almost completely German population, was removed from Germany and made into a semi-autonomous city state ruled by the League of Nations. This was done to give Poland access to the Baltic Sea, which would allow it to develop trade and a viable economy. Land to the west of Danzig was also granted to Poland and became known as the Polish Corridor. Both the Corridor and the Free City of Danzig separated a large province of Germany, East Prussia, from the main body of the country.

While many Germans were probably indifferent about the annexation of Austria or Czechoslovakia, neither of which had ever been part of the German state before 1938 and 1939, they certainly were not indifferent about the possibility of reacquiring parts of Poland which had been part of Germany just twenty years previously. After successes in Austria and Czechoslovakia, Hitler's government was under pressure to obtain the Polish Corridor and Danzig, if not more.

Polish Crisis 1938–9

As early as October 1938, just after the German occupation of the Sudeten, Germany requested negotiations with Poland regarding the building of rail and road links between the main part of Germany and East Prussia. If Poland agreed, Germany would agree to a 25-year non-aggression pact. Poland would be compensated with territory elsewhere, perhaps Memel (see the map on page 111) or other parts of Czechoslovakia. Poland and Germany had had relatively friendly relations since the implementation of the non-aggression agreement in 1934 (see page 151) and Germany allowed Poland to also help participate in the dismantling of Czechoslovakia. There were even suggestions that Poland and Germany should be allies within the Anti-Comintern Pact to oppose the Soviet Union. Germany now demanded that the League of Nations return Danzig to its control as well, something that required Poland's agreement and co-operation.

Of all German requests for territory, asking for access through the Polish Corridor and control of Danzig was the most logical of its demands. Both had only twenty years before been part of Germany and most of the residents in the Corridor and Danzig were Germans. Danzig has its own locally elected government and it too was dominated by the Nazi Party. Whether or not German demands were rational, the British and French

> What issues caused the Polish Crisis and why was resolution of these seemingly impossible?

public, however, were outraged, having been led to believe that Germany territorial requests ended with the Munich Agreement. There were overwhelming demands that their governments should not negotiate away Polish or League territory and confront Germany if required. Britain, afraid that an isolated France might make a diplomatic arrangement for its own security that would then isolate Britain, announced in February 1939 that Britain would support France militarily. This was the alliance that France had sought since the end of the First World War.

Guarantee of Poland's borders, March 1939

Poland, a heavily armed state, very simply stated that it was not interested in negotiating away any territory and eventually informed the League of Nations that if Germany attempted to annex Danzig, Poland would go to war to prevent this. Britain and France made a public, verbal declaration that they would guarantee Poland's borders on 31 March 1939. It was hoped that this would cause Germany to negotiate any changes in borders and not use military force. The declaration reinforced the decision by Poland's government not to negotiate since it was through negotiation that both Austria and Czechoslovakia had lost their independence. Poland believed that the British and French guarantee made it highly unlikely that Germany would attack. There was an agreement that Poland and Britain would begin talks to create a formal military alliance along the same lines as the alliance between Poland and France (see page 144).

Britain and France were now in an ever-strengthening position with regard to armaments. It was in the autumn of 1939 that both countries, if working together, would surpass the production and stockpiles of weapons of Germany and be able to field large, well-equipped armies, fleets of ships and thousands of aircraft. In April, Britain began conscripting soldiers as part of its military build-up. This dominance would mean that if Germany attacked Poland or France, it would have the option to respond militarily. It was with this in mind that Poland's borders were guaranteed. Britain now worked to create an anti-fascist network of alliances so that any conflict between it and Germany would drag other countries into the conflict. Mutual assistance agreements were signed with Greece and Romania after Italy's invasion of Albania (see page 131) and later with Turkey.

Although they proclaimed an alliance with Poland, both Britain and France refused to send weapons or supplies as they argued that nothing could be spared during their own rearmament. When Poland asked for loans to buy weapons elsewhere, both nations stated that their own financial problems prevented this. Both Britain and France feared that arming Poland would either lead to Poland attacking Germany in a pre-emptive strike or provoke Germany into attacking Poland. Regardless of the reasons, failure to supply Poland with armaments meant that Poland was not as well prepared for war as it could have been. Formal military talks between Poland and Britain were only finalized on 25 August 1939.

Britain and France negotiate with the Soviet Union

Britain and France finally made overtures to the Soviet Union. They presented the case that it was in the Soviet Union's best interest to help prevent a war between Germany and Poland. Britain and France pointed out that a war could be prevented if the Soviet Union would join their anti-German coalition because surely Germany would pause if faced with war by Britain, France, Poland and the Soviet Union.

SOURCE T

Excerpt from *The History of Poland* by M.B. Biskupski, published by Greenwood Press, Connecticut, USA, 2000, p. 93. Biskupski is a prominent historian on central European history and a professor at Central Connecticut State University, USA.

In the last months of peace, the Germans and the Western powers pursued some understanding with the Soviets in anticipation of imminent hostilities: the Germans to avoid a major conflict in the east and to isolate Poland, assuming Western inactions; the allies to present Hitler with so daunting a prospect of a two-front war that he would quail, or, if the worst came, have a major eastern foe in the form of the Soviet Union. For their part, the Soviets hoped for mutually destructive struggle among capitalist states and had little interest in rescuing Britain and France from the German threat, certainly none in aiding the despised Poland. Soviet negotiations with the West were pointless from the start and were conducted in bad faith. The Soviet insistence that their troops be allowed complete discretion to enter Polish territory should they join against the Germans, which the Poles rejected as compromising their sovereignty, was never a serious issue despite the attention later given to it by many historians. The Soviets raised the issue merely to draw the Western powers, isolate Poland, and up the ante in their simultaneous negotiations with Germany.

The only enticement that Britain and France had to offer was that they would agree to preserve the borders of eastern Europe as they currently stood, in mid-1939. From the British and French perspective, the Soviets should be thankful that they were now being made part of international diplomacy and that they should appreciate that Britain and France would finally go to war against Germany, whose Nazi Party opposed communism and was a long-term threat to the Soviet Union. The Soviets, however, had lost territory at the end of the First World War, from which various states had been created. These included Finland, Poland, Estonia, Latvia, Lithuania and part of Romania. The Soviets believed that these should be returned to the Soviet Union at some point in the future. What Britain and France expected was for the Soviets to essentially endorse these old losses and fight to preserve these small states.

To further complicate alliance talks, Poland refused to allow any Soviet army to cross into its territory to fight Germany in the event of war, even if Germany had already invaded Poland. Poland was more concerned with the Soviets than with Germany. This meant that in the case of any war, the

> Why were negotiations with the Soviet Union over Poland bound to fail, according to Source T?

Soviets would only be able to fight Germany in Poland if they received Polish permission. Since this permission was unlikely to be granted, the Soviets would be left to fight Germany only when the Germans were close to the Soviet border or already in their territory. This seemed irrational and unfair, and was proof to the Soviets that they were only a tool to be used, not a real alliance partner. Negotiations were not helped by the British and French, who continued to send low-level diplomats instead of important officials who could make decisions; this insulted the Soviet leadership. Negotiations continued until Germany and the Soviets announced that they had come to a separate agreement (see page 175).

Germany's response

Hitler never believed that Britain and France would actually go to war over Poland. Part of this belief stemmed from his earlier success over the Sudeten Crisis, and part was based in his thoughts on democratically elected governments (see page 150). He continued to believe throughout the crisis that the citizens of those countries would oppose any military intervention and that fear of war made these states fundamentally weak.

?

Why did Hitler believe that any conflict with Poland would be limited, according to Source U?

SOURCE U

Excerpt from *The Road to War* by Richard Overy and Andrew Wheatcroft, published by Penguin Books, London, UK, 1999, pp. 64–5. Overy is a prominent modern historian and professor at Exeter University, UK. Wheatcroft is a professor at City University London, UK.

On 3 April Hitler definitely resolved to attack Poland and bring the disputed territories, rich in coal and agricultural resources, into the Greater Reich [German Empire] by force. On 23 May he called the military together again to his study in the Chancellery [office]. 'The Pole is not a fresh enemy,' he told them, 'Poland will always be on the side of our adversaries ... It is not Danzig that is at stake. For us it is a matter of expanding our living-space in the east and making food supplies secure' ...

... The war could be isolated only, Hitler continued, as 'a matter of skilful politic.' His experience of Western appeasement in 1938 convinced him that neither Britain nor France would seriously fight for Poland. This conviction dominated Hitler's thinking throughout the crisis which led to war. The decision to attack Poland can only be understood in the light of this conviction. The war with the West, if it came to war, would come not in 1939, but in three or four years as planned, 'when the armaments programme will be completed.' ...

... Hitler saw the contest with the West as a contest of wills: 'Our enemies have men who are below average. No personalities. No masters, men of action ... Our enemies are little worms. I saw them at Munich.' Democracy had made the west soft.

In April, just weeks after the announced British and French guarantee of Poland and at the time Britain began conscription, Hitler ordered Germany's army to prepare plans for an invasion of Poland; this plan was called Case White. These plans took into consideration only Poland's forces and not those of Britain and France. On 28 April, Germany withdrew from the Polish–German Non-Aggression Pact (see page 151) as another way to threaten Poland so that it would negotiate away its territory; Poland did not respond.

Pact of Steel, May 1939

Germany also responded to British and French pressure by creating a formal alliance with Italy. The Rome–Berlin Axis (see page 159) had only been a statement of mutual support. The Pact of Steel required each state to:

- follow similar, closely co-ordinated foreign policies
- support the other in war
- make war plans together
- work together economically
- co-ordinate their press, news and other propaganda.

Historians such as A.J.P. Taylor have successfully argued that the Pact of Steel was essentially meaningless. There was little co-ordination of foreign policy and no mutual war plans. There was practically no economic co-operation either. It may be that Germany never intended on this alliance amounting to much other than to increase temporary pressure on France, which shared a border with Italy, and Britain. Italy's navy in the Mediterranean was large and could challenge British forces there. It may have been hoped that Britain and France, fearing a larger war, would force Poland to concede territory.

Nazi–Soviet Pact, 23 August 1939

Meanwhile, Germany began secret discussions with the Soviet Union. These talks essentially called for Germany and the Soviet Union not to fight each other, while allowing Germany to do whatever it wanted diplomatically, and otherwise, with the parts of Europe that had not belonged to the former Russian Empire, which the Soviets hoped to reclaim. Secret parts of the agreement made it clear that the parts of Poland that once belonged to Russia were now to be reabsorbed into the Soviet Union. This document, the Treaty of Non-Aggression between Germany and the Union of Soviet Socialist Republics (Soviet Union), commonly known as the Nazi–Soviet Pact, was signed on 23 August 1939, one week before Germany declared war on Poland on 1 September. Germany now had no fear of Soviet intervention on behalf of Poland and was convinced that Germany would now fight Poland without any outside interference.

What diplomatic initiatives failed to prevent the invasion of Poland by Germany?

Invasion of Poland, 1 September 1939

Throughout the crisis, Poland refused all negotiations. Britain and France, although working to prevent war by guaranteeing Poland's borders, hoped that Poland would grant Germany rail and road connections through the Polish Corridor and allow Danzig to rejoin Germany. This would not only prevent an immediate war, but also remove obstacles to future conflict. They also felt that it would help Poland by removing hundreds of thousands of Germans who did not want to be part of the country. Yet Poland refused and both Britain and France pledged that Germany would not be allowed to use war to settle conflicts, in line with the Locarno Treaties (see page 147) and the recent Anglo-German Declaration signed in Munich (see page 167).

Mobilization, 21 August 1939

Hitler had earlier ordered the military to create plans for Poland's invasion (see page 175). On 21 August, he ordered the military to begin mobilization for the implementation of Case White, the invasion plan, for 26 August. The announcement of the Nazi–Soviet Pact on 23 August removed any possibility of the Soviet Union intervening.

Invasion delayed, 25 August 1939

The 26 August invasion, however, was delayed. On 25 August, two separate issues emerged that caused Hitler to pause. These were:

- Britain and Poland announced that they had signed a formal military alliance, replacing the earlier verbal promises of mutual support.
- Mussolini asked to be released from obligations imposed by the Pact of Steel made just months earlier (see page 175).

Mussolini had hitherto been a supporter of Germany, hoping that by attaching his country to a powerful ally it too could benefit. It was hoped that a weakened, frightened France, for example, might grant Italy the island of Corsica and other southeastern French provinces; perhaps Italy could also obtain French colonies. Yet, it was clear that there was a real danger that Italy could be dragged into a war it was not prepared for and suddenly find itself facing the full might of Britain and France in Africa and the Mediterranean. Hitler granted Mussolini's request and the Pact of Steel was moderated so that Italy could play a supporting role but not yet a military or economic role.

On 25 and 26 August, Britain and France continued to work to prevent war. In talks with Britain's ambassador to Germany, Germany demanded that its military be allowed to move against Poland without interference. Germany pledged to respect the borders of the British Empire in return. This was an implicit threat to Britain and was immediately rejected. France's appeal for a negotiated settlement was also rejected.

On 28 August, Britain issued a formal warning to Germany not to violate Poland's borders. To underline the seriousness of the warning, all British ships in the Baltic and Mediterranean seas were ordered to leave those areas. The British government instituted emergency rationing of food and essential supplies. Hitler was still not convinced that Britain would go to war over Poland and Germany's forces continued to move into position for the invasion.

On 29 August, Germany made a final diplomatic gesture, perhaps to satisfy Britain and demonstrate that Hitler was reasonable to some degree. The offer was for the Polish government to send a representative with the authority to sign treaties to Berlin on 30 August. In this meeting, Poland would be required to agree that Danzig should be returned to German control, as well as the Polish Corridor – a new demand as earlier only transportation links through this land had been requested. Poland sent an ambassador to meet the German government on 31 August, but as he did not have authority to sign treaties for his government, the meeting ended almost immediately. Germany's radio stations announced that Poland had rejected negotiations.

Poland invaded, 1 September

On 1 September, a massive invasion of Poland began. Three large German armies attacked from the north, west and south of the country, numbering over 1.5 million men, and a smaller, Slovakian army entered from the south. Aircraft bombed military and civilian positions, disrupted roads and railways, destroyed bridges and attacked factories. Thousands of civilians were killed within hours as German bomber aircraft attacked towns and cities. Danzig's Nazi Party government announced that it was now merging with Germany.

International response to the invasion of Poland

Immediately, Britain and France called for a cessation of hostilities. Italy joined too and called for a Five-Power Conference on 2 September in which Germany, Italy, Britain, France and Poland would meet to resolve the crisis. Britain agreed to the meeting, but insisted that Germany remove itself from Poland as a condition. Germany rejected this demand.

On 3 September, both France and Britain declared war on Germany. By all accounts, Hitler was shocked as he never expected either country to come to the aid of Poland. The declaration of war meant that a localized war between Poland and Germany would now be a European war. He had gambled that neither Great Power would be willing to risk war and possible defeat over the borders of an eastern European state; he lost. What would become the Second World War in Europe and north Africa had begun.

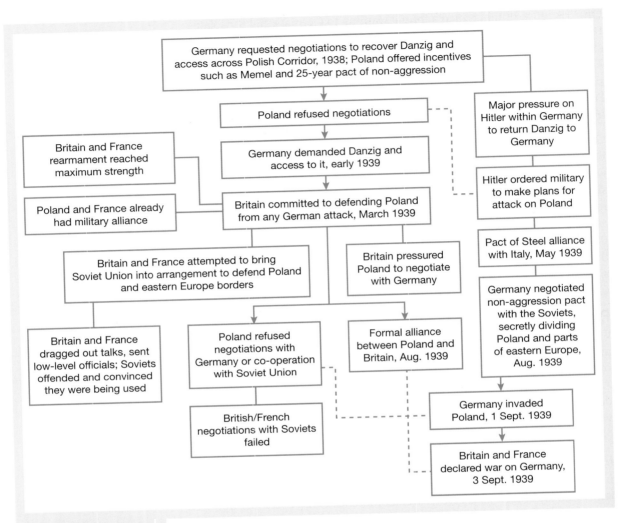

⑤ Key debate

▶ *Key question: Who should be blamed for the outbreak of an
international war in Europe in September 1939?*

Since 1939, historians have debated who and what caused the Second World
War in Europe. A few of those arguments are presented here.

Germany and Hitler

Historian A.J.P. Taylor wrote in *The Origins of the Second World War* that the
world blamed Hitler and his policies because he was gone, and someone in
Germany had to be found guilty for causing the war that left millions dead

and destruction throughout Europe. Taylor added that Hitler's foreign policies were actually quite similar to earlier German policies and those of other states throughout history, and that he was only being blamed because he was German.

SOURCE V

Excerpt from *The Origins of the Second World War* by A.J.P. Taylor, published by Penguin Books, UK, 1991, pp. 26–7. Taylor was a British historian who wrote many books on European history and was lecturer at many British universities.

Little can be discovered so long as we go on attributing everything that happened to Hitler … He would have counted for nothing without the support and cooperation of the German people. It seems to be believed nowadays that Hitler did everything himself, even driving the trains and filling the gas chambers unaided. This was not so. Hitler was a sounding-board for the German nation. Thousands, many hundred thousand, Germans carried out his evil orders without qualm or question. As supreme ruler of Germany, Hitler bears the greatest responsibility for acts of immeasurable evil: for the destruction of German democracy, for the concentration camps; and, worst of all, for the extermination of peoples during the Second World War … His foreign policy was a different matter. He aimed to make Germany the dominant Power in Europe and maybe, more remotely, in the world. Other Powers have pursued similar aims, and still do. Other Powers treat smaller countries as their satellites. Other Powers seek to defend their vital interests by force of arms. In international affairs there was nothing wrong with Hitler except that he was a German.

According to Source V, why was Hitler no different than leaders of other countries with regards to Germany's foreign policy?

Taylor goes on to say that the truth is much more complicated, and that Hitler and his government officials simply took the policies of former governments and expanded on them.

Nevertheless, many historians have held Hitler personally responsible as he seemed to make key decisions and conducted much of his foreign policy in the late 1930s personally. He was intimately involved in coercing Austria's government to capitulate to Germany in 1938. He was clearly active in the Sudeten Crisis, meeting with Britain's Chamberlain and other officials when working out the Munich Agreement. He personally ordered the mobilization of the Germany army and ordered it to attack Poland using plans created earlier on his command.

Yet, blaming Hitler alone for the Second World War is simplistic. There were certainly other factors, and actors, at work.

Poland

Several historians have pointed out that Poland absolutely refused to negotiate or compromise with regards to Danzig or the Polish Corridor, even when pressured by Britain and France. It was clear to Poland and other states that the areas in question had recently been part of Germany, and perhaps most people there desired reunification with Germany – a stronger, more prosperous state than Poland, where Germans were discriminated against. Poland's government probably assumed that any compromise with Germany would lead to its destruction, similar to the experience of Czechoslovakia. This was, however, an assumption and not necessarily based on fact. There may have even been a desire for war on the part of some in Poland's military.

According to Source W, what was Poland's stance regarding Germany?

SOURCE W

Excerpt from *The Myth of German Villainy* by Benton L. Bradberry, published by AuthorHouse, Indiana, USA, 2012, p. 319.

At around the same time, Poland's Marshall Rydz-Śmigły said, 'Poland wants war with Germany and Germany will not be able to avoid it even if she wants to.'

According to historians A.J.P. Taylor and Richard Overy, most Germans felt very strongly about the return of Danzig and the Polish Corridor. Hitler was under pressure to obtain these territories whereas he had been under almost no pressure whatsoever with regards to Austria and Czechoslovakia, since neither had ever been part of Germany. These two factors – of Poland's refusal (to negotiate what may have been a reasonable demand), and Hitler under pressure – presented a problem, whereby a solution had to be found, and this resulted in an invasion.

According to Source X, why were Germany's demands on Danzig reasonable?

SOURCE X

'Poland Caused WWII: Russian Report' by Mike Eckel, published in *The World Post*, July 2009. *The World Post* is an online news source and is associated with the Berggruen Institute of Governance. In this article, US-based reporter Eckel, quotes Colonel Sergei Kovalyov, a member of the Institute of Military History of Russia, a section of the Russian Ministry of Defence.

'Everyone who has studied the history of World War II without bias knows that the war began because of Poland's refusal to satisfy Germany's claims,' he writes.

Kovalyov called the demands 'quite reasonable.' He observed: 'The overwhelming majority of residents of Danzig, cut off from Germany by the Treaty of Versailles, were Germans who sincerely wished for the reunification with their historical homeland.'

Britain

Historian Richard Overy has stated that the Second World War in Europe erupted because Britain and France were threatened as world powers. In this interpretation, Germany could be allowed reasonable demands, such as rearmament for defence, annexation of German-speaking lands and so forth, but had to do so through negotiations. These negotiations were not accomplished with the states being directly affected, but with the Great Powers of Britain and France. Essentially, Germany would be allowed reasonable demands, but had to have British and French permission. It was when Germany no longer asked permission that it challenged the authority and position of Britain. If Britain were to remain a world power, it had to counter this.

SOURCE Y

Excerpt from *1939: Countdown to War* by Richard Overy, published by Allen Lane, London, UK, 2009, p. 117. Overy is a prominent twentieth-century historian who is a professor of history at Exeter University, UK.

The British and French decision for war has also to be seen against the background of growing fears in both populations that Germany in particular represented a profound threat to their existing way of life and the values that they wished to see observed in the conduct of international affairs. Although it is often argued, and with justice, that neither state cared very much to observe those values in the treatment of their empires, the two powers saw themselves as self-appointed guardians of a Western world assailed by internal anxiety and external threat. In Britain in particular there existed a strong sense of responsibility for keeping the wider world in order. 'Great Britain,' wrote the politician Oliver Harvey in April 1939, in a wide-ranging survey of the international order, 'is the greatest, richest and potentially strongest Power,' and should use that power to restore sanity to the world.

> What did Britain and France consider their international role in world affairs according to Source Y?

P.M.H. Bell holds Britain somewhat responsible for the outbreak of war. Britain's guarantee of Poland's independence in March 1939 was a challenge to Germany, and all but made war a certainty.

SOURCE Z

Excerpt from *The Origins of the Second World War in Europe* by P.M.H. Bell, Routledge, London, 2007, p. 297.

The precise significance of the guarantee has been much debated. It referred to Polish independence, not integrity, and thus left open the possibility of frontier changes; and in consequence it has been regarded as little more than appeasement under another name, with every chance of another Munich. On the other hand, it has been seen as making war virtually inevitable, by throwing down a challenge which Germany was bound to pick up … the guarantee was enough to bring Britain and France into war over Poland, but not enough to deter Hitler from launching one.

> What was the effect of Britain's guarantee of Poland's independence, according to Source Z?

A.J.P. Taylor also points out that the fight between Poland and Germany was only a local war, and that it only became a multinational conflict was when Britain and France declared war on Germany two full days later. While Germany might be blamed for a war on Poland, Taylor held that a larger war erupted when Britain and France declared war on Germany, not the other way around.

Historians use evidence to create arguments. Whose interpretations of evidence are more meaningful and trustworthy? (Reason, Emotion, Language, Ethics)

A note on the work of historians

Historians use evidence to support arguments. The historians above agree on many points, but differ on others. Each emphasizes particular pieces of evidence to support their views. While it is tempting to assign blame for historical events on a single person or event, history is usually much more complex and this produces debate and discussion. With regards to the origins of the Second World War, historians will continue to debate who or what was responsible and to what degree for centuries to come.

Chapter summary

German foreign policy 1933–40

Germany's foreign policy aims from 1933 to 1939 were essentially the same aims of German governments since the conclusion of the First World War. Hitler's government was unable to achieve much in terms of foreign policy success, other than withdrawing Germany from the League of Nations in 1933, since it was economically and militarily weak. Economic recovery allowed significant rearmament from 1935. As the economy grew, so did the strength of the military. This led to a more active foreign policy.

Hitler and his government enjoyed several rapid successes starting in 1935. A plebiscite in the Saar returned that territory to German rule. In 1936, the Rhineland was reoccupied by Germany without significant international response, and diplomatic isolation ended with agreements with Japan and Italy; and in 1938, Austria and Germany merged peacefully without international diplomatic difficulties.

German rearmament caused Britain and France to begin a similar programme of military preparations. Britain was particularly interested in resolving German demands that it considered sensible but both Britain and France believed that negotiations over borders and other post-First World War issues would mean an avoidance of war. German demands regarding the Sudeten region of Czechoslovakia, for example, were resolved peacefully in late 1938.

Further German demands for territories and treaty revisions at the end of the First World War led to problems between Germany and Poland. The British and French governments were under pressure from their citizens to oppose Hitler and Germany after the occupation of the remnant of Czechoslovakia in March 1939, leading to an impasse. Poland refused to negotiate away any territories while Britain and France pledged to defend Poland. Hitler believed that Britain and France would not actually go to war over Poland's borders and once a mutual assistance treaty had been signed between Germany and the Soviet Union, an invasion of Poland began on 1 September 1939. Two days later, Britain and France declared war on Germany, leading to a larger war in Europe.

Examination advice

Paper 1 Question 12: how to integrate sources and write a good essay

Question 12 is always an essay question. It requires you to write what you know while integrating the sources provided. The sources are there to support your own knowledge. Therefore, it is important that you prepare yourself for this type of question by knowing and understanding the history of Japanese, Italian and Germany foreign diplomacy in the 1930s that is presented in this book.

Question 12 is always worth 9 marks. This means it is worth 37.5 per cent of the overall possible mark. You should spend 30–35 minutes answering this question, using the first five to eight minutes of this time to summarize the sources and outline your response.

The essay in question 12 is assessed by examiners using a rubric called a markband. This can be found in the IB Guide.

> Remember that questions for Prescribed subject 3 will be numbered 9, 10, 11 and 12 in the Paper 1 exam.

How to answer
Summarize the sources and outline your essay
It is best to first list and summarize the sources to focus your thoughts. This should be done in about five minutes and should be in the form of short bullet points. Once you have summarized the sources, briefly outline your essay's structure. This outline should include some sort of introduction to your essay and a concluding answer to the question. Write your outline down on your examination paper, but put a line through everything that you do not want the examiner to mark.

Writing the essay
When you write your essay, make sure you follow your outline and use all the sources. This should take the remainder of your time, which should be at least 25 minutes.

You need to start with a good introduction to focus your essay and which defines anything that might be open to interpretation. Your introduction should conclude with a definite answer to the question. This should further serve to focus your essay. Usually you can introduce one or more of your sources in the introduction to support what you are going to cover.

All sources must be used at least once, but use them multiple times if they will help your essay. Remember: the sources should support your essay.

Finally, under no circumstances are you to actually just list the five sources and a couple of bullet points beneath each in a sort of preamble to a real essay. Sources need to be integrated and quoted to support your essay.

Your concluding paragraph should clearly answer the essay question, summarizing your main arguments. For example, if the question asks you 'to what extent', answer the question:

- 'to a great extent'
- 'to some extent' or
- 'to no extent'.

Your conclusion will then include a summary of your main points.

Example

This question uses Sources J, M, N and P found in this chapter:

Source J: see page 156
Source M: see page 159
Source N: see page 160
Source P: see page 166

> Using these sources and your own knowledge, evaluate the success of Germany's foreign policy between 1936 and the end of 1938.

First, very briefly summarize the sources just for your own information in five minutes or less.

Source J: Hitler remilitarizes Rhineland with inexperienced troops, shows nerve.

Source M: Rome–Berlin Axis announced by Mussolini, new centre of diplomacy.

Source N: Hitler understands Britain/France not willing to fight, Britain indicates possible border changes in Germany's favour, France backing down from commitments.

Source P: Cartoon showing British giving Czechoslovakia nothing but an olive branch.

Second, briefly outline in bullet points the main parts of your essay in five minutes or less.

Introduction: German foreign policy 1936–8.
- *Was successful*
- *Britain and France divided*
- *Italy becomes friendly*
- *More Germans come to join Germany*
- *Planted seed for future confrontation*

Paragraph 2: Successful for undoing Versailles and other treaties
- *Rearmament*
- *Rhineland demilitarized, remilitarized in 1936*

- *Anschluss forbidden, but accomplished in 1938*
- *Sudeten granted to Germany in 1938*

Paragraph 3: End of isolation
- *Rome–Berlin Axis*
- *Anti-Comintern Pact with Japan*
- *Negotiations with Britain/France over Sudeten*
- *Treated as a real state*

Paragraph 4/5: Seeds of the future
- *Britain and France begin rearmament*
- *Munich Agreement causes expectation of no more demands*
- *Poland witnesses the results of Sudeten, no negotiations*
- *Public demands British/French governments resist*

Paragraph 6: Conclusion

Third, write an answer to the question.

Germany's foreign policy between 1936 and 1938 was extremely successful in many of its goals. Hitler, Germany's leader, desired to undo all facets of the peace treaties created at the end of the First World War to restrict Germany. Additionally, he desired the implementation of many old ideas such as pan-Germanism and lebensraum. Finally, Germany wished to end its post-First World War isolation from international diplomacy. These were accomplished largely in this three-year period. At the same time, Germany's rapid series of successes alarmed the Great Powers of France and Britain, causing them to react in ways that would eventually lead to confrontation and then into war, something Hitler hoped to avoid.

The first paragraph outlines the main arguments that the essay will make.

It is clear that a series of foreign policy successes occurred for Germany between 1936 and 1938. These were most notably a reoccupation of the Rhineland in 1936, which had been demilitarized after the First World War, the merger of Austria and Germany in a process called Anschluss and the annexation of the Sudeten area of Czechoslovakia, both in 1938. One of Hitler's often-stated aims was to undo the decisions made at end of the First World War. All three of these conflicted in one way or another with decisions made in Paris in 1919. These decisions had been made either to

Sources are used and
underlined making it
easier for the examiner.

limit Germany, in the case of the Rhineland, as indicated in _Source J_, and Anschluss or to create a viable state, in the case of Czechoslovakia. All these were possible because Germany had launched a rearmament effort starting in 1935 which increasingly gave it the ability to act with little consideration of military consequences from Britain or France. Earlier, in 1934, when Anschluss was attempted, Italy threatened to use its military, demonstrating not just Germany's weakness, but its diplomatic isolation; it had no friendly, mutually supportive relations with any state.

Each paragraph is clearly
focused on one aspect of
the argument.

By 1936, Germany was also much less isolated. The Abyssinian Crisis had led to the isolation of Italy, one of the stronger states of Europe. Germany and Italy, both fearing isolation for economic, diplomatic and military reasons, came to an understanding that they would work together, forming an alternative to the axis of London and Paris, as stated by Mussolini in _Source M_, the capitals of Britain and France which seemed to dictate much of European diplomacy. Whether this Rome–Berlin Axis had any real substance or not, it did mean that Italy, which had opposed the 1934 merger of Germany and Austria, would now not prevent it; it was accomplished early in 1938. Germany's emergence from isolation was furthered with the Anti-Comintern Pact that was agreed with Japan in 1936 as well. Germany's increasingly active foreign policy also helped bring it out of isolation. Whereas Hitler had been primarily ignored before 1938, by 1938 he sat with the Prime Ministers of Britain and France to negotiate over the Sudeten territory of Czechoslovakia. This was a real triumph in German foreign policy. Germany was now seen as a reasonable state that could be trusted to create a lasting peace in Europe through negotiation. This was true to the extent that Britain and France agreed to undo treaties of alliance between Czechoslovakia and France, implied by _Source P_, as well as aspects of the Paris Peace treaties from 1919.

A deeper understanding
of Germany's foreign
policy and its
consequences indicates
depth of historical
knowledge and
understanding of cause
and effect.

Germany's successes in this short period also led to future difficulties. Germany's active foreign policy was possible because of its rearmament and the relative military weakness of both France and Britain. While the citizens really had no desire for war, perceived as weakness by Hitler, as stated in _Source N_, they could not have intervened in Germany if they had desired to do so. With rearmament in Germany, both Britain and France began rearmament. While Germany's rearmament was rapid, it would always be limited because of a lack of raw materials such as iron, oil and rubber. Britain and France could depend on worldwide empires to supply these materials and so were to be stronger in the long term. By 1939, both Britain and France were fully armed and at full strength, allowing them to increasingly resist. The seeds of this strength came from Germany's rearmament, so in effect, Germany's foreign policy successes would have necessarily been limited to the short time period between 1936 and 1938 if Britain and France decided to resist in 1939 – which they did.

Additionally, Germany's negotiations at Munich in 1938 that allowed it to receive the Sudeten area of Czechoslovakia led voters in Britain and France to believe that there would be no further demands. When Germany took control of much of the rest of Czechoslovakia a few months later, it led to public indignation and a demand for their governments to refuse future negotiations. It may be that many in the British government felt that they had been taken advantage of, since, as the cartoon in Source P indicates, Britain had done much to weaken Czechoslovakia in order to please Germany. Poland believed that negotiations could lead to the dismantling of their state, as it had Czechoslovakia. When Germany made a demand for territory of Poland, not only did Britain and France state publicly that they would defend Poland's borders, but Poland also refused any negotiations which might have resolved the crisis. In effect, Germany's actions in achieving success, especially in 1938 over the Sudeten Crisis, meant that it would be unable to continue this rapid success without resistance from the voters of Britain and France, as well as Poland. This resistance would lead to the outbreak of war in September 1939, something that Hitler clearly wanted to avoid, according to historian Richard Overy, at least at that date.

Germany had many successes between 1936 and 1938. These successes were the undoing of various treaties that limited Germany and kept it from expanding, as well as ending its diplomatic isolation. These successes, however, were necessarily short lived as they were completed at a time of military weakness of both Britain and France; once these powers were stronger, they would, and did, resist further German demands. Additionally, the resolution of the Sudeten Crisis, clearly a success for Germany, proved to be an obstacle to further successful German diplomacy since it led Poland to not negotiate in 1939 and caused an outraged British and French public to demand that their governments resist future German foreign policy success.

> The final paragraph summarises the argument and answers the essay question.

> The answer indicates that the question was understood. The response is clearly focused on the question. There are references to all four sources and they support the essay as evidence. Accurate, relevant knowledge of the topic is presented and there is a synthesis of knowledge and material from the sources. This essay would score in the upper markband of the Paper 1 examination for Question 12.

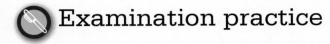

Examination practice

The following are exam-style questions for you to practise, using sources from the chapter. Sources can be found on the page references given.

The questions also reflect the numbering style of the exam (there are no questions 1–8; questions for The move to global war begin at question 9).

PAPER 1 PRACTICE QUESTIONS FOR CASE STUDY 2 (USING SOURCES FROM CHAPTER 3)

See Chapters 1 and 2 for advice on answering questions 9 and 10.

Source T: page 123

Source U: page 124

Source V: page 125

Source Z: page 128

9 **a)** What, according to Source U, was the importance for the Abyssinian Crisis for the League of Nations? [3 marks]

b) What message is conveyed by Source Z? [2 marks]

10 With reference to its origin, purpose and content, analyse the value and limitations of Source T for historians studying the Abyssinian Crisis. [4 marks]

11 Compare and contrast what Sources T and V indicate about the League of Nations. [6 marks]

12 Using the sources and your own knowledge, evaluate the results of the Abyssinian Crisis for the League of Nations. [9 marks]

PAPER 1 PRACTICE QUESTIONS FOR CASE STUDY 2 (USING SOURCES FROM CHAPTER 4)

See Chapters 1 and 2 for advice on answering questions 9 and 10.

Source B: page 144

Source C: page 146

Source D: page 147

Source G: page 151

9 **a)** What, according to Source D, were the results of Germany's announcement that it was rearming? [3 marks]

b) What message is conveyed by Source B? [2 marks]

10 With reference to its origin, purpose and content, analyse the value and limitations of Source C for historians studying Germany's rearmament in the 1930s. [4 marks]

11 Compare and contrast what Sources B and G indicate about Germany's rearmament programme. [6 marks]

12 Using the sources and your own knowledge, evaluate the significance of Germany's rearmament that began in 1935. [9 marks]

Activities

1 Create a large list of states involved in European diplomacy during the 1930s. These should include Britain, France, Italy, Germany, the Soviet Union, Czechoslovakia and Poland, but more could be included. For each of these countries, indicate their foreign policy goals in order of importance, conflicts with other states and any other issues that prevent resolution of international issues. For some it will be peace and maintenance of their empires, for others it will be to regain lost territories, and so forth. The job for you and your classmates will be to create a lasting peace that will satisfy as many of the states as possible on your list.

2 History is about making arguments using supportive evidence. Divide into four groups. Each group should take one of the four statements below and come up with evidence in support of the statement:

- Poland's refusal to negotiate led to the Second World War.
- Britain's guarantee of Poland's borders led to the Second World War.
- Germany's demands on Poland led to the Second World War.

Now, using your evidence, debate the following question in class: 'To what extent was the Second World War the result of the failure of British, German and Polish foreign policies?'

3 Locate a cartoon archive online that gives at least four countries' perspectives on the Munich Agreement or the crisis over Danzig. Create a display of these artworks, complete with explanations and analysis.

Case Study 2: Timeline

1922	Mussolini becomes prime minister of Italy
1928	Soviet Union begins mass industrialization in Five Year Plan, renews this in 1932
1929	**Oct:** Great Depression begins
1932	German unemployment at 26 per cent
1933	**Jan:** Hitler becomes Chancellor of Germany **Mar:** *Gleichschaltung* begins **Oct:** Germany leaves League of Nations
1933	Mussolini becomes minister of war, air, navy, interior and foreign affairs as well as prime minister
1934	**Jan:** Polish–German Non-Aggression Pact signed **July:** German attempt to annex Austria prevented by Italy
1934	New Plan for Germany's economy initiated; Soviet Union joins League of Nations
1935	**Jan:** Saar Plebiscite held **Mar:** Germany announces rearmament **Apr:** Stresa Front forms to ensure Germany's diplomatic isolation **May:** Franco-Soviet Treaty of Mutual Assistance **June:** Anglo-German Naval Treaty **Oct:** Italy invades Abyssinia; League of Nations imposes economic sanctions on Italy
1936–9	Spanish Civil War; Italy commits troops and weapons to helping Nationalist

1936	**Mar:** Germany remilitarizes the Rhineland **May:** Italy leaves League of Nations **Sept:** Four Year Plan for Germany's economy announced **Oct:** Rome–Berlin Axis announced **Nov:** Anti-Comintern Pact agreed by Germany and Japan
1938	**Mar:** Germany annexes Austria, confirmed by April plebiscite **Sept:** Munich Agreement grants the Sudeten areas of Czechoslovakia to Germany **Oct:** Poland seizes part of Czechoslovakia; Slovakia is granted autonomy; Germany requests negotiations for the return of Danzig **Nov:** Hungary seizes large areas of Czechoslovakia, mostly from autonomous Slovakia
1939	**Feb:** Britain announces military alliance with France **Mar:** Rump of Czechoslovakia occupied by Germany; Slovakia made independent; Memel returned to Germany from Lithuania; Britain pledges to defend Poland's borders **Apr:** Italy invades and annexes Albania **May:** Pact of Steel alliance signed by Italy and Germany **23 Aug:** Nazi–Soviet Pact announced **25 Aug:** Britain and Poland sign formal military alliance; Italy released from Pact of Steel obligations **1 Sept:** Germany invades Poland **3 Sept:** Britain and France declare war on Germany

Glossary

Annexed   Acquired by force.

Bayonet   A type of knife that is attached to the end of a rifle for stabbing enemies when fighting at close range.

Boxer Rebellion   An anti-foreign, anti-Christian revolt in China that was eventually joined by government soldiers with support from the Qing Dynasty. The revolt was put down by foreign troops.

Cabinet   Ministers of a government.

Capital ships   Large ships such as battleships and heavy cruisers.

Chancellor   A position equivalent to prime minister in most countries and the most powerful official in Germany.

Chiang Kai-shek (1887–1975)   Leading military and political ruler of China after 1925, dominating the Kuomintang political party.

Coalition   A government that includes multiple parties, often formed during times of national crisis.

Collectivization   The Soviet Union's policy of ending privately owned and operated farms by consolidating farmers, farm animals and equipment in state-managed farms.

Conscription   Required military service by a government for a specific length of time and usually for men only.

Coup d'état   An overthrow of a state's government by individuals within that state.

Deficit spending   When a government spends more money than it brings in through taxation, usually to stimulate a country's economy.

Embargo   A restriction on the import of specific items or from a specific country.

Enabling Act   Officially the 'Gesetz zur Behebung der Not von Volk und Reich' or 'Law to Remedy the Distress of the People and the State', this act allowed the government to rule by decree instead of through parliament, including the implementation of laws that contradicted Germany's constitution.

Fasces   A bundle of bound rods that included an axe that was carried by guards of important Roman officials, which eventually represented government authority and power.

Fascism   A term derived from the Fascist Party of Italy. It refers to a governing philosophy that glorifies the state, war and sacrificing oneself for the state while de-emphasizing individual rights and freedoms. This term is often used to refer to non-democratic, militaristic governments.

Fascists   Originally referring to Italy's ultranationalist Fascist Party, the term was eventually used to refer to most ultranationalist groups who advocated an end to or severe modification of republican forms of government in favour of authoritarian, nationalist single-party states.

Feudalism   Form of government in which nobility and their associates, such as warriors, hold substantial governing power.

Great Depression   A worldwide economic depression that led to massive unemployment, political instability, hunger and poverty, among other issues, starting from late 1929 and ending by the early 1940s, depending on the country or region.

Great Powers   In this period, primarily European states such as Britain, France, Germany and Russia, but sometimes meant to include the USA, the Austro-Hungarian Empire and Italy.

Gross national product (GNP)   The value of all goods and services produced by the citizens of a state over one year.

Guerrilla attacks   Military attacks by small groups, usually on a larger military force.

Heinrich Brüning (1885–1970)   Chancellor of Germany from 1930 to 1932.

Imperial preference   A system of commerce created by lowering import taxes between areas of an empire, while increasing taxes on imports from countries outside the empire.

Imperialism   Policy or system of a state gaining control of foreign lands for reasons of trade, prestige or military advantage.

Indemnity   A financial penalty.

International Settlement Area of Shanghai controlled by foreign governments where foreign-owned factories and other enterprises were located, and where many non-Chinese lived.

Josef Stalin (1878–1953) Authoritarian leader of the Soviet Union by the late 1920s.

Kuomintang China's main political group, also known as the Guomindang, or Nationalists.

Kwantung Army Japan's most elite military unit before the Second World War, stationed in the Liaodong Peninsula, next to Manchuria.

Lausanne Conference A conference in 1932 between Britain, France and Germany that suspended Germany's First World War reparations as a result of the world economic crisis.

League of Nations International organization that agreed to resolve international crises through diplomacy and not war that also established groups to address health issues, refugees, workers' rights and more.

Lebensraum German for living space, loosely defined as parts of eastern Europe.

Mandates Lands formerly held by Germany and the Ottoman Empire that were to be administered by Britain, France, Belgium, Australia, New Zealand and Japan after the First World War for the League of Nations.

Meiji Emperor Emperor of Japan between 1867 and 1912 in whose name modernizing reforms were instituted.

Meiji Restoration The creation of a new government of Japan after centuries of military government, in which Japan's Emperor held new powers and new, more modern systems of governance were created; it is named after the ruling emperor of that period.

Monarchy A government led by a king or queen.

Monopolies Companies that control entire sections of the economy, such as steel production or shipbuilding.

National Socialists Abbreviated name for the National Socialist German Workers' Party or Nazi Party, an ultranationalist group.

Nazi–Soviet Pact More correctly known as the Molotov–Ribbentrop Pact. Germany and the Soviet Union agreed that neither country would attack the other or help other states attack the other. Additionally, there were economic aspects and secret sections that divided parts of central and eastern Europe into Soviet and German spheres of influence.

Neutrality Acts A series of US government laws that generally imposed embargoes on the sale of weapons to states at war.

Open Door Policy Policy advocated by the USA that called for all nations to have equal access to China's markets.

Ottoman Empire Empire that once covered most of the Middle East, much of north Africa and the Balkan peninsula of Europe, with its capital at Istanbul.

Pact of Steel More formally known as the 'Pact of Friendship and Alliance between Germany and Italy', the Pact publicly stated that the two countries supported and trusted each other; secret clauses stated that there would be a union of economic and military policies, although these were never enacted.

Pan-Germanism An idea from the early nineteenth century that all German-language speakers should live in the same country.

Paramilitaries Military units that operate outside official control of a government.

Paul von Hindenburg (1847–1934) A highly decorated general and president of Germany from 1925 to 1934.

Plebiscite A national vote or referendum about one particular issue.

Privy Council Small government body of elites whose approval was required for laws, major political appointees and more; they controlled access to the Emperor of Japan and were heavily relied on by the Emperor owing to their prestige and experience.

Purge The removal of people, through loss of work, imprisonment or execution, who were deemed a threat by Soviet government authorities.

Qing Dynasty of China The ethnic Manchu family of rulers of China from 1644 to 1911.

Radical nationalism   An extreme form of nationalism which can include racism and other forms of discrimination and prejudice against those not part of the nation, which is usually narrowly defined; this belief often justifies violence to achieve certain goals.

Rapallo Treaty   Treaty signed in 1922 by the Soviet Union and Germany in which each renounced all claims against the other, recognized the other diplomatically and agreed to co-operate economically.

Reichstag   Germany's parliament.

Republic   Form of government consisting of elected representatives of voters.

Rome–Berlin Axis   Treaty of friendship between Germany and Italy in 1936, signalling an end to diplomatic co-operation between Italy and Britain and France.

Satellite state   A state that is closely associated with another and is unable to act independently in many areas such as in economic or foreign policies.

Semi-isolation   A policy of having limited involvement in international diplomacy.

Shōgun   Hereditary military governors of Japan from 1192 to 1867.

Shōwa Emperor   Grandson of the Meiji Emperor and often called by his personal name, Hirohito, outside Japan. He was preceded by the short reign of his mentally ill father, the Taishō Emperor.

Socialists   People who believe that society should be as equal as possible financially and in terms of political rights.

SS   An acronym for *Schutzstaffel*, a Nazi paramilitary group that later functioned as the state police and operated a large part of the German economy.

Stimson Doctrine   This policy stated that the USA would not recognize international border changes that resulted from war.

Sudeten German Party   A German political party in Czechoslovakia in the 1930s that was closely allied to and adopted many of the ideals of the Nazi Party of Germany.

Suez Canal   Major canal linking the Mediterranean and Red Seas and therefore the Atlantic and Indian Oceans.

Suffrage   The right to vote.

Synthetic oil   Oil produced from non-crude oil sources such as coal by-products and fish oils.

Synthetic rubber   Rubber made from petroleum by-products instead of tree sap.

Trade barriers   Means of restricting trade with other countries, usually by placing high taxes on foreign imports so that domestic goods can be sold more cheaply.

Treaty of Brest-Litovsk   A treaty signed between Russia (soon to be the Soviet Union) and Germany and Austria-Hungary in early 1918 in which Russia left the First World War, turning over huge territories to Germany and Austria-Hungary that would include today's countries of Poland, Ukraine, Lithuania, Latvia, Estonia and Finland, containing one-third of Russia's population and farmland and half its industry.

Treaty of Versailles   Treaty imposed on Germany in 1919 by the victors of the First World War, which included financial penalties, severe military reductions and loss of land.

Tributary   A state which presents gifts or funds to a stronger state for protection and/or as a sign of loyalty, respect and subservience.

Tripartite Pact   An alliance involving initially Germany, Italy and Japan, coming into effect in September 1940 and eventually joined by Hungary, Romania, Slovakia, Bulgaria and Independent Croatia.

Ultranationalist   A belief in which a person or state's nationality is considered superior to that of all others and usually involves racist and discriminatory beliefs against others not of the same nationality.

Vichy France   The common label for the southern part of France that was not occupied by German troops between 1940 and 1942, with its administrative centre in the town of Vichy. While it was allowed a certain degree of autonomy over its internal affairs, and allowed to oversee France's colonial empire, it had no meaningful independence from German authorities.

Wall Street Crash   A rapid decline of the US stock market, located on Wall Street in New York City, in October 1929, which led to an economic crisis throughout the world.

World Disarmament Conference   Conference held by the League of Nations which began in 1932, the aim of which was to reduce military sizes and weapons as a way to prevent future war.

Further reading

Works dealing with the interwar period generally

The Origins of the Second World War by A.J.P. Taylor. Penguin Books, 2001.
A famous book by one of the world's most famous historians that continues to inspire and provoke controversy.

Versailles and After: 1919–1933 by Ruth Henig. Methuen, 1984.
A very short work that reviews the period 1919–33 and summarizes events succinctly.

A Shattered Peace: Versailles 1919 and the Price We Pay Today by David A. Andelman. John Wiley, 2008.
A highly praised work that connects modern-day events to the Paris Peace Conference 1919.

The Origins of the Second World War in Europe by P.M.H. Bell. Pearson, 2007.
A highly useful and readable work that exhibits excellent scholarship on the interwar period.

The Road to War by Richard Overy and Andrew Wheatcroft. Penguin Books, 2000.
A work that expands on A.J.P. Taylor's earlier views.

From Sarajevo to Potsdam by A.J.P. Taylor. Thames & Hudson, 1966.
Reviews the interwar period through to the end of the Second World War.

The Causes of the Second World War by Anthony Crozier. Blackwell Publishers, 1997.
Contains interesting historiography regarding the outbreak of the Second World War.

The Origins of the Second World War by R.J. Overy. Longman, 2008.
Argues that the Second World War was the result of the decline of old empires and the rise of new ones.

The Making of the Second World War by Anthony Adamthwaite. Routledge, 1992.
Based on French, British, German and Soviet documents, publishing many for the first time.

The Lights that Failed: European International History 1919–1933 by Zara Steiner. Oxford University Press, 2005.
Argues that real political stability was achieved in Europe in the mid-1920s, only to be destroyed by the Great Depression.

Works concentrating on specific countries or regions

Japan

Emperor Hirohito and His Chief Aide-de-Camp: The Honjō Diary, 1933–36 by Honjō Shigeru, translation and introduction by Mikiso Hane. University of Tokyo Press, 1982.
A work by someone who worked directly with Japan's Emperor at a time of political crisis.

The Autobiography of Ozaki Yukio: The Struggle for Constitutional Government in Japan by Ozaki Yukio. Princeton University Press, 2001.
Ozaki was the longest serving member of Japan's Parliament in history and provides an intimate view of the internal wrangling of Japanese politics.

The Age of Hirohito: In Search of Modern Japan by Daikichi Irokawa. The Free Press, 1995.
A comprehensive work that includes much detail on Japan's policies and actions before the Second World War.

Shōwa: An Inside History of Hirohito's Japan by Tessa Morris-Suzuki. Schocken Books, 1985.
A detailed analysis of the political struggles and policies of Japan's government in the interwar period.

The Manchurian Crisis and Japanese Society, 1931–33 by Sandra Wilson. Routledge, 2002.
Provides unique perspectives of the Manchurian Crisis on Japanese society, including farmers, women and business groups.

Fifty Years of Light and Dark: The Hirohito Era. The Mainichi Newspapers, 1975.
A work created from comprehensive newspaper coverage since 1872.

The Wars for Asia, 1911–1949 by S.C.M. Paine. Cambridge University Press, 2012.
A work that includes the details and actions of Japanese and Chinese governments in military terms, including China's warlord period through the Second Sino-Japanese War and beyond.

War and Nationalism in China 1925–1945 by Hans J. Van De Ven. RoutledgeCurzon, 2003.
Focuses on the internal military struggle within China between factions, including the KMT and CCP.

A Modern History of Japan: From Tokugawa Times to the Present by Andrew Gordon. Oxford University Press, 2008.
Provides an academic and thorough review of Japan's history including the interwar period.

Italy

Italian Fascism, 1919–1945 by Philip Morgan. Macmillan, 1995.
A comprehensive overview of the entire period of Mussolini's rise and rule.

Italy: From Revolution to Republic, 1700 to the Present by Spencer Di Scala. Westview Press, 1998.
A thorough history of Italy, covering the interwar period in great detail.

Mussolini by R.J.B. Bosworth. Bloomsbury Academic, 2010.
A very focused study on Mussolini that has been well received.

Mussolini and his Generals: The Armed Forces and Fascist Foreign Policy, 1922–1940 by John Gooch. Cambridge University Press, 2007.
A focused study on Italy's military and Mussolini's foreign policy aims and achievements.

Germany

Germany: A Short History by Donald Detwiler. Southern Illinois University Press, 1999.
A very general history of Germany since ancient times.

Hitler: A Study in Tyranny by Alan Bullock. Harper & Row, 1991.
A candid review of Hitler that focuses only on proven facts, not entering into speculation.

Documents on Nazism 1919–1945 by Jeremy Noakes and Geoffrey Pridham. University of Exeter Press, 1995.
A supply of primary source materials regarding Nazism.

Hitler's Foreign Policy 1933–1939 by Gerhard L. Weinberg. Enigma Books, 2009.
A massive work by a German historian.

Hitler 1936–1945: Nemesis by Ian Kershaw. Penguin Group, 2000.
A work by one of the most prolific and noted historians regarding Nazi Germany.

Soviet Union

Russian's International Relations in the Twentieth Century by Alastair Kocho-Williams. Routledge, 2013.
A recent work detailing the foreign relations of Russia and the Soviet Union throughout the twentieth century.

Stalin: A Biography by Robert Service. Pan Books, 2005.
One of the most authoritative works regarding Stalin.

War and Peace in Soviet Diplomacy by T.A. Taracouzio. Macmillan, 1940.
A hard-to-find work that gives a unique pre-Second World War view of Soviet diplomacy.

Years of Russia, the USSR, and the Collapse of Soviet Communism by David Evans and Jane Jenkins. Hodder Education, 2008.
Thoroughly reviews the interwar period with statistics, primary sources and historiography.

Other countries

The Foreign Policy of France from 1914 to 1945 by Jacques Néré. Routledge, 2002.
A work that discusses French foreign policy in incredible detail.

Czechoslovakia in a Nationalist and Fascist Europe 1918–1948 edited by Mark Cornwall and R.J.W. Evans. *Proceedings of the British Academy*, vol. 140. Oxford University Press, 2007.
Part of a series of works that reflect modern research on Czechoslovakia after the First World War.

Poland, 1918–1945: An Interpretive and Documentary History of the Second Republic by Peter D. Stachura. Routledge, 2004.
One of the most thorough histories of modern Poland.

Eastern Europe in the Twentieth Century and After by R.J. Crampton. Routledge, 1997.
A political history of the entire region, including the interwar period.

The History of Albania from its Origins to Present Day, by Stefanaq Pollo and Arben Puto. Routledge & Kegan Paul, 1981.
An overview of Albania's twentieth-century history.

A work on the League of Nations including successes and failures

The League of Nations: Its Life and Times 1920–1946 by F.S. Northedge. Holmes & Meier, 1986.
The work is a very thorough overview of the history of the League of Nations.

A work on the Great Depression and its impact on political systems

The Global Impact of the Great Depression, 1929–1939 by Dietmar Rothermund. Routledge, 1996.
An invaluable work for studying the effect of the Great Depression on the world.

Internet and film sources

- A vast number of primary documents, including treaties, speeches, letters and so forth, can be found at Fordham University's Modern Internet History Sourcebook: www.fordham.edu/halsall/mod/modsbook.asp
- All treaties and much primary material of the period can be found at Michael Duffy's Firstworldwar.com: www.firstworldwar.com
- Political cartoons of the period from Britain may be found at the University of Kent's Cartoon Archive website: www.cartoons.ac.uk
- Many out-of-print books and period journals and magazines may be located with Google Books. Searches can be made for those works that provide a full view and can be saved in a personal library.
- British National Archives contain primary documents of all periods, but can be difficult to navigate given the sheer volume of data available: www.nationalarchives.gov.uk
- US National Archives also contain primary documents in vast quantities, but can also be difficult to navigate given the sheer volume of data available: www.archives.gov
- The British television documentary series *The World at War* contains interwar period material in its first volumes.

Internal assessment

The internal assessment is a historical investigation on a historical topic. Below is a list of possible topics on international diplomacy in the 1930s as covered in this book that could warrant further investigation. They have been organized by topic.

Japanese imperialism

1 To what extent did Japanese policies regarding Manchuria change between 1905 and 1931?
2 How successful was Japan's policy of settling Japanese colonists in Manchuria?
3 In what ways did Japan's rule of the South Seas Mandate differ from British rule of Mandates in Africa?
4 To what extent did Japan's economy benefit from the occupation of Manchuria between 1932 and 1945?
5 How similar was Japanese rule in Manchukuo to that of Mengjiang?
6 To what extent was Japan's imperialism driven by economic conditions in Japan?
7 Why was Japan's military able to take control of the government by 1932?
8 Were Japan's imperialist policies between 1919 and 1931 different from the period 1894–1918?
9 How did Japan's military actions in China between 1931 and 1936 affect its relationship with the Soviet Union?
10 How was Chinese religion affected by Shinto during the Japanese occupation of China between 1937 and 1945?

Italian imperialism

1 To what extent were Italy's colonies integrated into the Italian economy by 1939?
2 How was Italy's military affected by the Great Depression?
3 What were the most important changes in Ethiopia's architecture while under Italian rule?
4 How effective was political opposition in Albania to Italian rule?
5 To what extent did Italy's involvement in the Spanish Civil War affect Italy's economy?
6 To what extent did Italian–Yugoslavian relations improve between 1929 and 1939?
7 How effective was the Pact of Steel between 1939 and 1940?
8 To what extent did Italy benefit more from a closer relationship with Germany starting in 1936, than Germany benefited from Italy?
9 To what extent was the Catholic Church opposed to Mussolini's foreign policy?
10 How successful was Mussolini in achieving his foreign policy aims between 1922 and 1935?

German imperialism

1 To what extent was Germany's Four Year Plan different from the New Plan?
2 How different was Hitler's foreign policy between 1933 and 1935 from that of German chancellors between 1920 and 1933?
3 How was the Saar's economy affected by its reintegration into Germany in 1935?
4 To what extent was Danzig economically important for Poland?
5 How were Sudeten Germans affected politically by the Sudeten's annexation by Germany in October 1938?
6 To what extent was Poland's military stronger than Germany's between 1933 and 1939?
7 How did Hitler's *lebensraum* aim differ from that of earlier German leaders?
8 Why did *Anschluss* with Austria fail in 1934?
9 To what extent did Romania's economy benefit from Germany's economic revival between 1933 and 1939?
10 Why did Britain not protest the *Anschluss* between Germany and Austria in 1938?

Index

Acknowledgements:

Allen Lane, *1939: Countdown to War* by Richard Overy, 2009. AuthorHouse, *The Myth of German Villainy* by Benton L. Bradberry, 2012. Berg, *Germany, 1871–1945: A Concise History* by Raffael Scheck, 2008. Blackwell Publishers, *The Causes of the Second World War* by Anthony Crozier, 1997. Cambridge University Press, *Mussolini Unleashed 1939–1941: Politics and Strategy in Fascist Italy's Last War* by MacGregor Knox, 1982; *Social Darwinism in European and American Thought, 1860–1945: Nature as Model and Nature as Threat* by Mike Hawkins, 1997; *The Wars for Asia, 1911–1949* by S.C.M. Paine, 2012. Children and Youth in History, https://chnm.gmu.edu/cyh/primary-sources/136. Greenwood Press, *The History of Poland* by M.B. Biskupski, 2000. Hanover College Historical Texts Collection, http://history.hanover.edu/texts/1889con.html. Harper & Row, *Hitler: A Study in Tyranny* by Alan Bullock, 1962. Harvard University Press, *A Time of Crisis: Japan, the Great Depression and Rural Revitalization* by Kerry Smith, 2001. His Majesty's Stationery Office, *British War Economy* by W.K. Hancock and M.M. Gowing, 1949. *History Review*, 'The Nazi Economy – Was It Geared to War?' by Richard Overy, No. 31, September, 1998. Hogarth Press, 'Why the German Republic Fell' by Bruno Heilig in *Why the German Republic Fell and Other Lessons of War and Peace Upholding True Democracy through Economic Freedom*, edited by Arthur Madsen, 1941. Holmes & Meier, *The League of Nations: Its Life and Times, 1920–1946* by F.S. Northedge, 1986. I.B. Tauris, *Chronicle of a Downfall: Germany 1929–1939* by Leopold Schwarzschild, 2010. *Insight on the News*, Stephen Goode, 2003. Institute of Pacific Relations, *The Struggle for North China* by George E. Taylor, 1940. John Day Company, *The Collected Wartime Messages of Generalissimo Chiang Kai-Shek, 1937–1945*, Vol. 1, by the Chinese Ministry of Information, 1946. Little Brown & Co., *The European World: A History*, second edition by Jerome Blum *et al.*, 1970. Longman, Green & Co., *Japan Among the Great Powers: A Survey of Her International Relations* by Seiji Hishida, 1939. Macmillan, *Italian Fascism, 1919–1945* by Philip Morgan, 1995; *War and Peace in Soviet Diplomacy* by T.A. Taracouzio, 1940. Mainichi Newspapers, *Fifty Years of Light and Dark: The Hirohito Era*, 1975. Modern Age Books, *Japanese Terror in China* by H.J. Timperley, 1938; *You Might Like Socialism: A Way of Life for Modern Man* by Corliss Lamont, 1939. Nelson-Hall, *Haile Selassie I: Ethiopia's Lion of Judah* by Peter Schwab, 1979. New York University Press, *King Zog of Albania: Europe's Self-made Muslim King* by Jason Tomes, 2004. Oxford University Press, *A Modern History of Japan: From Tokugawa Times to the Present* by Andrew Gordon, 2014; *Hitler: Diagnosis of a Destructive Prophet* by Fritz Redlich, 1999; *Modern Japan: A History in Documents* by James L. Huffman, 2004. Pearson Education, *The Inter-War Crisis: 1919–1939*, second edition by R.J. Overy, 2007; *The Origins of the Second World War in Europe*, second edition by P.M.H. Bell, 1998. Penguin Books, *The Origins of the Second World War* by A.J.P. Taylor, 2001; *The Road to War* by Richard Overy and Andrew Wheatcroft, 1999. Praeger, *From Democratization and Expansionism: Historical Lessons, Contemporary Challenges* by Masayo Ohara, 2001. Princeton University Press, *Dilemmas of Growth in Pre-war Japan* edited by James William Morley, 1971; *The Autobiography of Ozaki Yukio: The Struggle for Constitutional Government in Japan* by Ozaki Yukio, 2001. Public Affairs Press, *From the Marco Polo Bridge to Pearl Harbor: Japan's Entry into World War II* by David J. Lu, 1961. Routledge & Kegan Paul, *The History of Albania from Its Origins to Present Day* by Stefanaq Pollo and Arben Puto, 1981. Routledge, *Emperor Hirohito and Shōwa Japan: A Political Biography* by Stephen S. Large, 1992; *Modern Germany Reconsidered, 1870–1945* by Gordon Martel, 1992; *The Foreign Policy of France from 1914 to 1945* by J. Néré, 2002; *The Making of the Second World War* by Anthony Adamthwaite, 1992; *The Manchurian Crisis and Japanese Society, 1931–33* by Sandra Wilson, 2002; *The Origins of the Second World War in Europe* by P.M.H. Bell, 2007. RoutledgeCurzon, *War and Nationalism in China 1925–1945* by Hans J. Van De Ven, 2003. Russo-Japanese War Research Society, www.russojapanesewar.com/sakuri-1.html. Schocken Books, *Shōwa: An Inside History of Hirohito's Japan* by Tessa Morris-Suzuki, 1985. Springer, *Sir Gerald Fitzmaurice and the World Crisis: A Legal Adviser in the Foreign Office 1930–1945* by Anthony Carty, 2000. The Free Press, *The Age of Hirohito: In Search of Modern Japan* by Daikichi Irokawa, 1995. *The World Post*, 'Poland Caused WWII: Russian Report' by Mike Eckel, July 2009. University of British Columbia Press, *Japanese Diplomacy in a Dilemma: New Light on Japan's China Policy, 1924–1929* by Nobuya Bamba, 1972. University of Exeter Press, *Documents on Nazism 1919–1945* by Jeremy Noakes and Geoffrey Pridham, 1995. University of Tokyo Press, *A History of Shōwa Japan* by Takafusa Nakamura, 1998; *Emperor Hirohito and His Chief Aide-de-Camp: The Honjō Diary, 1933–36* by Honjō Shigeru, translated by Mikiso Hane, 1982; *The Honjō Diary, 1933–36* by Honjō Shigeru, 1982. W.W. Norton & Co., *Lend Me Your Ears: Great Speeches in History* by William Safire, 2004. Yale Law School, The Avalon Project: Documents in Law, History and Diplomacy. Yale University, Lillian Goldman Law Library's The Avalon Project: Documents in Law, History and Diplomacy, http://avalon.law.yale.edu/imt/parti.asp.

Every effort has been made to trace all copyright holders, but if any have been inadvertently overlooked the Publishers will be pleased to make the necessary arrangements at the first opportunity.